FRANCIS
of A S S I S I

FRANCIS
of ASSISI

History, Hagiography
and
Hermeneutics
in the
Early Documents

Edited by
Jay M. Hammond

Foreword by
Joseph P. Chinnici, O.F.M.

New City Press
www.newcitypress.com

Published in the United States
by New City Press, 202 Cardinal Rd., Hyde Park, New York 12538

©2004 Jay M. Hammond

Cover design by Nick Cianfarani

Library of Congress Cataloging-in-Publication Data:

Francis of Assisi : history, hagiography, and hermeneutics in the early documents / edited
    by Jay M. Hammond.
          p.   cm.
    Includes bibliographical references and index.
    ISBN 1-56548-199-2
    1. Francis, of Assisi, Saint, 1182-1226.   2. Christian
saints--Italy--Assisi--Biography--Early works to 1800.   3. Franciscans--History--Sources.
I. Hammond, Jay M., Ph. D.

  BX4700.F6F7225   2004

                                        2003064875

Printed in the United States of America

Contents

Foreword

Joseph P. Chinnici

After the publication of Paul Sabatier's *Francis of Assisi* in 1894, anyone working in the field of Franciscan studies or medieval history has confronted the "difficult inheritance" of the Umbrian saint.[1] Containing within his own personality so many apparently paradoxical elements, bequeathing to the church and society of his time both a new intuition and a novel institution, and founding a fraternity of brothers who struggled to balance a commitment to living "without anything of one's own" with the realities of power, prestige, and influence which came with expanding popularity and social ascendancy, the "poverello" spawned a cottage industry of liturgical texts, *legendae*, poetry, legal commentaries, academic reflections, and general descriptions within the first hundred and fifty years of his life. One prominent contemporary historian has referred to this communal process of the "remembered" Francis as his "misadventure."[2] The extent of this phenomenon has remained largely unknown to English-speaking readers up to the present time. With the publication of the monumental three volume *Francis of Assisi: The Saint* (I), *The Founder* (II), and *The Prophet* (III), 1999–2001, medievalists and devotees of the saint now have available to them in English the most significant productions of this literary explosion.[3] The various works in their evolution and

---

1. Paul Sabatier, *Life of St. Francis of Assisi,* translated by Louise Houghton (New York, Scribner's Sons, 1894).
2. Jacques Dalarun, *La Malavventura di Francesco d'Assisi* (Milan: Edizioni Biblioteca Francescana, 1996). English translation, *The Misadventure of Francis of Assisi: Towards a Historical Use of the Franciscan Legends,* translated by Edward Hagman (Saint Bonaventure, NY: Franciscan Institute, 2002).
3. *Francis of Assisi: Early Documents,* vols. I–III, edited by Regis J. Armstrong, J. A. Wayne Hellmann, and William J. Short (New York: New City Press, 1999-2001).

inter-connection tell the story not only of Francis but also of the
communities of memory which used his inheritance to create their
own identities and argue for a place and a vision in the church and
society of their times. When studying this vast amount of material
or even viewing it on the shelf (!), the reader is often confronted
with the intellectual barrier separating medieval texts from contemporary understanding and a personally bewildering sense of "Where
do I begin?" or "How can I possibly make sense of all of this?" A
beginning guide is badly needed.

This timely work, edited by Dr. Jay Hammond, and composed of
essays by significant scholars in Franciscan theology, history, and
hagiography, may serve as this much needed beginner's guide. After
a general and fundamental survey of the time period covered by the
three volumes of texts, 1209–1365, the volume contains perceptive
essays on Francis's own spirituality and its subsequent development in various individual works from the first legend by Thomas of
Celano through the *Mirror of Perfection.* This historical trajectory
opens up the key issues at the heart of the "Franciscan question":
the novelty of Francis's own experience, the emergence of the
"textual community" around the early brothers and sisters, the
movement from a performative theology for the marketplace to a
more objectified caricature of the Christian life, the "misadventure"
of Clare in her various portrayals as "saint," "foundress," and
"prophet," the relationship between social location, the material
structures of the fraternity, communal identity formation, and the
changing image of Francis. While only a beginning excursion into a
very large field, the work serves as a fine introduction to some of the
possibilities and difficulties confronting the historian of medieval
texts and all members of the Franciscan family. Four significant
areas of development strike this reader as particularly important.

First, the essays presented here will prove valuable for scholars
not only in the way in which they begin to fashion a path through
the three-volume compilation of materials, but also through the
hermeneutic tools which are used to illuminate these sources.
Understanding texts holistically within their social, political, theological, and communal contexts; attending to the changing usages
of words and phrases; interpreting medieval narratives in their
simultaneous literal, allegorical, moral, and mystical significances;

tracing meaning through the analysis of rituals and symbols; identifying distinctive genres, their audiences, and their rhetorical rules of composition; connecting written with oral culture, material space with intellectual formulation. All of these methodologies are well illustrated and indicate paths of investigation for medievalists and members of the Franciscan family. Here is a rich resource for both the historian and the contemporary practitioner of Franciscan life.

Second, "Will the real Francis of Assisi please stand up?" While the essays in this volume do not purport to answer this question, they point in a direction that may dissolve some of the traditional answers. A careful reading will indicate to anyone traditionally reared on the various biographies by Thomas of Celano and Bonaventure the importance of interfacing the primary tradition of Francis's writings with the hagiographical developments that take their location from a different time and place within the community. The results may be startling, as for example, a person may discover the gradual movement from the personal, prophetic, and concrete biblical categories of the evangelical life in Francis's own writings to the preoccupation with an "ideology of perfection" through the acquisition of virtues and the imposition of authority in the *Mirror of Perfection*. In addition, a person may begin to realize that the underlying ecclesiology pervasive in Francis's writings, reflective as they are of dealing with an imperfect and limited institution within which one discovers a life of faith, mutates as the "life of a man" becomes subordinated to the "story of a saint" and the papal objectives for reform and renewal. On the practical level, these developments which emerge from careful reading and study may have particular implications for formation programs, the relationship between friars, sisters and laity, and the strategic planning by apostolate which undergirds an inherited but not necessarily authentic approach to the Order's role in church and society.

Third, emerging from this volume is the challenge *to study* sources in their development, *to see* the implications of the "misadventure" of Francis and Clare, and *to know* that the life of faith is a difficult inheritance which "follows in the footprints of Jesus Christ" by engaging a changing history within the context of a changing church. The themes cry out for further exploration and indicate the close connection that needs to exist between the academic develop-

ment of new tools of research and interpretation and the
self-understanding of Franciscan life itself. In this sense this volume
is closely connected with the retrieval of the Franciscan intellectual
tradition that is currently taking place in the community.[4] The
essays attempt to analyze major texts in the "vernacular" theological tradition which in parallel fashion to the scholastic project
insured the continued liveliness of Francis's spiritual experience.
Awaiting scholars and the whole Franciscan family are major reflections on how the vernacular and academic traditions overlap, how
communal life may be a precondition for interpreting texts, and
how various dimensions of life, which are often categorically
divided, intersect, reinforce, and sometimes modify each other.

Last, in the present volume, contemporary questions of religious
life, mysticism, sexual abuse, the formation of character, the methodology for pastoral care, and the appreciation of novelty form the
backdrop to revitalizing the often moribund texts of medieval
ancestors. From this perspective, a deeper penetration of texts,
history, and change will help describe religious communities of
memory and mission who reconstruct themselves so as to communicate a tradition of spiritual wisdom. A task and an intellectual
agenda for the present seem obvious corollaries. May the scholar
and popular reader enjoy this rich intellectual feast and be fired into
further exploration of Francis, *Saint, Founder, Prophet.*

Joseph P. Chinnici
Franciscan School of Theology
Berkeley, California

---

4. For example see *The Franciscan Intellectual Tradition: Washington Theological Union Symposium Papers, 2001*, edited by Elise Saggau (St. Bonaventure, NY: Franciscan Institute, 2001); *Franciscan Identity and Postmodern Culture: Washington Theological Union Symposium Papers, 2002*, edited by Kathleen Warren (St. Bonaventure, NY: Franciscan Institute, 2002); Kenan Osborne, *The Franciscan Intellectual Tradition: Tracing Its Origins and Identifying Its Central Components*, in Franciscan Heritage Series, vol. 1(St. Bonaventure, NY: Franciscan Institute, 2003); Ilia Delio, *The Franciscan View of Creation*, in Franciscan Heritage Series, vol. 2 (St. Bonaventure, NY: Franciscan Institute, 2003).

Editor's Preface

Jay M. Hammond

The idea for this volume came as I attended a session at the 36th International Congress on Medieval Studies celebrating the publication of the three volumes, *The Saint, The Founder, The Prophet* from *Francis of Assisi: Early Documents.* At the session there was excitement as everyone honored the new texts and their editors. I too was excited about their completion, but was even more thrilled about the myriad of new research possibilities spawned by the new editions. Having worked on the editions, especially the *Index,* I was keenly aware of two things: that these texts were a treasure trove of theological, spiritual, hagiographical, historical, and hermeneutical information, and that these texts, with their introductions, critical apparatus and detailed *Index,* provided keys to accessing the treasures therein.

Thus, I envision this collection of essays as keeping the work of the editions working by allowing new and renewed forays into the *Early Documents.* All eleven essays, in varying degrees, touch on the three organizing concepts of history, hagiography and hermeneutics, and each essay offers insightful and informative contributions beginning with the overviews of all three volumes by Hellmann and Peterson. The following essays continue chronologically spanning from Armstrong, Carney, and J. Hammond's studies of Francis's own writings, through those of Short and Cunningham on Thomas of Celano's *Life of Saint Francis,* and Cusato's analysis of *The Sacred Exchange,* to M. Hammond's focus on pivotal passages from *The Remembrance* and *The Legend of the Three Companions,* to Johnson's consideration of Bonaventure's *The Minor Legend,* and ending with an examination of *The Mirror of Perfection* by Michaels.

13

As the new millennium is under way this book is among the first waves of what will hopefully be several more waves ensuing from the seminal three-volume publication of Franciscan sources. As Chinnici mentioned in the *Foreword*, ". . . this volume is closely connected with the retrieval of the Franciscan intellectual tradition that is currently taking place." Thus, as this volume builds on the previous work of so many who have preserved and explained the Franciscan tradition, it continues the process of retrieval and revitalization by providing new insights for interpreting and understanding the early documents. In so doing, may it also inspire others, present and future, to reap the harvest of the rich Franciscan heritage. Just as all the contributors have taught me much about the Franciscan early documents, other readers will no doubt also benefit from their work.

Francis of Assisi: Saint, Founder, Prophet

J. A. Wayne Hellmann

Three subtitles, *The Saint, The Founder,* and *The Prophet*, identify the three volumes of *Francis of Assisi: Early Documents* and correspond to their chronological order. The first volume, *The Saint,* includes texts from the years 1209–1239, and in these the church proclaims a saint. The second, *The Founder,* offers texts from 1240–1272, and in these the brothers remember and identify the founder of their brotherhood. The third, *The Prophet,* is a collection of texts written between 1277–1365, and in these a select group of brothers claim a prophet as they critique late thirteenth and early fourteenth century developments.

The thirty or more texts collected in the three volumes, (not including the related documents), cover a span of more than 150 years. In preparing the three volumes the editors were struck by the great differences among the texts written over that span of time. Each of the texts on Francis had different historical contexts, and in many cases, radically different ones. This means that the reason or "why" each of these thirty texts was written differs, which in turn significantly impacts "how" each text is written. The effect, "what" is written about Francis, his image, role, and significance, changes from text to text as the contexts shift over this century and a half of evolution.

In order to highlight the need for understanding the historical and literary interconnections between the texts and their particular contexts, the editors chose to publish the texts in chronological

15

order with an eye to facilitating a reader's awareness of the important text/context relationship. To this end, the editors identified three chronological periods that contextually frame the differences among the "why," the "how," and the "what," as the literature on Francis expanded and changed. Each subtitle was chosen to help explain the texts' different characteristics in each of these three distinct historical periods. Such a division intends to make visually identifiable three specific historical periods between the years of 1209 and 1365. Each subtitle gives an indication of what image of Francis predominates in each volume; they are intended to offer the reader a catchword that can serve as a general hermeneutical tool for interpreting, understanding, and appreciating the uniqueness of each collection of texts found in the three volumes.

To illustrate the interconnections between the texts, their contexts, and the three subtitles, this essay is divided into three parts. Each part presents an initial overview of the different texts found in each of the three volumes, followed by a closer examination of particular texts to demonstrate the differences among the three volumes. A short conclusion offers a reflection on general positives and negatives of the three different approaches to the one man, Francis of Assisi, as a saint, a founder, and a prophet.

I. The Saint (1209–1239)

A. Overview of the First Volume

The Saint contains Francis's own writings as well as the first life of Francis written by Thomas of Celano (+1260): *The Life of St. Francis* (1228–1229). Two other lives based primarily on Thomas's text, *The Life of St. Francis* (1232–1235) by Julian of Speyer and the *Versified Life* (1232–1239) by Henri d'Avranches follow. The exhortatory and allegorical text, *The Sacred Exchange between Saint Francis and Lady Poverty* (1237–1239), is also included near the end of *The Saint*.

Francis's own writings allow the reader to enter into the inner workings of his spiritual journey, a journey recognized shortly after his death as the journey of a saint. When the church proclaimed

Francis a saint in 1228, Pope Gregory IX ordered a life of the new saint to be written. In *The Life of Saint Francis*, Thomas of Celano presents Francis as an example for the renewal of the whole church. Francis's holiness rings loud and clear throughout all of volume one. Even Lady Poverty in *The Sacred Exchange* takes on "the personification of biblical Wisdom and, at times of the church."[1] This means that Francis is proclaimed a saint for the sake of the whole church. Volume one also offers the earliest liturgical texts that celebrate him as newly listed in the calendar of saints: *The Legend for Use in the Choir* (1230–1232), *The Divine Office of Saint Francis* (1228–1232), *Sequences,* and *Masses in Honor of Saint Francis.*

B. Mixing and Casting the Dye: Interpreting Francis as Saint

In *The Saint*, the pivotal text is Thomas's *The Life of Saint Francis*. Its importance cannot be underestimated. Understanding its content, that is, its message and interpretation concerning Francis, however, cannot be done without appreciating its context. Why was this life written? Who decided it should be written? Who wrote it? It was, of course, written by Brother Thomas of Celano for the occasion of Francis's canonization at the request of Pope Gregory IX.[2] This context itself speaks volumes about the content, for it determines how Francis is presented.

First of all, the prime mover behind Thomas's text was Pope Gregory IX (1227–1241), earlier known as Cardinal Hugolino.[3] Who was this man? He had studied theology in Paris and canon law in Bologna, and shortly after his uncle, Innocent III, ascended the papal throne in 1198, Hugolino was named cardinal deacon and, later in 1206, cardinal bishop of Ostia. In this capacity he served not only as papal legate in Germany from 1207 to 1209 but he also

---

1. FA:ED I, 523.
2. For an overview of this text see Jacques Dalarun, *La Malavventura di Francesco d'Assisi* (Milan: Edizioni Biblioteca Francescana, 1996), 69–91. English translation, *The Misadventure of Francis of Assisi: Towards a Historical Use of the Franciscan Legends,* translated by Edward Hagman (St. Bonaventure, NY: Franciscan Institute, 2002).
3. His full name is Hugolino dei Conti di Segni, born in 1170. See *Vita Gregorii papae IX,* in L. A. Muratori, *Rerum Italicarum Scriptores,* III/1 (Bolona: n.p., 1932), 575–87.

helped prepare the agenda for the Fourth Lateran Council in 1215 and supported its call for crusade and reform. Influential for the 1216 election of his uncle's successor, Honorius III (1216–1227), Cardinal Hugolino then vigorously preached the crusade in Lombardy and Toscana. He was bent on recapturing the holy places. He had little patience for heretics and schismatics, but he extended his warm friendship and enthusiasm to orthodox religious groups.[4] He preached under the banner of church reform, and this eventually shaped the dynamic of his own papacy from 1227 to 1241. It was as a newly elected pope, schooled in the reform tradition of Innocent III and Honorius III, that Gregory IX, with the stroke of his pen, canonized Francis, called for a basilica in his honor to be built, and ordered a life to be written.

It is not surprising that Gregory IX's bull of canonization, *Mira Circa Nos*, is filled with reform imagery.[5] He describes Francis as the hope for reform: "For behold at the eleventh hour, he raised up his servant Francis, a man truly after his own heart. He was a beacon whom the rich viewed with contempt, but whom God had prepared for the appointed time, sending him into his vineyard to root out the thorns and brambles after having put the attacking Philistines to flight, to light up the path to our homeland."[6] Gregory's language and images follow the spirit and language of the Fourth Lateran Council and the same theological vision of his predecessor, Honorius III, who had earlier in the first known papal document described the new brotherhood in a similar vision: ". . . they go through the different regions sowing the seed of the word of God."[7] In his bull of canonization, Gregory is not so much interested in the

---

4. See Benedikt Zöllig, *Die Beziehungen des Kardinals Hugolino zum heil. Franziskus und su seinem I. Orden* (Münster i. Westfallen: Aschendorffschen Buckdruckerei, 1943), 2–10, 18–21. Zöllig documents Hugolino's friendship with the Cistercians, the Camaldolise, and the Dominicans. These, in effect, prepared him for his subsequent friendship with Francis. All of this indicates Hugolino was well connected with the different forms of religious life of his day. His relationship with Francis solidified after the death of Cardinal John of St. Paul in 1216, and Hugolino's direct and formal connection with the brothers began in 1218 when he came to the chapter at the Portiuncula. In 1220 he was formally named the Cardinal Protector.

5. See FA:ED I, 565–69. Also see Regis Armstrong, "*Mira Circa nos*: Gregory IX's View of Saint Francis of Assisi," *Laurentianum* 25 (1984): 385–414.

6. *Mira Circa nos* 2 (I, 566).

7. This citation is taken from the first known official document of the papal court concerning Francis's brotherhood, *Cum dilecti* (1219); see FA:ED I, 558.

personal aspects of Francis's holiness as he is in the significance of Francis's example for renewal and reform.[8]

The power and focus of Gregory's thirst for reform could not have been lost by Thomas, who was chosen by the pope for this task.[9] The spirit found in the bull of canonization provides the context which characterizes the manner in which Thomas writes. Francis is proclaimed a saint not just to edify but "to root out the thorns and brambles" and "to reconcile people to God by his zealous preaching."[10] Conversion and reconciliation by preaching are two goals identified in the bull of canonization. Thomas kept this in mind as he wrote about the new saint. Conversion forms a substantial part of the initial narrative, and the mission of preaching and the formation of the brothers in this mission for the sake of reconciliation shape much of the rest of the narrative.[11]

In the narrative's initial part, when Thomas writes about Francis's conversion and the virtues of his conversion, he employs the

---

8. Francis's canonization so soon after his death is to be considered in light of the developing practice of canonization in the early 13th century. Note the canonization of the following: Ombono da Cremona (+1197, can. 1199); Gilbert of Sempringham (+1189, can. 1202); Cistercian William of Donjeon, bishop of Bourges (+1209, can. 1218); Hugo, bishop of Lincoln (+1200, can. 1220); Anthony of Padua (+1231, can. 1232); Dominic of Caleruega (+1221, can. 1234); Elizabeth of Turingia (+1231, can. 1235); Edmond of Abingdon, archbishop of Canterbury (+1240, can. 1247); William of Pinchon, bishop of St. Brieuc (+1234, can. 1247). All of these, along with Francis, are presented to the church. Of these, beginning with Francis in 1228, Gregory canonized Anthony, Dominic, Elizabeth, Edmond and William. For all of these a life was required as part of the process. Finally, in 1237 Gregory IX reserved canonization of saints to himself. None of this is without significance on Thomas of Celano's *Life of St. Francis*. See Felice Accrocca and Roberto Paciocco, *La leggenda di un santo di nome Francesco* (Milan: Edizioni Biblioteca Francescana, 1999), 29–42.

9. Later as Gregory IX, in the first papal bull to interpret the Rule, *Quo elongati* of 1230, Hugolino acknowledges his relationship to Francis and his participation in the formulation of the *Later Rule* of 1223: "For as a result of the long-standing friendship between the holy confessor and ourselves, we know his mind more fully. Furthermore, while we held a lesser rank, we stood by him both as he composed the aforesaid Rule and obtained its confirmation" [*Quo elongati* 3 (I, 571)]. Given the history of this relationship, Thomas could not have written his life of Francis without attention to Gregory's agenda. Regarding this point see also: Accrocca and Paciocco, *La leggenda*, 165–74.

10. *Mira circa nos* 2 (I, 566).

11. In this context of reconciliation, Thomas emphasizes Francis as a messenger of peace; see Jay Hammond, "The Concept of Peace in Book One of Thomas of Celano's *Vita Prima*," *Miscellanea Francescana* 98 (1998): 348-58, and Jay Hammond and J. A. Wayne Hellmann, "Franciscan Spirituality," in *The New Catholic Encyclopedia*, Second Edition, vol. 5 (Washington: Catholic University of America press, 2002), 892a-97a.

long tradition of hagiography that he knew so well. Nuances allude
to conversions found in *The Life of Polycarp*, *The Life of Saint Antony*,
The Life of Saint Martin of Tours, the life of Benedict as presented in
Dialogue II, *The Life of Saint Anselm of Canterbury*, and *The Life and
Death of Saint Malachy the Irishman*.[12] The tradition of the saints,
especially in their conversion, comes into renewed life in Saint
Francis's conversion, and Thomas frames this conversion narrative
very much within light of the theology of Saint Augustine's *Confessions*.[13] Francis is the saint who like others before him "rooted out
the brambles and thorns" first within himself and who then after-
wards became an example for others.

Francis's mission "to reconcile people to God by his zealous
preaching" becomes very clear throughout the subsequent development of the entire text. Thomas accents that Francis's formation of
the brothers had one primary goal: "they go through the different
regions sowing the seed of the word of God."[14] In the hagiographical
tradition Thomas thus accents something new. Conversion moves
toward the mission of preaching. It is based on hearing the word of
God and comes to fruition in the preaching of the word to the whole
world, even to all creatures. It is no accident that Thomas frames
the first book, the longest narrative, in this manner. Francis's
conversion follows the traditional line of the saints before him, but
his conversion moves him forward into something new, into the
mission of preaching for renewal. In the earlier part of the first book,
Francis hears the gospel at Saint Mary of the Portiuncula, and after
having had it explained to him, he exclaims: "This is what I seek,
this is what I desire with all my heart."[15] At the end of the first book,
Francis "with full voice sings the holy gospel. Here is his voice: a
powerful voice, a pleasant voice, a clear voice, a musical voice,
inviting all to the highest of gifts."[16] As a result, in a vision a man
saw Francis approach the lifeless child in the manger and "waken
him from a deep sleep." Thomas then comments "nor is this vision
unfitting, since in the hearts of many the child Jesus has been given
over to oblivion. Now he is awakened and impressed on their loving

---

12. See footnotes in FA:ED I, 182–87, 190–92, 194–96.
13. See footnotes in FA:ED I, 182–202.
14. See 1C 29–31 (I, 207–10); quotation from *Cum dilecti* (I, 558).
15. 1C 22 (I, 201–02).
16. 1C 86 (I, 256).

memory by His own grace through His holy servant Francis."[17]
Renewal of the church through the gospel of the Word made flesh is
what Francis, the saint, is all about: this is very much why he was
canonized, why a basilica in his honor was built, and why a life was
written. This makes sense. A saint is proclaimed a saint, not for
private devotion or personal asceticism, but for promotion of holiness in the life of the church.

Even book two, which treats the mystical experience of the stigmata and his death, presents Francis as "a new Evangelist." Thomas
explains that "he preached the way of the Son of God and the
teaching of truth in his deeds. In him and through him an unexpected joy and a holy newness came into the world."[18] This is very
much in line with Gregory's vision and explains why he was so
anxious to canonize Francis. The third book that treats Francis's
canonization makes Gregory's whole purpose clear when he
himself, at that event, is described by Thomas in the following
manner: "He rejoiced and exulted, dancing with joy, for in his own
day he was seeing the Church of God being renewed with new
mysteries that were ancient wonders."[19]

The "holy newness" and the "new mysteries" exemplify the
renewal and reform for which Gregory longed, and this spirit forms
very much the context out of which Thomas wrote. His text is the
first to present Francis to the world, and it contains bibliographical
information about Francis and gives the specifics of places and
persons that appear in his life. However, Thomas's scope is to fit
this saint into the tradition of saints in a manner consistent with
something new, the agenda of Gregory for renewal of the church in
the early thirteenth century. In this sense, Thomas's *The Life of Saint
Francis* is an ecclesial document grounded in the tradition, but
shaped for the mission of church renewal through new and dynamic
preaching. Thomas is a master at crafting this image of Francis. He
presents Francis as a saint in the tradition of saints, but he is a saint
for a new time and a new mission that is to pour out "the streams of
the gospel in a holy flood over the whole world."[20]

---

17. 1C 86 (I, 256).
18. 1C 89 (I, 259–60).
19. 1C 121 (I, 291).
20. 1C 89 (I, 259).

II. The Founder (1240–1272)

A. Overview of the Second Volume

The Founder takes the reader twenty to forty years forward into
the middle of the thirteenth century and therefore into the second
generation of brothers. By this time the brotherhood had spread
throughout most of Europe and had drastically grown in numbers:
from around 3,000 to 5,000 a decade after the death of Francis in
1226 to an estimated 30,000 at the time Saint Bonaventure
(+1274) was elected Minister General in 1257.[21] In the texts of the
second volume there is general focus on the gathering of memories
about the saint. This became necessary as the brotherhood
continued to expand through the different regions of Europe and
beyond. Different memories were brought forward by those with
different personal experiences and with different perspectives on
the nature of the life of the brotherhood.

There are various and different kinds of memories in the second
volume. The first two texts, *The Anonymous of Perugia* and *The Legend
of the Three Companions* are the earliest (e.g. 1240's) and are unique
among the collection of texts in volume two. These two texts focus
not so much on Francis but on the memory of the earliest days of
the fraternity, precisely as it was formed in Assisi. These two texts
set precedence for the significance and normative value of the early
companions' experiences and identify those experiences as worthy
of remembrance. The early companions therefore help define the
origin and identity of the new brotherhood.

Other texts in volume two focus more exclusively on the memory
of Francis himself. *The Assisi Compilation* is just as it is entitled, a
random compilation of memories. A second text, *The Remembrance of
the Desire of a Soul,* brings Thomas of Celano back on the scene. Only

---

21. See Dominic Monti, *Saint Bonaventure's Writings Concerning the Franciscan Order*, in
Works of Saint Bonaventure, vol. V (St. Bonaventure, NY: Franciscan Institute,
1994), 1 and 13; also see Kajetan Esser, *Origins of the Franciscan Order* (Chicago:
Franciscan Herald Press, 1970), 37–40, and John Moorman, *A History of The
Franciscan Order* (Oxford: Clarendon Press, 1968), 62–74.

this time he does not offer a carefully constructed hagiographical text describing a saint, but rather he brings forward in this text of the mid-1240's a collage of memories about Francis. The longest part of *The Remembrance* is in book two where Thomas catalogues and develops memories already compiled (many apparently taken from *The Assisi Compilation*) into a kind of treatise that categorizes numerous and varied memories from Francis's life. This text helps cultivate a new and formative collective memory for the many new brothers who never knew Francis. Then in his *Treatise on the Miracles,* Thomas crafts a new focused memory of Francis as a "miracle worker." Moved by the ever spreading popular devotion to Francis,[22] Thomas compiles one third of the 157 miracles from his own earlier works, and he draws the remaining from other unknown sources. Both of Thomas's writings in the second volume contribute to the formation of a collective memory. He emphasizes "miracles that touch more on the inner dynamic of Francis himself or on that of his brothers, the founding of the fraternity, the stigmata, the miraculous power he had over creatures, and the arrival of Lady Jacoba at his death."[23]

Finally, when Bonaventure enters the scene as Minister General in 1257, the Chapter of Rome commissioned him in that year to compile "one good" legend of Saint Francis based on those already in existence.[24] Bonaventure fulfilled his task by writing a new life of Francis based on Thomas of Celano's *The Life of Saint Francis, The Remembrance of the Desire of a Soul,* and the *Treatise on the Miracles.* Nuances from Julian of Speyer's *The Life of Francis* and his various liturgical texts can also be found. Using this earlier material, Bonaventure again presents the accumulated memory of Francis. However, he does so in a fashion that also articulates something new, namely, a developed and systematic theological understanding of Francis's experience. At the heart of Bonaventure's

22. Evidence of this growing popular devotion can be found in the explosion of various artistic representations of Francis. See William Cook, *Images of St. Francis of Assisi: In Painting, Stone and Glass* (Florence: L.S. Olschki, 1999). In fact, in the later 13th century, Francis became the first medieval figure to be represented within grand narrative cycles as first found in the Basilica of Saint Francis in Assisi.
23. FA:ED II, 397.
24. See Jay Hammond, "Bonaventure, St.," in *The New Catholic Encyclopedia,* Second Edition, vol. 2 (Washington: Catholic University of America Press, 2002), 482a.

theological vision of Francis is the cross. The mystery of Christ crucified was at work in Francis, and the brothers can connect with Francis because this same mystery is at work in the life of every Christian. Bonaventure interprets and broadens the memory of Francis within the wide scope of a theological vision so that it can be applicable for new generations of brothers, wherever they may find themselves in their spiritual journey and ministry.

B. Activating and Forming the Brothers' Memory: Interpreting Francis as Founder

While the second volume contains eight texts about the life of Saint Francis, the context is no longer the proclamation of a saint; rather, the new context of the 1240's through the 1260's is the attempt by the second and third generations of brothers to foster a shared memory of Francis, not in view of his canonized mission for the church, but in view of understanding and interpreting their own lives as Lesser Brothers. The first volume looked outward toward the broader life and needs of the church; the second volume looks inward toward the internal life of the developing fraternity. Thus, the identity of the new brotherhood is not primarily based on the remembrances about the canonized saint, but more generally as the initiator and founder of their new way of life.

It is important to remember that the texts in volume two are written after the crisis of 1239, that is, after Brother Elias was deposed and Albert of Pisa was elected. Part of the problem that caused the crisis under Brother Elias was a lack of clear legislation regarding the government of the brotherhood. During the first thirty years, from 1209 to 1239, government of the brotherhood had a basically autocratic character. Chapters were called, but most authority was invested in the Minister General. After 1239 this changed; new legislation strengthened the authority of the chapters. In the tensions of these mid-thirteenth century legislative developments the memories about Francis are often connected to questions of authority. New to the texts after 1239 are ideal descriptions of the Minister General, stories about chapters, problems with the provincial ministers, tensions over Francis's resignation and other legislative debates, particularly concerning the *Rule*.[25] These are also the years of new commentaries on the *Rule*.[26] In Thomas's *The Remembrance of the Desire of the Soul*, for example, there are twenty references to the *Earlier Rule* and nearly as many to the *Later Rule*. Questions about the *Rule* are one perspective from which this and other texts of volume two can be read.

Thus the general context or reason for collecting these memories came from the shifting landscape of the 1240's. Within this specific context, the new Minister General, Crescentius of Iesi, elected in 1244, "directed all the brothers to send him in writing whatever they could recall about the life, miracles, and prodigies of blessed Francis."[27] There was great interest in recapturing the memory of Francis, especially from the perspective of his interactions with the brothers. It is precisely in the memory of his relationships with the brothers that Francis is identified as the founder of their way of life. Their collective memory shapes their identity. In this sense volume two, at least in notable part, moves away from the mission of the ecclesial reform found in volume one and into the cultivation of virtue and inner personal holiness that is to structure the brothers' daily life. Remembrance of Francis is the shared means by which the brothers can identify themselves and move forward in their continual reform. With their remembrances the brothers look back to Francis as they advance on their own spiritual path and deal with the new issues of organization and identity that face them.

Such a shift can be seen with Thomas of Celano's *The Remembrance of the Desire of a Soul*. First, an important difference between this text and his earlier *The Life of Saint Francis* is the simple fact that Thomas now writes in response to the request of his brothers rather than to that of the pope. Accordingly, his reason for and purpose in

---

25. See Jacques Dalarun, *Francesco d'Assisi: Il potere in questione e la questione del potere.* (Milan: Edizione Biblioteca Francescana, 1999), 66–91.

26. For example, in response to the crisis of 1239, the 1241 "Chapter of Definitors" at Montpellier called for commissions in each province to settle disputed points of the *Rule*. The four master theologians (Alexander of Hales, John de La Rochelle, Odo Rigaldus and Robert of Brescia) at Paris responded with their *Exposition of the Rule* in 1242; see FA:ED II, 15. Ten years later in 1252 Hugh of Digne completed another *Commentary on the Rule*.

27. See "Chronica XXIV Generalium," in *Analecta Franciscana sive Chronica Aliaque Varia Documenta ad Historam Fraturm Minorum III* (Quaracchi: Collegium S. Bonaventura ad Claras Aquas, 1897), 262.

writing about Francis a second time is very different. His *The Remembrance* is just what he identifies it to be: a remembrance that cultivates the deepest desire of the soul. For only out of deep desire can the brothers authentically live a life shaped and based on the memory of Francis and his *Rule*. Examples of Francis's life are therefore recalled, treasured and developed in order to move the brothers' hearts toward renewal and reform in their own lives.

Second, *The Remembrance* is pivotal for this purpose because its division into two books captures the two earlier traditions important to the development of memories about Francis at this time. On the one hand, the shorter book one of *The Remembrance* flows out of the earlier *Legend of Three Companions* (and thereby out of its primary source, *The Anonymous of Perugia*), which focuses on the development of the early fraternity and the brothers' interactions with each other. Here Francis is one of the brothers identified as "these evangelical men" and attention focuses on "the form of their holy way of life."[28] It also develops the stories of Francis's conversion from these two earlier accounts (*The Legend* and *The Anonymous*), and differs significantly from the conversion narrative Thomas had earlier written at the request of Gregory IX.[29] In this second conversion narrative Thomas does not narrowly focus on Francis's solitary developmental experiences, nor does he attempt to fit him into the church's long tradition of conversion narratives. Rather, he now presents Francis's interactions with his contemporaries as part and parcel of the conversion narrative. He writes that Francis was the "ringleader of Assisi's frivolous young crowd"[30] and Thomas shows Francis's interactions with his "embarrassed friends."[31] Furthermore, Francis's conversion story is now directly connected to the conversion of Brother Bernard, who "became a son of perfection, . . . thanks to the example of the man of God."[32] Finally, the first book, again accenting the relationship of Francis with the brothers, ends

---

28. L3C 34 (II, 88).
29. The conversion narrative in the 1228 *Life of St. Francis* is constructed in the context of the earlier rich hagiographical tradition; see Dalarun, *Francesco d'Assisi*, 66-91.
30. 2C 7 (II, 246).
31. 2C 8 (II, 247).
32. 2C 15 (II, 253–54).

with the vision of the small black hen, which Francis himself interprets: "I am the hen...the chicks are the brothers."[33]

On the other hand, the memory of Francis's relationship with the brothers takes a different twist in the longer book two of *The Remembrance,* which draws mostly from *The Assisi Compilation* and its emphasis on individual remembrances that are more direct, unique, and personal experiences of Francis. Here Thomas categorizes the collected individual memories according to the different virtues operative in Francis's life. In this manner, Thomas illustrates for the brothers that the memory of Francis is to serve their own growth in virtue. Francis is clearly presented as the model the brothers are to follow. Francis is the founder to the extent that he is remembered as the model of virtue that they all hold in common and are all to strive to follow. *The Remembrance* thus offers a decidedly different approach to Francis of Assisi. He is no longer the saint raised to lofty heights and held up as model for renewal in the church. Rather he is now presented as one of the brothers and as one who exemplified extraordinary virtue in the common ordinary experiences of fraternal life with the brothers. That these two different texts find their way into the one work of *The Remembrance* reflects the brothers' mid-1240 effort to synthesize two different traditions into a single remembrance of their founder: insofar as Francis was collectively related to the brothers and insofar as he was individually part of the fraternity.

Around twenty years after the completion of *The Remembrance,* Bonaventure of Bagnoregio, like Thomas of Celano, was asked by the brothers at the Chapter of Rome in 1257 to write a new legend in order to bring the earlier stories of Francis into a deeper synthesis.[34] Three years later, the brothers gathered for the General Chapter in Narbonne to codify the legislation of the previous eleven general chapters. Just as the accumulated legislation was to be codified, so also were the accumulated lives of Francis to be brought forward into a new unifying text for dissemination among the

---

33. 2C 24 (II, 260).
34. See Hammond, "Bonaventure, St.," 482a. Like the request from Crescentius of Iesi a few years after Elias was disposed, Bonaventure too was asked by the brothers to write a new life of Saint Francis after the removal of John of Parma as Minister General in 1257.

brothers.[35] Thus the context reveals a desire to codify and clarify the earlier hagiography along with the previous legislation. Bovaventure completed the *Major Legend of Saint Francis* by 1263 when he presented it to the General Chapter of Pisa which was then distributed to all the provinces of the Order. A new life for the brothers again stresses Francis as a founder whom the brothers are called to follow.

Bonaventure had taken seriously the directive that this new life of Francis was to be based on earlier texts. For example, throughout his legend Bonaventure incorporates nearly two hundred references to Thomas's *The Life of Saint Francis* and again as many references to Thomas's *The Remembrance*. Although he draws from both Thomas's earlier and later works, the spirit with which Bonaventure wrote follows the line of the *The Remembrance*. Bonaventure's purpose, in the spirit of the General Chapter of Rome, flowed out of the initial vision of remembering that was fostered by Crescentius of Iesi in 1244. Thus, like Thomas's *The Remembrance*, Bonaventure collects and reorganizes his sources for the purposes of fostering a collective memory of Francis for an increasing number of brothers.[36] Only in this case, Bonaventure now introduces a new dimension to the memory of Francis. He remembers not only specific deeds of Francis, but perhaps more importantly he recalls "the grace of God Our Savior" that "appeared in his servant Francis."[37] Bonaventure shifts the focus toward a contemplative stance of remembering how Francis was a "messenger of God—worthy of love by Christ, imitation by us, and admiration by the world."[38] Francis was the founder not only of a new group in the church but also the origin of a new order of grace appearing in the world. The brothers connect on a

---

35. The context suggests a complementary emphasis between the Chapter of Rome's effort to synthesize the earlier stories of Francis and the Chapter of Narbonne's effort to codify the earlier legislation. Moreover, as the new Constitutions of Narbonne were published at the Chapter of Narbonne in 1260 the old ones were to be destroyed. A similar decision was made by the Chapter of Paris in 1266, and so the lives of Francis prior to Bonaventure's were likewise to be destroyed; see FA:ED II, 503; Dalarun, *Francesco d'Assisi*, 110–11; and *La Malavventura*, 160–175.

36. As his purpose was toward the fostering of a unifying collective memory on a more contemplative level, Bonaventure leaves out of his narrative divisive controversial issues of the 1240's regarding money, study, and rigid poverty. See Dalarun, *La Malavventura*, 170–71.

37. LMj prol.1 (II, 525).

38. LMj prol.2 (II, 527).

much deeper level to the memory of their founder when they seek and search out a life that is to share in the order of grace that transforms one into the very image of Christ crucified. True memory of Francis is also remembrance of the mystery of Christ crucified. In this rich memory the brothers are, in the very struggles of their journey, to share in the mystery of Christ that the example of their founder exemplified and continued to inspire.

III. The Prophet (1277–1365)

A. Overview of the Third Volume

The Prophet introduces readers into a new world of texts that reflect the thinking of a specific group of fourteenth century brothers formed in rural areas of central Italy. Despite the limited circle from which these texts arose, they nevertheless influenced subsequent fifteenth century Italian reformers such as Bernadine of Sienna (+1444) and John of Capistran (+1456). Thus, the influence of these fourteenth century texts on the subsequent tradition was enormous. Although Thomas of Celano had earlier introduced the notion of prophet as a way of describing Francis,[39] and Bonaventure later expounded Francis's "spirit of prophecy,"[40] the notion of prophet in the third volume develops further and becomes the prominent motif for interpreting and re-presenting the memory of Francis. *The Prophet* texts present Francis in an operative biblical framework that is primarily apocalyptic and thereby approaches him in eschatological terms.

The late thirteenth and early fourteenth century fascination with the apocalyptic views of Joachim of Fiore (+1202) contributed extensively to this development of Francis as a prophet. Much of their Spiritualist perspective is framed in apocalyptic and eschato-

---

39. 1C 26–28 (I, 205–07), 2C 27–54 (II, 263–84), and see FA:ED II, 264, footnote a.
40. LMj 11.1-3 (II, 613-14).

logical terms based on Joachim's earlier theology of history.[41] As
certain brothers responded to the unending troubles and tribulations of the fourteenth century they found in Francis a prophetic
figure who exemplified the critical role they were to play in salvation
history. In view of their prophetic critique, Francis became *the*
prophet who leads the church beyond corruption into the final age
of salvation history. In effect, Francis had ushered in Joachim's
sixth age of salvation history. Those who follow him are to keep
alive the gospel of Christ in the age of the final tribulation that had
come upon them. The way to persevere through the final tribulation
is the way of gospel poverty; poverty leads to the richness of the
final age when all will be fulfilled in the kingdom of God.

Within this charged context of Joachimist thought the authors in
the third volume move with the conviction that a new age is
dawning. Characteristic of this manner of thinking is a sense of
urgency that a crisis is about to break and the new way of life of the
brothers holds the key to the future. History had already focused on
Francis and given him a unique mission. Key to Francis's focus and
mission was absolute poverty. The image of Francis, already earlier
acknowledged by Bonaventure as the "Angel of the Sixth Seal" of
the Apocalypse,[42] identified him as the prophet that embodied the
ideal of life in a new and final age in which all were to be drawn into
the *status evangelicae perfectionis.*[43] The eschatological task of

---

41. The 1240's saw the introduction of a group of Joachimist thinkers within the
    brotherhood. Salimbene gives the first indication thereof. See Salimbene, *Chronicle
    of Salimbene de Adam*, edited by Joseph Baird (Binghamton: Medieval &
    Renaissance Texts & Studies, 1986), 174, 224, 231, 233, 236, 238-39. In
    Provence Hugh of Digne (+1257) introduced Joachimist thinking, but it was
    Peter John Olivi (+1296) who, influenced by Hugh's thinking, developed a
    theology of history that later impacted Angelo Clareno (+1337). In 1254/55 at
    Paris, Joachimist thought had entered broader theological circles with the
    publication of the *Introduction to the Eternal Gospel* by the Franciscan Gerard of
    Borgo San Donnino (+1276). During the same time, John of Parma was most
    likely asked to resign his position as Minister General in 1257 because of his
    adherence to Joachimism. Bonaventure replaced him; yet he did not shy away
    from employing the quasi-Joachimist title "Angel of the Sixth Seal" in LMj prol.1
    (II, 527).
42. LMj prol.1 (II, 527).
43. See Marjorie Reeves, *The Influence of Prophecy in the Later Middle Ages: A Study of
    Joachimism* (Oxford: The Clarendon Press, 1969), 175–90; also see *Prophecy and
    Millenarianism: Essays in Honor of Marjorie Reeves,* edited by Ann Williams (Essex:
    Longman House, 1980), and Bernard McGinn, *Visions of the End: Apocalyptic
    Traditions in the Middle Ages* (New York: Columbia University Press, 1979).

converting the whole world was entrusted to Saint Francis and his brothers. Thus, his *Rule* was bound up with the consummation of the whole of history.[44] Such an apocalyptic vision springs from and responds to the confusions and challenges of their own day.

Two principal authors in the third volume, Ubertino of Casale (+c.1325) and Angelo Clareno (+1337), represent the tradition of the rural Spiritualist movement that developed in central Italy. As such they take on a social critique of the corruption they find in the church and the brotherhood itself. They identify what they see as abuses of power caused by the deliberate suppression of the gospel message of poverty, and they hold forth the example of Francis of Assisi and his *Rule* of gospel poverty to provide a prophetic response that points the way toward restoration and completion of God's kingdom.

Ubertino of Casale's 1305 *The Tree of the Crucified Life of Jesus* is the earliest fourteenth century text in volume three. Following the apocalyptic thought of his mentor, Peter John Olivi (+1298), Ubertino presents Francis as initiating a new beginning in the life of the church. Francis is "the angel of the sixth age"[45] who charges his followers to take on the same apocalyptic mission of the angel. Francis and his true followers are to manifest, by their lives of poverty, a "clear knowledge of God and of his entire City, and an extraordinary opening into and knowledge of the work of our redemption and of Christ Jesus."[46] The fourteenth century mission of Francis and the brothers is now clearly a prophetic one. Every aspect of their lives is framed within this vision of offering Francis's new and clear knowledge.

Angelo Clareno in his work, *The Book of Chronicles or of the Tribulations of the Order of Lesser Brothers,* continues Ubertino of Casale's apocalyptic perspective on Francis, but he radicalizes this perspective even more because his main focus is precisely on "tribulations." As Angelo reflects back on the first century of the life of the brotherhood, he sees only suffering and persecution (i.e. tribulations), beginning with the first rejection of Francis's *Rule* in 1220–21, while he was away in the Near East. Through tribulation, Angelo

---

44. See Reeves, *Prophecy*, 199.
45. See FA:ED II, 20 and III, 142; TL 422a21–423a42 (III, 149–52).
46. TL 442b17 (III, 193).

writes, one is transformed into Christ. In his vision, Francis and the brothers are, like the prophets of old, the persecuted ones. Angelo's own experience of suffering, first encountered at the hands of Boniface VIII, who suppressed his separatist group, the Poor Hermits, and his later harsh treatment by the Minster General Michael of Cesena and by John XXII, all impacted his whole vision of Francis and characterized how he understood what it meant to follow Francis. Angelo sees the Order only in diminishment and decline. Those victimized in this process become the genuine prophets of the sixth age.

Two other texts that speak of the prophetic tradition are the *Mirror* texts, the Sabatier edition and the Lemmens edition. Throughout much of the medieval tradition mirror texts were a literary form that offered examples or mirrors for upright living.[47] This form took a turn with Bernard of Clairvaux when his mirror texts took on the role not only to inspire a manner of life but also to purify the reader's life of any imperfection. It is in this context that the two *Mirror* texts are written. They are to "help the reader scrutinize and amend their lives according to the example of Francis."[48] These two *Mirror* texts can be called prophetic texts insofar as they claim prophetic insight into the way the *Rule* is to be interpreted and lived. Not only do the examples of Francis confirm their underlying position, but even the voice of Christ, over and against the voices of the ministers, proclaims: "And I want the Rule observed in this way: to the letter, to the letter, to the letter, and without gloss, without gloss, without gloss."[49]

The first genre of prophet texts by Ubertino and Angelo addresses the prophetic role of Francis and his brothers in the eschatology of salvation history. And the second genre of prophetic texts, the *Mirror* texts, addresses the interpretation and implementation of the *Rule* as a prophetic text. These four prophetic texts form the heart of volume three, but the other texts, for example *The Deeds of*

---

47. See Rita Mary Bradley, "Background of the Title *Speculum* in Medieval Literature," *Speculum* 29 (1954): 100–15, and Margot Schmidt, "Miroir" in *Dictionnaire de Spiritualité Ascétique et Mystique: Doctrine et Histoire* 10 (Paris: Beauchesne, 1980), 1290-1303; also see the essay by Daniel Michaels, "*Speculum*: Form and Function in the *Mirror of Perfection*" in this collection of essays.
48. FA:ED III, 208.
49. 2MP intro. (III, 254).

Blessed Francis and His Companions and its reworked and translated form *The Little Flowers*, share in the same prophetic spirit. This can be demonstrated by the manner in which the editor/translator of *The Little Flowers* rearranges the material of *The Deeds* to form four of the five *Considerations of the Holy Stigmata*. The stigmata becomes prophetic because "through these the height of Francis's teachings can shine forth."[50] Even the final text, *The Kinship of Saint Francis*, although it begins what is later to become the fifteenth century tradition of a new literary form of "conformities," still connects to the fourteenth century tradition of Ubertino and Angelo when it states that "in the sixth age, almost on the sixth day, came a human being, Francis, made in God's image and likeness."[51]

B. Restoring and Completing God's Kingdom: Interpreting Francis as Prophet

As just mentioned, the third volume takes on a double prophetic thrust. The first hints at the final *status* of history, which is in turn echoed in the second thrust, the *status* of the individual soul. The first, through Ubertino's *Tree of the Crucified Life* and Angelo's *Tribulations*, emphasizes the prophetic role of Francis and his brothers in the eschatology of salvation history moving toward the final *status* of history. The second, through the two *Mirror* texts, addresses the interpretation and implementation of the *Rule* as a prophetic text showing the brothers the way to purify their own personal lives and move toward the *status* of gospel perfection. The first focuses on the example of Francis's poverty as the way of the future while the second focuses on the text of the *Rule* as the way of perfection.

Underlying these two prophetic dimensions the reader finds a new notion introduced into the literary tradition of the third volume. This new notion, not found in the first two volumes, is "the intention" (*intentio*) of Francis. It first appears in the *Collection of Sayings* and appears again in the Lemmens's edition of *The Mirror* and in Angelo's *Tribulations*. It also appears in *The Deeds* and finally

---

50. *The Divine Office of the Feast of the Stigmata* (III, 669).
51. KnSF intro. (III, 679).

in the last text, *The Kinship*.[52] With this concept that attempts to identify the intention behind Francis's life and the *Rule*, the authors introduce a new abstraction that begins a new type of speculation and thereby a new interpretation. The *"intentio"* provides a new conceptual and hermeneutical base to develop and sustain the apocalyptical, eschatological, and ascetical notions that emerge in volume three. This development actually goes so far as to identify the "intention" of Francis with the "will of Christ."[53] Unlike earlier texts that are more open and free flowing, these fourteenth century texts exude an absolutist tendency.

Along with the new abstract concept of "intention" other new abstract notions also appear. For example, the texts of the third volume likewise introduce the notions of "perfection" and "observance." These rather static terms do not capture the creativity and dynamic found in the earlier texts, rather, the two texts of Ubertino, Angelo and the two *Mirror* texts are replete with these new notions of perfection.[54] For example in Angelo's *The Tribulations* the emphasis on the intention of Francis in writing certain passages of the *Rule* is described thus: "In order to preserve purely and completely the perfection of the highest evangelical poverty revealed to him by Christ, Francis,...strictly orders:..."[55] Intention is about perfection. Thus, in the Sabatier *Mirror* text the focus is on the "perfection of every virtue"[56] and the "the purity of perfection, that is, how all the brothers fervently and zealously observed holy poverty in all things."[57]

The notion of "perfection" flows into an expanded notion of "observance." Although the notion of observance is not in Francis's writings, nor in the earliest lives found in volume one, *The Legend of the Three Companions* and *The Assisi Compilation* in volume two introduce the notion. Both texts do so in terms of the gospel, i.e. "obser-

---

52. See FA:ED III, 214, 409, 451, 709, 713-14; also see 255 and 262 where this term also appears in the Sabatier *Mirror* text, but only in editorial subtitles.
53. 1MP (III, 214).
54. The notion of perfection does occur sporadically in FA:ED II. For example 2C 26 (II, 263) refers to Francis as "the holiest mirror of the holiness of the Lord, the image of his perfection." In no place in the earlier volumes, however, does it state that the brothers are to live in perfection.
55. HTrb 149 (III, 386).
56. 2MP 113 (III, 362).
57. 2MP 71 (III, 316).

vance of the gospel."[58] However, in volume three this notion is expanded and identified in the following manner: "observance of the gospel and the *Rule* and the *Testament* of the blessed father."[59] Observance of the gospel becomes linked to observance of the *Rule* and *Testament*, raising thereby the *Rule* and *Testament* to a new hermeneutical level. The *Testament*, in particular, offers Francis's intention as the highest spiritual insight. It "embodies the *spiritualis intelligencia* and stands on a par with the scriptures."[60] In this expansion of the notion of observance, the followers of Francis begin to be identified as his "imitators," again the introduction of a new notion to explain relationship to Francis. In volume three the true disciples of the saint are no longer "followers" but rather "imitators" acting on an intention, an intention that is directed toward the perfection of observance.

"Oh, what a true prophet Francis was!"[61] This exclamation of Ubertino in the third chapter of *The Tree of the Crucified Life* captures the general presentation of the Francis in volume three. He is presented as a prophet condemning the corruption of the life in the church and in the brotherhood. What is important about a prophet is inner disposition and clarity of insight. Therefore the prophet's intention is most important. In view of understanding Francis as a prophet who addresses the evils of the day (in this case the day of the fourteenth century), his intention is for the perfection of life that overcomes all corruption. This perfection that overcomes evil is found in the observance of the gospel, but more immediately and concretely in the *Rule* and the *Testament*. Francis, assuming almost a "cosmic role of Christ Himself to wage war on the Anti-Christ,"[62] announces this perfection and clarifies it, especially in his intentions that can be applied in multiple circumstances. His perfection is thus to be imitated, and this is what observance is all about. In all of this, Francis is no longer presented as an example of conversion. In fact in volume three there is no mention of conversion. Francis is already converted and perfected. Thus the life of the brothers is only about achieved perfection or perfection that is to be achieved.

58. L3C 45 (II, 95), AC 102 (II, 206).
59. TL 423a35 (III, 152).
60. See Reeves, *Prophecy*, 186.
61. TL 424b1 (III, 156).
62. Reeves, *Prophecy*, 198.

The ample conversion narratives of the earlier literary tradition found in the first two volumes are simply dropped, and so the emphatic and one-sided presentation of Francis as a prophetic eschatological figure addressing the evils of corruption is a new perspective. The result of this is that Francis is abstracted into new theological and ascetical categories that give a much different reading of the earlier tradition, albeit, for the much different times and troubles of the fourteenth century.

Conclusion: Three Contexts, Three Interpretations

In the first volume, *The Saint*, Thomas of Celano's *The Life of Saint Francis* is the predominant text that impacts the other two lives found in that volume. Together they speak of Francis as a canonized saint. That is why Thomas wrote his text and this determined his approach. Gregory's reform and renewal concerns become his concerns as he writes about Francis. The positive result is found in his emphasis on Francis's mission for the renewal of the life of the church through a new way of gospel living and through a dynamic preaching of the gospel. That is one of the reasons Gregory canonized Francis so soon after his death. A negative aspect could well be the almost super-human image Thomas presents of Francis, especially in the conversion narrative where he incorporates much of the earlier hagiographical tradition. All in all, the texts of volume one celebrate a saint who offers new life, hope and promise for the whole assembly of Christian believers.

In the second volume, *The Founder,* the texts of Thomas along with Bonaventure tend toward center stage. Thomas in *The Remembrance* occupies a central place insofar as he draws from the two earlier texts of *The Three Companions* and *The Assisi Compilation*. Here, at the request of the brothers, he incorporates in a new fashion the memory of the brothers about the early brothers and about the one who inspired their life and *Rule.* Twenty years later Bonaventure receives the same charge to write a life that incorporates all of the previous written memories into one text. Thomas incorporates earlier memories in view of the virtues they exemplify and Bonaventure synthesizes them all within his theological-christological framework. All this is requested *by* the brothers for the sake *of* the brothers as they seek to understand and apply the way of life they inherited from Francis. The focal point of volume two is the way of gospel life, particularly as it is articulated in the *Rule*. In one sense the texts of the second volume are about the canonization of a memory insofar as it identifies a new way of life in the church. The positive is that these texts provide refreshingly new and diverse stories about Francis. In these texts he is not raised on high but discovered in the multiple and inconsistent characteristics of his humanity as experienced by those who were with him. The framework of the virtues offered in *The Remembrance*, and the theological interpretation presented by Bonaventure, provide different perspectives for integrating those diverse memories into a unified pattern that allows for interpretation and application of those memories toward a way of life. In this manner the brothers are provided tools to connect and reconnect with their founder. The negative side of this approach is the tension that evolves between the individual and somewhat domestic memories of the founder and the more unified attempts at the integration thereof. All in all, the texts of volume two provide a rich treasury of diverse memories of the brothers articulated in such a manner that are to apply concretely to the lives of those who have embraced his way of life.

In the third volume, *The Prophet*, a new and different age has dawned. The apocalyptical schema of Joachim of Fiore has entered into the thinking of some brothers who are behind the texts found in this volume. The reference point for their reading of the first century of texts dramatically changes and becomes decidedly eschatological. Ubertino of Casale's *Tree of the Crucified Life* and Angelo of Clareno's *The Tribulations* as well as the two *Mirror* texts are ultimately all about dealing with preparation for the end of time. These texts are not about celebrating newness of life and mission in the church, as in volume one, nor are they about remembering the events in the life of Francis, as in volume two. They are more about preparation for the end of life, that is, for the final *status*. Francis, as the prophetic angel of the sixth seal, has already achieved that final *status* and he provides the example that all might achieve that final *status* of history. What is therefore important about him is not his conversion and development, nor his many human experiences. It is his final intention that is important because his final intention touches the final age the authors depict. This is primarily about the observance of perfection that is proper for the final age. Francis shows the way to embrace the end of life in a life-giving way, the way of Christ Crucified. All in all, the texts of volume three provide an example of how the earlier texts can be interpreted and applied to meet new and demanding times. In the tragedy and confusion of the fourteenth century, when many believed the end was near, the focus on Christ Crucified, as both the point of departure and the final goal of all Christian life, captured and applied the significance of Francis's stigmata as the primary seal marking those who followed him. The positive of these texts is that they sort through the earlier tradition and put in relief an important interior principle upon which Francis's life and mission was based. The negative aspect of the texts is that they are very selective in their use of the earlier tradition. Their emphasis on Francis's "intention" and the final *status* can be very static, even absolutist, missing the dynamic and development of conversion that imbue most of the earlier texts of volumes one and two.

The subtitles of *Saint*, *Founder*, and *Prophet* for the three volumes are not intended to identify each and every text in each of the volumes, but they are intended to assist readers to sense the general spirit and approach found in each of the volumes. The editors believed the three catchwords could give some indication of why and how the principal texts in the three volumes were written. Some might debate this, but what is important in all of this is to note that the Francis who we receive in each of the more than thirty different texts, is a Francis refracted thirty different ways and colored with numerous interpretations spanning many contexts. This fact alone proclaims Francis very significant for Christians living in past, present and future contexts.

Clare of Assisi: Hidden Behind Which Image of Francis?

Ingrid Peterson

The titles of the three volumes, *Francis of Assisi: Early Documents*, designate three images of Francis as he was portrayed in the first 150 years after his death. Initially, Francis was presented as *The Saint*, a model of holiness for the entire world. *The Founder* demonstrates how Francis and his primitive fraternity presented examples of the gospel way of life for his late followers. *The Prophet* illustrates how Francis's life and teaching provide a new way of holiness for a church in need of reform. The presentation of the role of Clare and the Poor Ladies of San Damiano changes behind these shifting portraits of Francis of Assisi.

As *Francis of Assisi: Early Documents* reveals the issues surrounding Francis in following Jesus by being "simple and subject"[1] to all, so does *Clare of Assisi: Early Documents* demonstrate Clare's desire, along with her sisters, to "embrace the poor Christ"[2] and his poor mother. *Clare of Assisi: Early Documents* provides the raw historical and hagiographic materials for studying the origins of the Order of Saint Clare in the same way that *Francis of Assisi: Early Documents* provides primary sources tracing the conversion of Francis and the development of the Order of Friars Minor. Consequently, while *Francis of Assisi: Early Documents* present stories about Francis that portray him as saint, founder and prophet, they also provide, even though omitting a great deal of information about Clare found else-

---

1. Test 19 (I, 125).
2. 2LAg 18.

where, valuable nuggets that are essential in showing how Clare too may be imaged as saint, founder, and prophet. Together these two collections of primary sources help complete an understanding of how Clare and Francis drew both women and men to new ways of following in the footprints of Jesus.

"The Writings of Francis of Assisi" include Francis's *Later Rule* (1223), which became a foundational document for what has come to be known as the Order of Saint Clare and the Third Order of Brothers and Sisters. However, Francis wrote three documents specifically for Clare and the Poor Ladies: *The Form of Life Given by Francis to Clare and Her Sisters* (1212–1213), *The Canticle of Exhortation for the Ladies of San Damiano* (1225), and *The Last Will Written for Clare and the Poor Ladies* (1226). The first volume, *The Saint*, includes *The Canticle of Exhortation for the Ladies of San Damiano*,[3] and the other two documents written for Clare are found in *Clare of Assisi: Early Documents*.[4]

Episodes in the legends and other primary sources of *Francis of Assisi: Early Documents* concerning Francis and the Poor Ladies appear in key events where their lives intersect. The three volumes include incidents about Clare revolving around: 1) Francis's prophecy, rebuilding and foundation of San Damiano; 2) Francis's death and burial; and 3) occasional mention of events involving the relationship of Clare and the Poor Ladies to Francis and the primitive fraternity. Discussions of each of these general three subjects will follow the chronology of the texts that consider them. The diverse texts mentioning Clare and the Poor Ladies will be discussed to illustrate how the images of Clare appear in the early sources. While Clare cannot be overlooked in reporting the history of Francis, the reasons given to introduce her into Francis's story vary greatly. Thus the question is: which images of Francis is Clare of Assisi hidden behind throughout *Francis of Assisi: Early Documents*?

3. FA:ED I, 115.
4. Regis J. Armstrong, *Clare of Assisi: Early Documents*, rev. (Saint Bonaventure, NY: Franciscan Institute, 1993).

I. Francis's Prophecy, Rebuilding, and Foundation of San Damiano

Four of the early biographies of Francis introduce Clare in the context of his prophecy about the Poor Ladies, the rebuilding of San Damiano, and the order for enclosed women that was founded there. These primary sources include the *Life of Saint Francis* by Thomas of Celano (1228), *The Life of Saint Francis* by Julian of Speyer (1232–35), *The Legend of the Three Companions* (1241–1247) and *The Remembrance of the Desire of a Soul* by Thomas of Celano (1245–1247).

1) The Life of Saint Francis by Thomas of Celano

Thomas of Celano begins his *Life of Saint Francis* with a series of stories about Francis's conversion. Thomas interrupts his narration about how Francis repairs the church of San Damiano by inserting an extensive eulogy about Clare and her virtues as well as the virtues of the Poor Ladies who came to live at San Damiano. Establishing a new religious foundation for women and the holiness of the lives of its members are presented by Thomas as testimony of how Francis renewed the church. The Poor Ladies are established there "through" the instrumentality of Francis. Since Thomas's point is that Francis renewed the church, the sanctity of Clare and the Poor Ladies and their recently acquired ecclesastical status is concrete evidence of how Francis restored the ancient church.

Thomas illustrates how the first work Francis undertook as a builder of the church was the repair of San Damiano. He devotes one sentence to San Damiano as a place:

> This is the blessed and holy place where
> the glorious religion and most excellent Order
> of Poor Ladies and holy virgins
> had its happy beginning,
> about six years after the conversion of the blessed Francis
> and through that same blessed man.[5]

---

5. 1C 18 (I, 197). All translations are taken from *Francis of Assisi: Early Documents*, vols. I–III, edited by Regis J. Armstrong, J. A. Wayne Hellmann, and William J. Short (New York: New City Press, 1999, 2000, 2001).

Jacques Dalarun points to the importance of the information in Thomas's statement, "about six years after the conversion of blessed Francis." If Francis's conversion is established as 1206, then Clare's foundation at San Damiano took place in 1212.[6]

Next Thomas introduces Clare as a saint, proclaiming her holiness in an embellished tribute:

> The Lady Clare
> a native of the city of Assisi,
> the most precious and strongest stone of the whole structure,
> stands as the foundation of all the other stones.
> For
> after the beginning of the Order of Brothers,
> when this lady was converted to God
> through the counsel of the holy man,
> she lived for the good of many
> and as an example to countless others.
> Noble by lineage, but more noble by grace,
> chaste in body, most chaste in mind,
> young in mind, mature in spirit,
> steadfast in purpose and most eager in her desire for divine love,
> endowed with wisdom and excelling in humility,
> bright in name, more brilliant in life,
> most brilliant in character.[7]

Thomas, in telling of Francis's return to San Damiano at the time of his burial, enlarges on this image of Clare as the foundational stone and speaks of the foundation itself as a work of living stones. Thomas reiterates the sequence of events, so frequently repeated by Clare: first Francis began an Order of Brothers, and then she was converted through him to that same Order which in 1209 received ecclesial approbation. In Thomas's version, Clare is Francis's "most precious and strongest stone." Having intimately identified Clare with Francis, the founder, Thomas proceeds to describe her as saint, using standard hagiographical references to Clare's nobility, purity,

---

6. Jacques Dalarun, *The Misadventure of Francis of Assisi: Towards a Historical Use of the Franciscan Legends*, translated by Edward Hagman (Saint Bonaventure, NY: Franciscan Institute, 2002), 76.
7. 1C 18 (I, 197).

desire for God, fidelity, wisdom, humility, and the brilliance of her example.

At this point Thomas shifts his attention from Clare to the Order of San Damian, the new order established by Pope Gregory IX in 1228, the year of Thomas's composition. As the Poor Ladies former protector, Gregory IX was well aware of the growing numbers of women's groups living as religious communities, their difficulties and their danger of being taken into heretical groups. Consequently, he established an Order inscribing all of them, including Clare and the Poor Ladies, under the 1228 Rule of Gregory IX, naming his new project the Order of San Damian.[8] Thomas eulogizes the merits of Gregory's effort, the pope who commissioned the *Life of Saint Francis*, by beginning with the classical modesty topos in which the author proclaims his inability to do justice to the dignity of the subject. Thomas begins:

> A noble structure of precious pearls rose above this woman,
>   whose praise comes not from mortals but from God,
> since our limited understanding is not sufficient to imagine it,
>   nor our scanty vocabulary to utter it.[9]

Since Thomas is writing in 1228, Dalarun claims he "automatically thinks of the nuns who were living there when he was writing." Thomas names seven virtues that characterize the new Order of San Damian: charity, humility, virginity, abstinence, silence, patience, and contemplation. After specifying that forty or fifty of them lived in one place, the remainder of the narrative refers to them in the plural and characterizes how they lived as a community.

Thomas concludes his laudatory digressions with the reminder that he was appointed to write about Francis and the early brothers, not Clare and the Poor Ladies or the Order of San Damian:

> For the moment
> let this suffice
> concerning these virgins dedicated to God

---

8. See the two articles dealing with the Order of Saint Damian: Beth Lynn, "What Difference Does a Rule Make? Clare's 'Poor Sisters' and Gregory IX's Nuns," *Magistra* 5.1 (1999): 25–42, and Maria Pia Alberzoni, "San Damiano in 1228: A Contribution to the 'Clare Question,'" *Greyfriars Review* 13.1 (1999): 105–23.

9. 1C 19 (I, 197).

and the most devout servants of Christ.
Their wondrous life
and their renowned practices received from the Lord Pope
Gregory,
at that time Bishop of Ostia
would require another book
and the leisure in which to write it.[10]

Thomas reiterates that Pope Gregory IX is the founder and lawgiver of "these virgins dedicated to God." Here Clare and the Poor Ladies are encompassed in the overarching image of the Order of San Damian, Pope Gregory's nuns.

Giovanni Miccoli credits Thomas's diplomacy as his reason for inserting such a long section on the Poor Ladies early in his story of Francis.[11] While Clare and her sisters could not be omitted in a biography of Francis, the relationship between the brothers and sisters at the time of Thomas's writing was dramatically different than the relationship beginning with Francis and Clare and their first followers. As the fraternity expanded instead of a genial and frequent association, many of the early wandering brothers did not want to be tied down to Assisi and Clare as promised by Francis. Furthermore, Hugolino's 1218–19 Rule for Clare and Francis's 1223 Rule restricted much of their close contact. Thomas avoids dealing with these later bitter developments by crediting Francis with Clare's conversion and indirectly with the foundation of the Poor Ladies at San Damiano. Rather than bring the story up to date, Thomas describes the good days of their early relationship, associating the material repair of San Damiano with the spiritual reconstruction of the church.

2) The Life of Saint Francis by Julian of Speyer

For Julian of Speyer, as for Thomas of Celano, Francis is associated with Clare through the commonality of San Damiano and the virtue of the Poor Ladies. Julian, writing four to seven years after

---

10. 1C 20 (I, 199).
11. Giovanni Miccoli, "Postfazione," in Jacques Dalarun, *Francesco: un passaggio* (Rome: Viella, 1994), 195–97; also see Dalarun, *Misadventure*, 83–84.

Thomas, refers to the Poor Ladies but does not name Clare in his account of the rebuilding of San Damiano. Julian overlooks the personal sanctity of Clare in favor of that of the Poor Ladies. He condenses Thomas's list of the virtues of the Poor Ladies by acknowledging that they were "of considerable perfection."[12]

Clare, the foundation of the Poor Ladies, and the widespread reputation of their holiness are presented by both Julian and Thomas as proof of Francis as saint. The holiness of the Poor Ladies is one of the fruits for which Francis's sanctity is celebrated. For Julian, Clare is never in the foreground. Dalarun notes that all Julian adds to Thomas's account is to say that the movement of women followers had spread throughout Italy, a confirmation of the list of twenty-four monasteries mentioned by Cardinal Rinaldo in 1228.[13]

3) The Legend of the Three Companions

In giving their version of the rebuilding of San Damiano, the three companions add the incident in which Francis prophesies that the church will be a place where God will be glorified. The companions introduce their account by telling how Francis went through Assisi begging for oil for the lamps in the church of San Damiano. Overcoming his shame to beg, Francis broke into a group of party-goers where he "for the love of God, begged in French for oil for the lamps of that church."[14] Their text paraphrases Thomas's statement of the importance of San Damiano as the place where the foundation of Poor Ladies began, but adds Francis's prophetic words:

> "Come and help me in the work of the church of San Damiano which, in the future, will be a monastery of ladies through whose fame and life our heavenly Father will be glorified throughout the church."[15]

---

12. LJS 13 (I, 378).
13. Dalarun, *Misadventure*, 77.
14. L3C 24 (II, 83).
15. L3C 24 (II, 83). Dalarun, *Misadventure*, 79–80 refers to the suggestion of Pio Rajna that Francis's prophecy corresponds to four verses in French:
    Come and help me in the work of the church of San Damiano (*Damien*)
    Which, in the future, will be a monastery of ladies (*dames*)
    Through whose fame and life throughout the church (*fame*)

Clare's *Testament* (1253), like *The Legend of the Three Companions*, includes the exact words of Francis's prophecy. Bartoli suggests that the three companions and those who contributed remembrances to Thomas's second life may have received their recollections from Clare.[16] Dalarun holds that because the first mention of a prophecy occurs between 1241 and 1247, it cannot be argued that Francis thought of a community of women before he created a fraternity.

Relying on Miccoli's commentary, Dalarun argues that while the three companions had no document to prove Francis's vision of an early form of life for women, they knew from their initial experience of fraternity that women were included.[17] Accordingly, the early companions give credence to an early movement of men and women by relating the story of Francis's prophecy. Dalarun refers to the evidence that shows the close relationship between Clare and Francis's first companions, including Leo, Philip, Juniper, Angelo, and Elias. He argues that these are the authorities that must be trusted for an accurate portrait of their relationship, not the second and third generation of authors, such as Thomas of Pavia who condemns Philip, or Ubertino of Casale who condemns Elias.[18]

The three companions point out that Francis is a prophet foretelling what has come to fruition through the sanctity of the Poor Ladies of San Damiamo: "See how, filled with the spirit of prophecy, he truly foretold the future!"[19] Clare is not mentioned by the three companions, and the Poor Ladies are mentioned as the subjects of Francis, the prophet. The three companions note how Francis was instrumental in the conversion of the Poor Ladies, Gregory IX, in approving their way of life, and the papacy in confirming Gregory's work while serving as Cardinal protector. The incident has little direct bearing on Clare's image, except to foreshadow her sanctity and that of the Poor Ladies of San Damiano.

---

16. Dalarun, *Misadventure*, 85.
17. Dalarun, *Misadventure*, 85.
18. Dalarun, *Misadventure*, 85–86.
19. L3C 24 (II, 83).

4) The Remembrance of the Desire of a Soul by Thomas of Celano

Toward the beginning of *The Remembrance of the Desire of a Soul*, Thomas includes a section explaining how Francis overcame his feelings of shame. Thomas illustrates his point by telling the story of Francis's prophecy about the Poor Ladies. Thomas's new account differs from his version of the repair of San Damiano in *The Life of Francis* by mentioning the oil lamps and Francis's shame in begging. Whereas the companions presented the words of Francis, Thomas adds details of the incident:

> One day the man of God was going through Assisi begging oil to fill the lamps in the church of San Damiano, which he was then rebuilding. He saw a crowd carousing by the house he intended to enter. Turning bright red, he backed away. But then, turning his noble spirt toward heaven, he rebuked his cowardice and called himself to account. He went back immediately to the house, and frankly explained to all of them what had made him ashamed. Then, as if drunk in the Spirit, he spoke in French, and asked for oil, and he got it. He fervently encouraged everyone to help repair that church, and in front of everyone he cried out in French that some day that place would be a monastery of Christ's holy virgins.[20]

Thomas gives his rendition a more prophetic tone than the companions, by crediting Francis's use of French to the fire of the Holy Spirit, explaining:

> Whenever he was
> filled with the fire of the Holy Spirit
> he would speak in French,
> bursting out in fiery words,
> for he could foresee
> that he would be honored
> with special reverence by that people.[21]

---

20. 2C 13 (II, 252).
21. 2C 13 (II, 252).

Toward the end of the *Remembrance*, Thomas again emphasizes the role of the Holy Spirit in strengthening the Poor Ladies as models of holiness for the brothers who follow the way of poverty and for the entire church. However, Thomas's second life of Francis transfers the focus from Francis as founder to the Holy Spirit as the primary agent in drawing persons to committed lives in God:

> It would not be right to pass over in silence
> the memory of a spiritual building,
> much nobler than that earthly one,
> that the blessed father established in that place
> with the Holy Spirit leading
> for the increase of the heavenly city,
> after he had repaired the material church.[22]

Later in the legend, Thomas adapts his image of Clare as the strongest stone of San Damiano to include the Poor Ladies as "a polished collection of living stones." Again, Thomas notes the prophetic element associated with the Poor Ladies because of Francis's prophecy:

> But, as earlier foretold by the Holy Spirit
> an Order of holy virgins was to be established there
> to be brought one day
> as a polished collection of living stones
> for the restoration of the heavenly house.[23]

Thomas concludes the *Remembrance* by reporting how Francis promised his fidelity and that of his followers to the Poor Ladies, "saying that one and the same Spirit had led the brothers and those Poor Ladies out of this world."[24]

Although more than thirty years pass between Thomas's first and second life of Francis, Clare remains in the role of saint and founder. At the time of the 1228 *Life of Saint Francis*, Clare and the Poor Ladies had only lived at San Damiano for about fifteen years. By the time of Thomas's second life in 1247, they were well established and their reputation highly respected. Thomas may have been

---

22. 2C 204 (II, 377–78).
23. 2C 204 (II, 378).
24. 2C 204 (II, 379).

urged to include the story by those who contributed recollections for his second life, or he may have felt greater confidence in proclaiming their greatness in the church since, in fact, they had fulfilled Francis's prophetic statement. For whatever reason, Thomas associates Clare with a prophetic image in the *Remembrance* while reinforcing her portrait as saint and founder.

II. The Exhortation to Clare and the Burial of Francis

The greatest number of texts linking Clare and Francis through a single incident concern Clare's desire to see Francis before his death, his response to her wish, and the scene at San Damiano at the time of his burial. Seven separate accounts treating aspects of Francis's forthcoming death and burial involve Clare. These sources are found in the *Life of Saint Francis* by Thomas of Celano (1228), *The Life of Saint Francis* by Julian of Speyer (1232–35), *The Assisi Compilation* (1244–1260), *The Remembrance of the Desire of a Soul* by Thomas of Celano (1245–1247), *The Major Legend of Saint Francis* by Bonaventure of Bagnoregio (1260–1263), *The Mirror of Perfection* (1318, Lemmens edition), and *The Mirror of Perfection* (1318, Sabatier edition).

1) Life of Saint Francis by Thomas of Celano

The only sections in *The Life of Saint Francis* by Thomas of Celano that treat Clare and the Poor Ladies concern the repair of San Damiano and Francis's death at the Portiuncula. After depicting a series of incidents preceding Francis's death, Thomas tells of the crowds who come to mourn Francis and accompany the funeral cortege from its beginnings at the Portiuncula, through its stopover at the monastery of San Damiano, and on to its final resting place in San Giorgio. He shows the Poor Ladies in mourning and includes some of their outcries of grief.

Thomas creates a family scene with Francis coming home to San Damiano, Clare, and the Poor Ladies. He employs warm and pastoral language alluding to the biblical imagery of the shepherd and his flock. Francis is like a father lovingly laid to rest by his sons in the intimacy of his family. Francis seems to belong to the Poor Ladies and they to him as the window of the grille is open, and the coffin is open so Clare and her sisters have access to Francis's body, touching his body and the wounds of his stigmata:

> With the sons carrying their father and the flock following the shepherd who was hastening to the Shepherd of them all, he arrived at the place where he first planted the religion and the Order of the consecrated virgins and Poor Ladies. They laid him out in the church of San Damiano, home to those daughters he gained for the Lord. The small window was opened, the one used by these servants of Christ at the appointed time to receive the sacrament of the Lord's body. The coffin was also opened: in it lay hidden the treasure of supercelestial powers; in it he who had carried many was now carried by a few.[25]

While Francis is imaged as the "planter" of the Order of Poor Ladies, Thomas's focus remains on Francis and his stigmata. The work of Francis, the founder, is completed. Then Thomas reintroduces Clare, briefly recalling her holiness which he had expounded upon in such detail earlier in his *Life of Francis*. Great attention is given to their grief, for the Poor Ladies seem to all but wash Francis body with their tears. Before Francis was taken away "they kissed his most splendid hands" in a gesture of anointing.

2) The Life of Francis by Julian of Speyer

Julian of Speyer shortens Thomas's account of Francis's death, stating that his body is taken to San Damiano where the Poor Ladies grieve with "the first seedling of that Order, 'Clare' in fact and in name." [26] One by one, they kiss Francis's hands as a sign of farewell. Julian adds one statement singling out the unique place of Clare in the story of Francis: "For her, among all mortals, the solace of which she was deprived was so certainly irreplaceable." While

---

25. 1C 116 (I, 285).
26. LJS 72 (I, 417).

Julian adds nothing new to the image of Clare, he acknowledges that the loss of Francis is greater for her than anyone.

3) The Assisi Compilation (1244–1260)

Gathered during Clare's life and after her death, *The Assisi Compilation* reports two accounts of the song that Francis composed for Clare as his death neared. Francis "composed some holy words with chant for the greater consolation of the Poor Ladies of the Monastery of San Damiano. He did this especially because he knew how much his illness troubled them."[27] The text states that because the Poor Ladies were converted through Francis's example and preaching, he wanted to proclaim these words instructing them that now and always they should be of one mind and live in charity. Because Francis knew they were freely living a strict and poor life, "his spirit was always moved to piety for them."

The *Assisi Compilation* concludes with a paraphrase of *The Canticle of Exhortation*:

> With these words, then, he begged them that, as the Lord had gathered them as one from many different regions in holy charity, holy poverty, and holy obedience, so in these they should live and die. And he begged them particularly to provide for their bodies with discernment from the alms which the Lord would give them, with cheerfulness and thanksgiving. And he especially asked them to remain patient: the healthy, in the labors which they endure for their sick sisters; and the sick in their illnesses and the needs they suffer.[28]

The text reads like a last will in which Francis instructs the Poor Ladies urging both the sick and the healthy to persevere in their religious commitment. The canonical vows of poverty, chastity and obedience have not previously been mentioned as part of Francis's legacy to Clare or her sisters. The compiler expounds about the importance of the Poor Ladies to the brothers and to the church:

---

27. AC 85 (II, 188).
28. AC 85 (II, 189); for *The Canticle of Exhortation* see FA:ED I, 115.

"Their conversion and manner of living is the glory and edification not only of the religion of the brothers, whose little plant they are, but also of the entire church of God." While the passage never mentions the name of Clare, but only the Poor Ladies in general, it demonstrates high regard for them by Francis, the brothers, and the entire church.

Another version of the incident in *The Assisi Compilation* gives specific attention to Clare and captures how fear of her own death sparks her longing to see Francis. It illustrates the tender, human aspects of their relationship, their awareness of their limitations, as well as their genuine concern for the emotional needs of one another. It is a portrait of mutual affection and compassion while specifying that this is the work of God in them:

> [Clare] feared that she would die before blessed Francis. She wept in bitterness of spirit and could not be comforted, because she would not be able before her death to see her only father after God, that is, blessed Francis, her comforter both internally and externally, and her first founder in God's grace.
>
> She sent word of this to blessed Francis through one of the brothers. Blessed Francis heard this and was moved to piety, since he loved her and her sisters with fatherly affection because of their holy manner of living, and especially because, a few years after he began to have brothers, she was converted to the Lord through his advice, working with the Lord . . . To console her, he wrote his blessing in a letter and also absolved her from any failings, if she had any, regarding his commands and wishes or the commands and wishes of the Son of God. Moreover, so that she would put aside all her grief and be consoled in the Lord, he, or rather, the Spirit of God speaking through him, spoke to the brother she had sent. 'Go and take this letter to Lady Clare, and tell her to put aside all her grief and sorrow over not being able to see me now. Let her be assured that before her death, both she and her sisters will see me and receive the greatest consolation from me.'[29]

---

29. AC 13 (II, 128-29).

The account relates how Francis's promise is fulfilled after his death and how Clare and the Poor Ladies are consoled when his body is brought to San Damiano:

> The iron grille was removed from the window through which the servants of Christ usually receive communion and sometimes hear the word of God. The brothers lifted his holy body from the stretcher and, raising him, in their arms, they held him in front of the window for over an hour. By then the Lady Clare and her sisters had received the greatest consolation from him, although they wept profusely and were afflicted with great grief, because, after God, he was their one consolation in this world.[30]

This rendering physically separates Francis from Clare and the Poor Ladies by a wall, so that they only have a peek at Francis, and this through the benevolence of the brothers who hold him with raised arms for more than an hour. The scene is painted with cold, disquieting images, using terms like "iron grille" and "stretcher." There is no sense of an intimate relationship between Francis and the Poor Ladies. In fact, appeasing their desire to see Francis for a last time appears to be a great burden to the brothers, who stand stiff-armed while the Poor Ladies weep inside. It is two different worlds, perhaps reflective of the historical reality during which it was composed: one of brothers and one of sisters. The sisters are shown as a burden to the brothers, as indeed they were perceived by the time of its composition when ministering to them conflicted with their lives as mendicant preachers.

The Assisi Compilation portrays the enclosure of Clare according to the church's later rigid agenda for women and cloister. *The Form of Life* given to Clare by Hugolino in 1218–19, its renewal by Gregory IX in 1228 and Innocent IV in 1247, all contain juridical regulation for enclosure that are circumvented in 1253 by Clare's *Form of Life*. Nonetheless, Francis continues to communicate with his body after his death through the small window they used to receive the Eucharist.

---

30. AC 13 (II, 129).

Despite this treatment of how Clare and the Poor Ladies mourned Francis, *The Assisi Compilation* presents an image of Clare's holiness and her perseverance in following the poverty of Jesus in the way of Francis. Not at all hidden behind Francis and the brothers, Clare and the Poor Ladies are shown to be examples of community life for the brothers and for the church. Thomas's *The Remembrance of the Desire of a Soul* places the story of Clare's role in Francis's death and burial as illustrations of the significance of Francis's example. Accordingly, those passages and their discussion will be placed below in Part III.

4) The Major Legend of Saint Francis by Bonaventure of Bagnoregio

Bonaventure devotes all of Chapter Thirteen of the *Major Legend* to Francis's stigmata. He verifies the wounds on Francis's hands, feet and sides by reporting that fifty brothers, Clare and her sisters, as well as innumerable lay persons saw them after his death. Bonaventure writes: "Many of them kissed the stigmata out of devotion and touched them with their own hands to strengthen their testimony . . ."[31] Later in Chapter Fifteen on Francis's canonization and the transferral of his body, Bonaventure describes once again the appearance of the stigmata, its newness and miraculous nature. *The Major Legend* ends with Bonaventure's testimony to the authenticity of the stigmata. He points out that, "A great number of the citizens of Assisi were admitted to contemplate those sacred marks with their own eyes and to kiss them with their lips."[32] Clare and the Poor Ladies were among the eyewitnesses to the stigmata:

> As they passed he church of San Damiano, where the noble virgin Clare, now glorious in heaven, was then living enclosed with the virgins, they stopped for a while so that those holy nuns could see and kiss his sacred body, adorned with its heavenly pearls.[33]

---

31. LMj 13.8 (II, 636).
32. LMj 15.4 (II, 646).
33. LMj 15.5 (II, 647).

That Bonaventure refers to Clare and the Poor Ladies as he accumulates evidence to establish the authenticity of the stigmata indicates the breadth and quality of her reputation. Choosing Clare as a witness to verify the new miracle of Francis's stigmata indicates her wide credibility about the mysterious ways of God.

5) The Mirror of Perfection, Lemmens edition

The compiler of the Lemmens fourteenth-century mirror text primarily draws from *The Assisi Compilation*. Accordingly, it describes Clare as "the first plant of the Order of Sisters, the abbess of the Poor Sisters of the monastery of San Damiano in Assisi, who emulated Saint Francis in observing always the poverty of the Son of God."[34] While *The Assisi Compilation* described Clare as "abbess" the phrase "Order of Sisters" had not been previously introduced. The account reports that Clare could not be comforted in her desire to see Francis before one or the other of them would be taken by death. Drawing from the earlier sources, *The Mirror* recalls that Francis, eager to console Clare, sends a letter with his blessing and promises that before her death she will see him and be consoled. Although Francis died that same night, his body was carried "to San Damiano at the Lord's will, in order to fulfill that word which the Lord had spoken through his saint to console his daughters and servants."[35]

This later re-telling in *The Mirror* stresses the prophetic nature of Francis's promise, and points out that it is God who works through Francis to bring consolation to Clare. The first part of the account mentioned that Francis was "her comforter both internally and externally." The section describing how Clare and her sisters, despite their grief, received consolation from seeing the body of Francis, borrows from *The Assisi Compilation* which names Francis as Clare's "only father after God," and "after God, he was their one consolation in this world" re-appears in Clare's *Testament* as "after God, our one consolation and support."

---

34. 1MP 18 (III, 228).
35. 1MP 18 (III, 229).

6) The Mirror of Perfection, Sabatier edition

Chapter Nine in the Sabatier edition of *The Mirror of Perfection* also relates the story of Clare's desire to visit Francis before her death.[36] The compiler of the longer *Mirror* text relies on similar accounts from *The Assisi Compilation* and the shorter edition of the *Mirror*. As noted in examination of the texts involving Francis's prophecy, the rebuilding of San Damiano, and the establishment of the foundation of Poor Ladies, the later texts in *Francis of Assisi: Early Documents* point to Francis in a prophetic role. Mention of Clare draws her into Francis in a prophetic role, although she does not appear as the voice of the prophet, but rather the subject of the prophecy. The incident described here tells of her desire for consolation from Francis, Francis's certitude of its accomplishment, and the fulfillment of the prophecy even after his death. Because prophecy is a work of the Spirit, Clare's participation in the events are further evidence of her extraordinary sanctity.

III. The Relationship between Clare, Francis, and the Sisters and Brothers

Six texts demonstrate various aspects of the relationship between Clare and Francis and his brothers and between Francis and the Poor Ladies. These sources are the mid-thirteenth- and four-teenth-century texts: *The Remembrance of the Desire of a Soul* by Thomas of Celano (1245–1247), *The Major Legend of Saint Francis* by Bonaventure of Bagnoregio (1260–1263), *The Mirror of Perfection* (1318, Lemmens edition), *The Mirror of Perfection* (1318, Sabatier edition), *The Deeds of Blessed Francis and His Companions* by Ugolino Boniscambi of Montegiorgio (1328–1337), and *The Little Flowers of Saint Francis* (after 1337). Although these later texts include various incidents, their historical reliability is more uncertain than the recollections given by eyewitnesses or first generation brothers and sisters of Francis and Clare.

---

36. 2MP 108 (III, 357–58).

1) The Remembrance of the Desire of a Soul by Thomas of Celano

Thomas of Celano's last words on the Poor Ladies in 1245–47 present Francis as an example for his brothers and is entitled "How to have dealings with them."[37] Unlike the praise given Clare and the Poor Ladies at the beginning of the 1228 *Life of Francis*, Thomas is silent about Clare until near the end of his *Remembrance*. Confident that Francis was not directed by God to "repair a crumbling and perishable building" but to restore a heavenly one, Thomas refers to Francis's prophecy that San Damiano would become the place where the Poor Ladies manifest perfection through poverty and virtue. According to the *Remembrance*, having established them Francis maintained his affection for them although he "gradually withdrew his bodily presence from them." Accordingly, Francis promised them perpetual help and advice "saying that one and the same Spirit had led the brothers and those little poor ladies out of this world." Francis explained his actions to his brothers by repeating the words of Jesus at the foot washing on Holy Thursday: "I am giving you an example, that as I do, so should you also do."[38]

Then Thomas illustrates how Francis served as an example at a time, when staying at San Damiano, he was urged to preach to Clare and the Poor Ladies. Acquiescing, he began in a posture of prayer by lifting his eyes to heaven. "Then he had ashes brought and made a circle with them round himself on the floor, and then put the rest on his own head."[39] After a period of silence, instead of a sermon, Francis recited the penitential Psalm Fifty-one and departed. Considering themselves ashes, Clare and the Poor Ladies are moved to contrition, knowing "that nothing else was close to his heart except what was keeping with that view."

Thomas explains the point of Francis's *exemplum* by adding:

> This was his way of behaving with holy women;
> this was his way of visiting them
> rare and constrained but very useful!

37. 2C 204 (II, 377–79).
38. 2C 205 (II, 379).
39. 2C 207 (II, 380).

> This was his will for all the brothers,
> whom he wanted to serve
> for the sake of Christ, whom they serve;
> that they might always, like winged creatures,
> beware of the nets before them.[40]

The story illustrates how Francis instructed Clare and the Poor Ladies about penance. Thomas interprets it as Francis's example of decorum for the brothers. No previous reference had been made in the written texts of the necessity to beware the temptation of women, the Poor Ladies or Clare. Thomas's use of the incident appears to reflect issues in the fraternity during his time.

2) The Major Legend of Saint Francis by Bonaventure

Two stories that appear later report a strong spiritual affinity between Francis and Clare. Chapter Twelve of Bonaventure's *Major Legend* on the effectiveness of Francis's preaching begins by telling how Francis called on Brother Sylvester, who spent all his time in prayer, and Clare to help him decide about "how he could more effectively arrive at the summit of perfection."[41] Francis asked Sylvester and "Clare to consult with the pure and simplest of the virgins living under her rule and to pray herself with the other sisters in order to seek the Lord's will in this matter." Through what Bonaventure describes as a "miraculous revelation of the Spirit, they came to the same conclusion: that it was the divine good will that the herald of Christ should preach." Bonaventure uses the story to illustrate that "Francis was not ashamed to ask advice in small matters from those under him."

3) The Deeds of Blessed Francis and His Companions by Boniscampi of Montigiorgio

The fourteenth-century *Deeds of Blessed Francis* presents another version of this story of Francis's struggle and doubt about God's

---

40. 2C 207 (II, 380).
41. LMj 12.2 (II, 623).

will. Francis's uncertainty is highlighted, rather than his desire for perfection, as framed by Bonaventure. The *Deeds* poses two choices for Francis: "should he spend his time in constant prayer, should he sometimes go out preaching."[42] The story points out that it is because of Francis's humility that he directs Masseo first "to go to Clare, and tell her for me that she, along with one of her spiritual companions should beg God on bended knee to show me whether I should sometimes preach or constantly spend time in prayer." When Masseo goes to Sylvester on Mount Subasio, Sylvester "immediately received an answer from God that Francis should preach. Clare and her companion received a similar answer. Certain of God's will, Francis sets out for Cannara and Bevegna to begin his preaching career before a flock of birds. The incident in *The Deeds* is not used for a didactic purpose as it was by Bonaventure but to illustrate how Francis chose the path of preaching. In both versions, Clare is incidental to the author's central point.

4) The Mirror of Perfection, Sabatier Edition

The longer *Mirror* text includes a poem that is unique to this text and which presents a positive view of Clare as the founding mother of the brothers. In this excerpt, the compiler points out the sacred nature of Saint Mary of the Angels as the place where the Lesser Order was born and where Clare consecrated herself to God:

> The bride of God, Clare,
> here shed her hair,
> the world's pomp refused,
> and her Christ pursued.
>
> Thus a sacred mother
> to ladies and to brothers
> gives forth a brilliant birth
> for whom she brings Christ on earth.[43]

---

42. DBF 16 (III, 468).
43. 2MP 84 (III, 331).

The verses are part of a passage reporting "prerogatives granted by the Lord" that happened at Saint Mary of the Angels. Many previous incidents associate Clare with Francis at San Damiano. However, this is the first time she is named in connection with her conversion at Saint Mary of the Angels. The account concludes by saying this is a sacred place where the truth of God is revealed. The author suggests that Clare is both saint and founding mother of Francis's fraternity.

5) The Deeds of Blessed Francis and his Companions and The Little Flowers

In mid-fourteenth-century, *The Deeds of Blessed Francis and his Companions* and its more literary re-writing, *The Little Flowers of Saint Francis*, bring back *florilegium*, or flowery legends from the oral tradition of Clare and Francis and introduce them into the written tradition. Both the *Deeds* and the *The Little Flowers* present three new stories of Clare. Two of them, the mystical picnic at the Porticuncula, and Clare's vision of the Christmas liturgy, indicate her relationship to Francis. Both of these sources also retold the story of Clare and Sylvester. The other story tells about Pope Gregory's visit to San Damiano and the miracle of Clare's blessing bread.

The account of Clare's visit to the Portiuncula in the *Deeds* begins by saying of Clare that Francis "frequently visited her with his words of sacred encouragement."[44] The story in *The Little Flowers* begins, "While Saint Francis was staying in Assisi he visited Clare many times, giving her holy instruction."[45] Both versions tell of Clare's desire to see Francis, and his reluctance tempered by the advice of his companions, who on the appointed day, accompany Clare and her companion. When Clare arrives she visits the altar of Mary where she received the tonsure and veil, and then tours around the place as Francis and his brothers prepare the table on the bare ground. The writer of *The Little Flowers* portrays Clare and Francis enveloped by their companions:

---

44. DBF 15 (III, 466).
45. LFl 15 (III, 590).

When it was time to eat they sat down together: Saint Clare with Saint Francis; one of the companions of Saint Francis with the companion of Saint Clare; then all the other companions gathered humbly at the table. And as a first course Saint Francis began to speak of God so sweetly, so deeply, and so wonderfully that the abundance of divine grace descended upon them, and all were rapt into God.[46]

The radiance of their conversation draws the people of the surrounding area to Saint Mary of the Angels, for to them, "It seemed that a great fire was consuming the church, the place and the forest together." Although the neighboring folks came intending to put out a fire, they soon realized that it was not material fire "which God made appear miraculously to demonstrate and signify the fire of divine love, burning in the souls of these holy brothers and holy nuns." The townspeople depart "with great consolation in their hearts and with holy edification." Francis and Clare, felt themselves "well comforted by spiritual food." Meanwhile at San Damiano, the Poor Ladies were glad when Clare and her companion returned because they were afraid that Francis might send her to another monastery, as he had directed Clare's sister Agnes to go to Monticello in Florence. The author concludes the story by identifying Clare "as a daughter of holy obedience," confirming that she was willing to go wherever she was sent.

Clare's Christmas eve vision of the liturgy at the Basilica of Saint Francis appears in the *Deeds of Blessed Francis*, Chapter 41,[47] and in Chapter 35 of *The Little Flowers*.[48] While the year is not indicated, Clare is seriously ill "so that she could not go to say the Office in church with the other nuns."[49] Yet Clare through a vision experiences the celebration at the church of Saint Francis. Upon their arrival home, Clare assures the sisters who attended that she was present "for by the intercession of my father Saint Francis and by the grace of our Lord Jesus Christ, with the ears of my body and spirit I heard the whole Office and the music of the organ there in

---

46. LFl 15 (III, 590).
47. DBF 41 (III, 515–16).
48. LFl 35 (III, 626).
49. LFl 35 (III, 626).

that very place I received Holy Communion."[50] The story indicates
how, after Francis's death, he remains with Clare, spiritually
assisting her on earth.

The only place in the primary documents recounting the story of
Clare blessing the bread with Pope Gregory IX are the two accounts
in *The Deeds*[51] and *The Little Flowers*.[52] At the beginning *The Little
Flowers* identifies Clare as "a most devoted disciple of the Cross and
noble plant of Sir Saint Francis." Having anchored Clare's story in
Francis, the author asserts that her extraordinary holiness drew
bishops, cardinals, and even the pope to view her with great affection and to visit her. On one such occasion when the pope went to
the monastery, having finished their conversation, Clare asked him
to remain with them for a meal, and to bless the bread placed on the
table. Instead, the pope asked Clare to bless the bread, but she
deferred claiming her unworthiness. The pope responded,
commanding her "under holy obedience to make the sign of the
most holy Cross over this bread and bless it in the name of God."
When Clare obediently blessed the bread, the sign of the cross
miraculously appeared cut into each loaf. They ate some of the
loaves, but because of the miracle the sisters kept some of the bread
and the Holy Father took some of it with him.

Conclusion

As the historical distance increases, so does the mythological
nature of the stories about both Francis and Clare. Both the incidents of the mystical conversation and the bread are miracles that
manifest sanctity. In the legends of Francis during the 150 years
after his death, Clare, too, is portrayed as saint, founder, and
prophet. Rather than disappearing from the stories about Francis in
the fourteenth-century texts, her presence is magnified so that the
story of Clare and the miracle of the bread is included, although it
takes place after Francis's death in the presence of Pope Gregory IX.

50. LFl 35 (III, 626).
51. DBF 42 (III, 516–17).
52. LFl 33 (III, 624).

If the episodes dealing with Clare in *Francis of Assisi: Early Documents* are pitted against those about Francis in terms of numbers, then Clare is dwarfed. After all, as Thomas of Celano says of his *Life of Francis*, the story is about Francis, not Clare and the Poor Ladies. But if the central images of Clare as saint, founder, and prophet are considered, Clare is not at all hidden. While the scenes about her in the early sources are appropriately fewer, the portrait of Clare is clear. Clare's virtues and those of the Poor Ladies are repeatedly cited. She is described as a saint from her earliest appearance in Francis's restoration of San Damiano to her Pieta-like presence weeping inconsolably over the body of Francis. She is assigned a dual position as founder in that she is credited with establishing an order for enclosed women as well as being named the mother of Francis's fraternity. Clare is identified with Francis as prophet through her fulfillment of the prophecy of San Damiano, and she is cited as an exemplar for the entire church.[53] Together Francis and Clare emerge from the writings of the early documents as saints, founders and prophets of a new age.

---

53. In *The First Franciscan Woman, Clare of Assisi and Her Form of Life* (Quincy, IL: Franciscan Press, 1993), 227–28, Margaret Carney demonstrates that a founder is innately prophetic.

"If My Words Remain in You . . ."

Foundations of the Evangelical Life

Regis J. Armstrong

The chronological approach to *Francis of Assisi: Early Documents* was logical at the beginning. It also seemed simple. As it unfolded, however, such an approach revealed educational opportunities that caught us by surprise. Succeeding generations of texts brought to light lessons that taught as much about the development of the Franciscan tradition as about the life of its Founder. Evidence that only an index could reveal later confirmed such lessons. For example, the development and refinement of a "Franciscan" vocabulary as well as images or concepts currently taken for granted that actually came to light much later in the tradition.

One of the unexpected discoveries was the depth of the rich biblical spirituality that emerges throughout all the texts of the first two volumes, which span Francis's life until Bonaventure's death, that is, from 1207 to 1274. The texts of the third volume, which cover 1285 to 1365, have some definite biblical strength, e.g., in the texts of Ubertino of Casale, Angelo Clareno, and Arnald of Sarrant, but, for the most part, do not clearly reflect the biblical mentality of the earlier authors. Bereft of the biblical images or phrases that seem to flow naturally from the authors of the first two volumes of *Francis of Assisi: Early Documents,* those of the third seem forced or inserted to bolster a line of thought rather than inspiring it. They tend to focus on the Franciscan values and vocabulary and seem eager to accentuate their correct nuances or degrees of perfection.

The Mirror of Perfection compilations, for example, almost exaggerate the "most austere" asceticism of Francis, the "most perfect" nature of his poverty, and his unrelenting drive for perfection.

The educational journey of the Index to *Francis of Assisi: Early Documents* confirmed a deep-rooted insight of biblical spirituality. The Index's thirty-eight pages also brought to light a pleasant surprise, what might be termed the "biblical originality" or the "biblical imagination" of Francis. A contemporary reader might expect to find a profound biblical approach in Bonaventure's writings, as would be normal for a theologian of thirteenth century Paris. Yet, the unique, insightful, and challenging biblical passages in Francis's rules, exhortations, admonitions, and prayers verify what both Thomas of Celano and Bonaventure later wrote of him: "Where the knowledge of teachers stands outside, the passion of the lover entered."[1]

From the perspective of the variety of biblical citations and allusions that characterize the early portraits of *Francis of Assisi: Early Documents,* in particular *The Saint* and *The Founder,* it may be profitable therefore, to revisit the discussion of Franciscan life through the lens of the evangelical life. Questions naturally arise. Are reflections on the evangelical life focused on the early Franciscan literature? Are conversations about the evangelical life more historical than existential? Do they neglect the dynamic of the word of God in which Francis found his identity and strength? Or do they mirror the same mentality of those fourteenth-century writers who focused myopically on preserving their own ascetical values while the society around them crumbled? The answers to these and many other questions are not simple. Once found they typically inspire others. Nevertheless, the Scriptures remind us repeatedly: the word of God is relentless, ever new, and incisive.

The Evangelical Life

Discussion of the evangelical life undoubtedly arose in 1983 when three documents became widely discussed, two within the universal church: the new *Code of Canon Law* and a statement of International Union of Superiors General, *Apostolic Spirituality in*

---

1. 2C 102 (II, 314), LMj 11.1 (II, 612).

View of the Kingdom; and a third within the United States, *Essential Elements in the Church's Teaching on Religious Life as Applied to Institutes Dedicated to Works of the Apostolate*. In order to assist the American bishops in ministering to the religious of their jurisdictions, *Essential Elements* conveniently looked at those of consecrated life as belonging to either institutes of monastic life or to those engaged in apostolic activities. Practically such a twofold perspective enabled bishops to deal with religious in a more comprehensible way, to resolve questions of jurisdiction more efficiently, and to understand more clearly the unique thrust of each community. What it did not take into consideration, however, was the encouragement of *Perfectae caritatis* to return to the spirit of their founders and the repeated calls of Paul VI to emphasize their charisms. In other words, as men and women of consecrated life were grappling with their own uniqueness,[2] the 1983 documents were attempting to categorize religious communities.

In 1984 Joseph Chinnici, at a gathering of the Provincials of the American Franciscan jurisdictions, responded to the defects of the statement of the Superiors' General. He encouraged his audience to "reflect on our common Franciscan tradition, to discover what, if anything, is unique about our experience and self-understanding."[3] Chinnici examined the contours of the twelfth-century debate over the *vita vere apostolica* [truly apostolic life] and its existence in light of the *vita monastica* [monastic life]. The perspectives of medieval historians Marie Dominique Chenu, Caroline Walker Bynum, and Lester K. Little,[4] undoubtedly broadened Chinnici's appreciation of

2. A perfect example of this is the struggle of the Capuchins who, in 1982, submitted their third post-conciliar revision of their Constitutions, and, to their dismay, saw it challenged because of its declaration that they were all brothers and, therefore, eligible to be major superiors. Were they clerical or non-clerical? Such was the question posed by the Sacred Congregation for Religious and Secular Institutes. To it the Capuchins responded: They are neither.
3. Joseph Chinnici, "Evangelical/Apostolic Tensions," in *Our Franciscan Charism in the World of Today*. Proceedings Super Conference IV, edited by Alcuin Coyle (Clifton, NJ: Franciscan Advertising and Media Enterprises, 1987), 96–121.
4. Marie Dominique Chenu, *Nature, Man, and Society in the Twelfth Century*, preface by Etienne Gilson, selected, edited and translated by Jerome Taylor and Lester K. Little (Chicago: University of Chicago Press, 1981); Caroline Walker Bynum, *Docere Verbo et Exemplo: An Aspect of Twelfth Century Spirituality* (Missoula: Scholars Press, 1979), and *Jesus as Mother, Studies in the Spirituality of the High Middle Ages* (Berkeley: University of California Press, 1982); Lester K. Little, *Religious Poverty and Profit Economy in Medieval Europe* (Ithaca: Cornell University Press, 1978).

the choices available to the early thirteenth-century Francis of Assisi as he attempted to guide his first followers. The rediscovery of Franciscan sources invaluably assisted in identifying the uniqueness of his inspiration that was such a phenomenon in the late Seventies and early Eighties. Chinnici's articulation of Francis's unique perspective was well received due to a large extent to Kajetan Esser's publication of a critical edition of Francis's writings, of the scholarly editions of the relatively unknown sources for his life such as *The Anonymous of Perugia,*[5] *The Legend of the Three Companions,*[6] and *The Assisi Compilation,*[7] and the explosion of translations in the European and even Asian and African languages.

At the time of Chinnici's critique of the monastic and apostolic paradigms of religious life, there were two in-depth studies of the *Earlier Rule.* The popular *The Birth of a Movement* by David Flood and Thadeè Matura looked at the document in its historical, socio-economic contexts. It was immediately successful in providing a new lens through which to examine its contents.[8] Shortly thereafter, Walter Vivianis wrote his doctoral dissertation that examined the document from a more biblical perspective, furthering some of Flood's hypotheses.[9] Both of these works opened the door, in 1986, for Dino Dozzi's more profound study of Francis's exegetical method as seen through the *Earlier Rule.*[10] Overall the three studies agreed that the original *proposal of life* of 1209 was in some way the foundation of the *Earlier Rule.* On its underpinnings Francis's followers built, clarified, expanded, and, in light of the Fourth Lateran Council, modified the description of their daily life and mission.

5. Lorenzo Di Fonzo, "L'Anonimo Perugino Tra Le Fonti Francescane del Secolo XIII: Rapporti Letterari e Testo Critico," *Miscellanea Franciscana* 72 (1972): 117–483.
6. Théophile Desbonnets, "Legenda Strium Sociorum: Edition Critique," *Archicum Franciscanum Historicum* 67(1974): 38–144.
7. Marino Bigaroni, "Compilatio Assisiensis" dagli Scritti di fr. Leone e Compagni su S. Francesco d'Assisi. Dal Ms. 1046 di Perugia. Il edizione integrale reveduta e correta con versione italiana a fronte e variazioni (Assisi: Publicazioni della Biblioteca Franciscana Chiesa Nuova, 1975).
8. David Flood and Thadee Matura, *The Birth of A Movement: A Study of the First Rule of St. Francis,* translated by Paul Schwartz and Paul Lachance (Chicago: Franciscan Herald Press, 1975).
9. Walter Viviani, *L'Ermeneutica di Francesco d'Assisi. Indagine alla Luce di Giovanni 13-17 nei Suoi Scritti* (Roma: Editrice Antonianum, 1983).
10. Dino Dozzi, *Il Vangelo nella Regola non Bollata di Francesco d'Assisi* (Roma: Istituto Storico dei Cappuccini, 1989).

If historians or analysts of Christian spirituality were to look for a document that would exemplify Francis of Assisi's choice of a gospel or evangelical way of life in contrast to the monastic or apostolic options open to him, they would only need to read his *Earlier Rule.* More than the other writings of Francis, the *Earlier Rule* reflects a lived-document. It has roots in the proposal Francis and his first followers brought to Pope Innocent III in 1209, shows the impact of a cataclysmic ecclesial event of the Fourth Lateran Council in 1215, reveals the resolution of tensions between ideal and reality between 1209 and 1221, and exemplifies fraternal minority as a hermeneutic of the gospel applicable for daily life.

Furthermore, theoreticians or animators of Franciscan spirituality were to look for a document in the Franciscan tradition that would assist in deepening a contemporary expression of that evangelical way of life; they would also need only to reflect upon Francis's *Earlier Rule.*[11] More than a historian's delight, more than a most personal expression of the Founder's vision, each of its twenty-three chapters reveals a gospel foundation upon which Francis's disciples not only fashioned the contours of their primitive fraternity, but responded to their society and reached out to all peoples.

These authors showed that the *Earlier Rule,* in other words, may be the ideal document to provide contemporary followers of Francis the tools with which to develop a pastoral plan in light of their charism, for intensifying their Franciscan approach to spiritual growth, to ministry among the poor, nonbelievers, or the unchurched, or for reflecting on "incarnating the healing charism through forgiveness and peace." Perhaps no other writing is more insightful into Francis's unique approach to life and to ministry than the *Earlier Rule.* Without a doubt a medieval document, it provides a dynamic more than any formula, it is more than a set of guidelines for expressing a valid gospel life in today's world, it is an operative principle.[12]

---

11. See FA:ED I, 63-86.
12. One might argue that Francis's 1LtF, a primary text and an interpretive tool for
    understanding the Franciscan tradition, is more appropriate. This may be so,
    especially when it is examined in light of its re-working in the 2LtF. *The Earlier Rule,*
    however, reflects the gospel foundations for their lives, the historical struggles of
    the primitive fraternity between 1209 and 1221, and how they were practically
    reconciled.

However, in their analysis of the *Earlier Rule*'s twenty-second chapter, there was a divergence. Flood and, after him, Viviani interpreted it as a statement of Francis's final counsel prior to his departure to embrace martyrdom at the hands of the Saracens, in other words, a type of last will and testament. Its initial encouragement to follow Christ's example in embracing one's enemies as "friends" and its concluding use of John's Last Supper Discourse provided ample reason for acceptance of such a theory. Dozzi, however, was not so convinced and preferred to see it as written *after* Francis's return in 1221 from his trip to the Middle East, that is, at the same time as the *Commonitorum and Exhortation to All the Faithful*. The themes and phrases are, in many instances, similar, as is his use of the Last Supper Discourse. Dozzi sees this twenty-second chapter as key to Francis's gospel-centered life written to provide his anxiety-filled confreres, who have now had a taste of life without him, with an approach to resolving the inevitable tensions between gospel ideals and mundane reality. From this perspective, it provides, in other words, the dynamic of the evangelical life and is a foreshadowing of the words Francis uttered on his deathbed: "I have done what is mine; may Christ teach you what is yours!"[13]

Setting the Bar High

"Let us pay attention," Francis begins, "to what the Lord says: *'Love your enemies'* and *'do good to those who hate you,'* for our Lord Jesus Christ, Whose footprints we must follow, called his betrayer a friend and willingly offered Himself to His executioners."[14] Nothing could be more typical of Francis of Assisi than this dramatic focus on the Lord, Jesus Christ, in the opening sentence of the twenty-second chapter of the *Earlier Rule*. It shows Francis's understanding of the underlying message of the Beatitudes, love, and his appreciation of how Christ so graciously embodied it in his regard of and benevolence toward his offender. Consistency is undoubtedly what Francis discovered in the life of Jesus, a consistency between his teaching and his behavior. Simultaneously, this

---

13. 2C 214 (II, 386).
14. ER 22.1–2 (I, 79).

opening sentence ever so gently expresses the Founder's understanding of the challenge that faces every follower of Jesus: to follow
in his footprints. To know them and to follow them is also a call to
consistency, one that Francis immediately expresses in words that
reflect his own day-to-day life with his brothers. "Our friends," he
states, "are all those who unjustly afflict upon us distress and
anguish, shame and injury, sorrow and punishment, martyrdom
and death. We must love them greatly for we shall possess eternal
life because of what they bring upon us."[15]
      There is a profound call to conversion in these opening words, a
call to identification with the attitudes and with the deeds of Jesus.
These initial four verses of the twenty-second chapter of the *Earlier
Rule* present the challenge of a life of penance, *metanoia* or conversion in the same way as do the opening three verses of Francis's
Testament, the embrace of the leper.[16] Francis articulates an
incarnational approach to Christian life, one that demands an
ongoing search for the "lepers" or "enemies" of life and, having
found them, to go among them, to show mercy to them, to see them
as friends, and to offer one's very being to them. Francis sets the bar
quite high, that is, he demands a life of penance modeled on the
example of Jesus. There is no neat formula, no conformity to any
standards beyond those seen in Jesus and described in the gospel.
      Penance has always been seen as a preliminary disposition that
must be adopted in the journey to God. The *conversatio* (daily life) of
monastic life cannot be embraced without a *conversio* (conversion)
from a sinful life. The monastic tradition of religious life described
life in the world as living in the region of unlikeness in which
humans suffer the effects of sin; entrance into a monastery is seen as
the embrace of an otherworldly, angelic, or heavenly life. The active
apostolic life also viewed conversion as a prerequisite, as the *Spiritual Exercises* of Ignatius of Loyola clearly demonstrate. During the
first two weeks of the *Exercises,* Ignatius describes the struggle of the
human soul in terms of dealing with the ravages of sin and with the
subtle, deceiving ways of emotions. Unlike Benedict and Ignatius,
Francis describes penance in the interpersonal language of dealing

---

15. ER 22.3–4 (I, 79).
16. Test 1–3 (I, 124).

with lepers.[17] He sees it in terms of relationships or as a struggle of the human heart. "And let us hate our bodies with its vices and sins,"[18] he writes.

> . . . Because by living according to the flesh (cf. Rom 8:4), the devil wishes to take from us the love of Jesus Christ and eternal life and to lose himself in hell with everyone else. Because, by our own fault, we are disgusting, miserable, and opposed to good, yet prompt and inclined to evil, for, as our Lord says in the Gospel: *From the heart proceed* (Mk 7:21) *and come* (Mt 15:17) *evil thoughts, adultery, fornication, murder, theft, greed, malice, deceit, licentiousness, envy* (Mk 7:21–22), *false witness* (Mt 15:19), *blasphemy, foolishness* (Mk 7:22). *All these evils come from within, from a person's heart,* and *these are what defile a person* (Mt 15:20).[19]

For the most part these few lines echo the teaching of the gospels. Only the opening phrase — "we must hate our bodies with its vices and sins" — comes uniquely from Francis, reflecting his conviction that we were created by God's goodness but, through our own vice and sin, now travel through life burdened with undesired baggage. Once we have been freed from evil, we are free to enter the struggle of the heart, the struggle of penance. By coupling the concept of "the body" — understood elsewhere in his writings as "made in the image of God"[20] — with "vice and sin," Francis wonderfully links poverty with the pursuit of penance.

While each of these three approaches to the spiritual life — monastic, apostolic, and evangelical — lead to the same reality, the embrace of penance, what is striking is the practical goal of that penance. From the monastic perspective, conversion enables one to enter a new way of life or into a monastic setting resembling paradise or, as the early monastic describes it, an angelic life. Art, architecture, liturgy, music: all these threads of the rich fabric of monastic spirituality speak of heaven but can be appreciated only

---

17. A succinct understanding of these various approaches may be found in Zachary Grant, *Paths to Renewal: The Spirituality of Six Religious Founders* (Staten Island, NY: Alba House, 1998).
18. ER 22.5 (I, 79); also see 1LtF 2 (I, 41), 2LtF 37 (I, 48).
19. ER 22.5–8 (I, 79).
20. Adm 5.1 (I, 131).

through the embrace of conversion. The apostolic understanding considers penance as freeing one for the kingdom of God and for dedicating one's life to its establishment on earth. In Francis's evangelical view, penitential journey of the heart leads to the intimacy of discipleship. While he uses the vocabulary of monasticism to describe that journey, "Now that we have left the world," he then states emphatically: " . . . we have nothing else to do but to follow the will of the Lord and to please Him."[21] The challenges of the spiritual life, in his view, can be reduced to two points: to follow God's will, and to give one's self to God's pleasure. And to achieve this, he counsels his followers: "Let us be very careful that we are not earth along the wayside, or that which is rocky or full of thorns, in keeping with what the Lord says in the gospel: *The word of God is a seed*" (Lk 8:11).[22]

The Life-Giving Seed of God

This simple statement places Francis's followers at the very heart of an evangelical life, that is, it defines his and their call as attentive recipients of God's word. He elaborates this through a collage of passages from the Synoptic parable of the sower and the seed inter-woven with Francis's nuances. Each passage reflects a different reflection on the earth, that is, the heart into which the seed of God's word falls. The gospel passages fall on almost deaf ears as Francis's synthesis is too commonplace or familiar. Interiorizing and fleshing out the word of God is, in essence, the life Francis envisions. Once Francis's interpretation is read in light of his preference for the Gospel of John, however, it takes on new meaning. Two points, in particular, are worthy of note: Francis's concept of the seed or the word and the soil, or the human heart, into which the seed falls.

An image used by Francis provides a glimpse into his understanding of the word as a seed. It emerges in a sermon of Odo of Cheriton (+1246/47) who tells of him identifying himself as a "woman whom the Lord impregnated with his word."[23] The passage

---

21. ER 22.9 (I, 79).
22. ER 22.10–11 (I, 79).
23. Odo of Cheriton, FA:ED I, 591.

is reminiscent of 1 Peter 1:23: "You have been born again, not from a perishable but an imperishable seed, through the living and abiding word of God." This generative dimension of the word — *sperma* according to the Greek — is beautifully nuanced in Bonaventure's portrait of Francis at the Portiuncula "conceiving and bringing to birth" in the shadow of she who had "conceived and brought to birth *the Word full of grace and truth* (Jn 1:14)."[24] The word's life-giving qualities, however, are only one dimension of the word's activities. When seen through the lens of the Old Testament, it is easy to appreciate Francis's encouragement to focus solely on God's word. For the Hebrew Scriptures, the "word," *dabar,* signified a dynamic entity or a channel of vitality or energy; it was an expression of the creative, life-giving power of God.[25] The Letter to the Hebrews expresses it well: "The word of God is living and effective, sharper than any two-edged sword . . . (Hb 4:3)." Thus opening himself to the words of Jesus gave Francis life. They provided the source of his inspiration as his frequent use of John's Gospel suggests, e.g., John 6:63: "my words are spirit and life." For the later Greek texts, however, the "word," *logos,* was an instrument or expression of thought; it was ordered or measured and provided form. Focusing on the words of Jesus now provided Francis direction. In this light a strong case could be made that Francis's understanding of discipleship is captured in John 8:31–32: "If you remain in my words, you are truly my disciples; then you will know the truth, and the truth will set you free."[26]

Realizing that Word and Wisdom were often interchangeable in the Hebrew scriptures, especially in the chronologically later books, reflecting on the traits of Hebrew scriptures, Wisdom leads a more profound appreciation of Francis's biblical spirituality. The Book of Wisdom is most helpful in this regard:

> For within [Wisdom] is a spirit, intelligent, holy, unique, manifold, subtle, active incisive, unsullied, lucid, invulner-

---

24. LMj 3.1 (II, 542).
25. This nuanced understanding of "word" in its Hebrew and Greek expressions is based on that of Alexander Jones, *God's Living Word* (Glen Rock, N.J.: Paulist Press, 1965), 16-17.
26. For a thorough understanding of John's theology of Jesus' word, see Rudolph Schnackenburg, *The Gospel of John,* vol. II (New York: Seabury Press, 1972), 483ff.

able, benevolent, sharp, irresistible, beneficent, loveable, steadfast . . . She pervades and permeates all things. She is the breath of the power of God . . . the untarnished mirror of God's active power . . . herself unchanging, she makes all things new (Wis 7:22-27).

All these attributes of Wisdom, God's word, act as a preparation for the theology of the Trinity that will unfold in the writings of Paul and John where a theology of Wisdom gives rise not only to a theology of the Word, but to a theology of the Spirit as well. John 6:63 articulates: "my words are spirit and life . . ." The Spirit-laden words of Jesus then emerge in light of the Old Testament as creative, prophetic, eschatological, transcendent, healing. They are the food of the poor, the executor of judgment, the law of the heart.

In reading Francis's biographies, it is nearly impossible to over-look the energy that drove this "new evangelist," as Thomas of Celano describes him.[27] Greccio alone reveals the wonder of Fran-cis's gospel imagination as he celebrated the Nativity and, as Thomas writes, brought about "a new Bethlehem."[28] His compan-ions, those who identify themselves as "we who were with him,"[29] tell one story after another in which Francis's gospel "imagination" emerges. The words of Jesus propelled his pursuit of God and the good of his fellow human beings, so that, even on his death-bed, he found and gave new expressions of their "spirit and life" as he listened — with his brothers — to John's account of the last hours of Jesus' death.[30] As he described the "passion of the lover," Bonaventure perceived the source of that drive in Francis's never-ending desire to penetrate the depths of Scripture, so that "through his imitation of Christ he carried in his activity the perfect truth contained in [the Scriptures] . . . "[31] To absorb Francis's zest for gospel life, therefore, demands embracing daily God's word and letting it confront our lives with questions, challenges, and restless-ness. Even a superficial glance at the sacred text will reveal the full implications of having the energy of God's word at the center of our

---

27. 1C 89 (I, 259).
28. 1C 85 (I, 255).
29. See FA:ED II, 118, footnote b.
30. 1C 110 (I, 278).
31. LMj 11.1–2 (II, 612–13).

lives. It is creative, prophetic, forward-looking or eschatological. It is food for the poor, life-giving, the executor of judgment, a two-edged sword. It is attractive, compelling, and healing.

The Central Place of the Heart

From that perspective, it is important not to lose sight of the heart, the soil into which the word of God so gently falls. The verses that follow Francis's call to be attentive to the seed of God's word are sufficient to alert any of his followers to the sharp focus he gives to the human heart. As in the Synoptic telling of the parable, the "that which . . . " becomes "those who . . . " The seed of the word, that is, demands expression — in varying degrees — through the human heart. One might easily claim that, in this light, Francis understood his evangelical life to be a call to transparency. The image of the heart appears fifty-five times in his writings, one of the most frequently used words by Francis, which signals his concern for it. In most instances, he uses it in the biblical sense as *the* symbol of the depths of the human person, the center of one's being that can become hardened, capricious, vulnerable, and, paradoxically, one's greatest strength.[32]

Articulators of the evangelical approach to Franciscan spirituality have been attempting to delineate its evangelical approach vis-à-vis the monastic and apostolic. In doing so, however, they seem to formulate its unique characteristics within the vocabulary of the Franciscan tradition, leaving even the casual reader to question if they have adequately defined or delineated the essence of the evangelical life Francis envisioned. Its very foundation is the Word, the Spirit, the Wisdom that is "subtle, active, incisive . . . unchangeable, yet making all things new." While monastic religious life envisions entrance into a world shaped and molded by the Word, apostolic religious life burns with the desire to proclaim the Word to all peoples. In the final analysis the evangelical approach to the spiritual life is a response to God's Word, as is the monastic and

---

32. Two books that are helpful in developing this perspective are: André Louf, *Teach Us to Pray*, translated by Hubert Hoskins (Chicago: Franciscan Herald Press, 1974), especially 16–22; and Jan G. Bovenmars, *A Biblical Spirituality of the Heart* (New York: Alba House, 1991).

apostolic. What makes the Franciscan approach so unique is its focus not on structure or activity, place or time, occupation or status, but simply on the human heart where the Word dwells. Francis expresses his appreciation for this Indwelling, the result of keeping or nurturing the word within, as John 14:23 reminds us, in the last half of the twenty-second chapter of the *Earlier Rule*. "Let us make a home and a dwelling place for Him,"[33] he writes and then proceeds to describe a life caught up in relationships.

The evangelical life is quite simple because simplicity is its hallmark. It consists in cultivating the heart so that it becomes the perfect soil in which God's seed can thrive and bear fruit. Turning attentively to the writings of Francis, and to Clare his perfect follower, a student of the evangelical life finds three primary forces that continually plow the landscape of the heart: penance, poverty, and prayer.

The penitential heart of Francis was caught up in a journey of the heart, one begun by God's heart and continued by the one whose heart has been touched. "It seemed too bitter for me to see lepers," he writes, "and the Lord Himself led me among them, and I showed mercy to them" (*et feci misericordiam cum illis*).[34] Etymologically *misericordia* means: a heart sensitive or tender to misery. In the Hebrew scriptures it is close to the Hebrew word *rahamîm,* an instinctive attachment of one human being for another, and to *hesed,* a deep response of love to the plight of another. In anthropomorphic terms, God's heart becomes the perfect expression of that as, in the New Testament, the heart of Jesus.[35] Francis, sensing the touch of God's heart in his own life, *feci misericordiam cum illis,* demonstrated a heart sensitive to the misery of others. Thus was shaped Francis's heart. Always sensitive to his own misery or sinfulness, and to God's never tiring heart, Francis was restless to address his own love-touched heart to the misery of others. *Cum illis* defines where Francis's followers most belong, with the miserable, the poor, downtrodden, broken hoards of humanity.

---

33. ER 22.27 (I, 80).
34. Test 1–2 (I, 124).
35. See *Dictionary of Biblical Theology,* edited by Xavier Léon-Dufour, translated by Joseph Cahill (Montreal: Palm Publishers, 1967), 309.

"Enlighten the darkness of my heart,"[36] Francis prays with this relentless call of penance. Eventually it leads him to the Portiuncula, to the Mother of mercies as Bonaventure describes it,[37] where his heart becomes filled with the word of poverty. This too was the beginning of a journey that begins with the gospel call to the poverty of missionary itineracy, gradually becomes a poverty touching life in fraternity, and ends with the poverty of mysticism, a life *sine proprio,* without anything of one's own. One has only to read the *Earlier Rule* as a historical unfolding of Francis's intuition to see how the seed of the word was interiorized and expressed in hearts that struggled mightily to be poor. New situations demanded new insights. New challenges demanded new ideals. With each new turn, with each new encounter, evangelical poverty strengthened its roots. Whereas the journey of penance had been traversed for centuries and its travelers had left tour guides strewn on the paths of those who embarked upon it, the road of poverty was relatively unknown. The *Sacred Exchange* provides ample evidence of the struggles to avoid its pitfalls. At each fork in the road, it is obvious that the gospel was always the guide. Until Francis shares a challenging insight into Matthew 22:21 — *render to Caesar what is Caesar's and to God what is God's* — and, in doing so, probes the direction of the heart's energy.[38]

The final and most prominent furrow of Francis's heart was the one formed by his prayer. In essence, it was a mirror of Paul's: Francis's spirit and God's Spirit together cried out as children of God, "Abba! Father!" (Rom 8:15–6). One might say that prayer was, more than anything, an activity of the heart for it was the work of love, always striving to see the Beloved, the Friend, the Consoler face to face. Because Francis understood prayer to be an activity of the Lord's Spirit, he described prayer, in Chapter 5 of the *Later Rule*, as the Spirit's first and continuing activity always demanding purity of heart. With an evangelical spirit he taught, "All temporal things must contribute to it,"[39] for prayer was the air he breathed. To penetrate the depths of Francis's prayer is to penetrate his very heart.

---

36. PrCr (I, 40).
37. LMj 2.8 (II, 540–41).
38. Adm 11.1–4 (I, 133).
39. LR 5.2 (I, 102).

What then is the evangelical life Francis proposed? It was a life open unceasingly to the gospel word of God that the Lord is continually scattering on the landscape of our hearts. It is a life dependent on the heart. If those hearts belong to people who are penitent, poor, and pulsing in prayer, then God's word is heard in ways different from the hard-hearted, affluent, and indifferent. It is heard as decisive, determining, and definitive. To find life's fulfillment, there is no preoccupation with the atmosphere of a monastery or with a self-giving through ministry. No, for Francis — as for John the Evangelist — life consists quite simply in the Word and in the words spoken by Him. Toward the end of his life, Francis reminded his followers of this. "Listen . . . " he writes in the *Letter to the Entire Order*, "Incline the ear of your heart and obey the voice of the Son of God . . . whoever belongs to God hears the words of God."[40] And in an encouragement reminiscent of his earlier writings, he writes: "I admonish all my brothers and encourage them in Christ to venerate, as best they can, the divine written words wherever they can find them . . . honoring in the words the Lord who spoke them."[41]

In the final analysis, in his focus on the gospel sower and the seed, Francis proposes a spirituality that is as ancient as monasticism itself, that of the *lectio divina.* His approach to this "sacred reading," however, could easily be that of a hermit. It is essentially a spirituality lived by an individual, one that Francis describes in the first thirteen verses of his *Testament* as he writes of his call to penance and faith in the church, priests, the eucharist, and the "most holy divine words."[42] After describing this "solitary" life, however, Francis attributes the call to brotherhood to the Lord himself. While he does not describe the divine influence as he does in terms of Odo of Cheriton's quote — "the woman whom the Lord with His word,"[43] he emphatically declares that the Lord showed him that theirs was to be a gospel life: "And after the Lord gave me some brothers, no one showed me what I had to do, but the Most High

40. LtOrd 5–6, 34 (I, 116–17, 119).
41. LtOrd 35–36 (I, 119).
42. Test 13 (I, 125).
43. FA:ED I, 591.

himself revealed to me that I should live according to the pattern of the Holy Gospel."[44]

"The Lord Gave Me Brothers . . . "

Challenged by living with brothers, Francis could have turned to a Benedictine/Cistercian monastic paradigm or to one of an Augustinian community. He rejected both even when urged to do so[45] and turned confidently — almost boldly — to the gospel. How *he* was to live was according to the gospel. Christ became the paradigm, or the Word incarnated through him became the paradigm. How essential that is in understanding the Franciscan approach to fraternity is verified in the historical contours of the *Earlier Rule.* Obstacles arose at nearly every turn challenging the brothers in their daily life. *Itineracy:* how to maintain the bonds of union when "on the road?" *Poverty:* how to provide for the sick, for the hermits, for those in need? *Human frailty:* how to live with one another, with the spiritually immature, with the recalcitrant? *Success:* how to cope with popularity, with generosity, with 'having arrived'? The answers were always found in the gospel. The *Earlier Rule* shows how together the brothers wrestled with the new situations or problems confronting them and, as each chapter shows, found the formulas for their daily lives in the gospel.

A reference 1 Peter 1:22 is frequently overlooked in Francis's writings.[46] The Latin Vulgate of Francis's time states: "Purifying your souls in an obedience of love, a love of fraternity, love one another more attentively from a simple heart." The modern Latin Vulgate, redone in light of the original text, has two differences. It describes obedience not as ". . . of love," but ". . . of truth;" and to the phrase "a love of fraternity," it adds and translates *anhypokriton* as *non fictum* (insincere). Both the medieval and the modern editions, however, see this Petrine consideration of obedience within the context of fraternal charity. One has to wonder if the modern

---

44. Test 14 (I, 125).
45. AC 18 (II, 132–33).
46. See Optatus van Asseldonk, "Le Lettere di S. Pietro negli Scritti di S. Francesco," *La Lettera e Lo Spirito,* vol. II, Dimensioni Spirituali VI/VII (Roma: Editrice Laurentianum, 1985), 429–41.

Vulgate with its accent on truth would have influenced Francis's vision of obedience as a virtue of love, a *sine qua non* of life in fraternity. If obedience were understood as *ob-audire* (to listen to another), as opposed to *obedire* (to incline one's will), there would be little practical difference in the two texts. Listening to another in the one would be done out of love, in the other out of respect for the truth. In both instances, obedience would be undertaken *in amore fraternitatis non fictum* (in a love of fraternity that is sincere).

The modern Vulgate edition of this passage may well be closer to Francis's biblical intuition, for as Bo Reicke observes in *The Anchor Bible,* the passage could well be translated: "Purifying your souls in an obedience to the Gospel, in a love of fraternity that is sincere, love one another more attentively from a simple heart."[47] Francis's evangelical fraternity finds its vitality in this text. Inclining one's ear to the gospel purifies the individual and strengthens the fraternity. As such it inspires a more attentive love of the other and does so with a simple, forthright heart. The fraternal crucible of everyday life, in other words, provides a school of Christ the Brother in which each student may study the gospel and learn from it how to deepen and express an authentic love for one another.

How this loving obedience is carried out is expressed in words taken directly from the gospel: ministry, service, patient suffering, laying down one's life. Absent from the *Earlier Rule* are the seventy-two chapters of *The Rule of Benedict* with its carefully articulated administrative vision. Absent from *The Earlier Rule* is the stress of *Essential Elements in Church Teaching on Religious Life* with its concern for "communion" expressed "in stable and visible ways through community life." What is present in the *Earlier Rule* is the gospel recognition that we are, in fact, related to one another and, in light of the mystery of Christ, how to relate to one another. Once again, the First Letter of Peter offers a perspective on how Francis translated this gospel-centered life into action. In the context of exhorting his readers to use their gifts for one another "as stewards of God's manifold grace," Peter writes "*whoever* speaks, let him do so

---

47. See *The Epistles of James, Peter and Jude* in *The Anchor Bible,* translated with introduction and notes by Bo Reicke (Garden City, NY: Doubleday & Co., Inc, 1964), 86. Quotations from New Vulgate from *The Navarre Bible: The Catholic Epistles,* translated by Michael Adams (Dublin: Four Courts Press, 1992), 95.

as the words of God. Whoever ministers, let him do so as of the strength that God administers." He concludes: "so that in all things God may be honored through Jesus Christ (1 Pt 4:10–11)." Peter's directive, then, envisions serving one another out of a consciousness of one's giftedness and that of another as the fundamental Christ-centered disposition and from it flow two unique attitudes: ministry and speaking as if with the words of God.[48]

In the first place, there is a definite awareness that many of the brothers will spend much of their time *in via*, as "pilgrims and strangers," and, therefore, without a fixed abode. "Wherever the brothers may be," Francis directs, "and in whatever place they may meet, they should spiritually and attentively see one another anew and honor one another *without complaining* (1 Pt 4:9)."[49] Thus visiting one another, showing hospitality to one another, and treating one another "as members of one family": these became salient virtues of Francis's brothers.

While the primitive fraternity was relatively small, the development of such an "intimate" brotherhood may have been easily achieved especially in the aura of Francis's presence. By 1217, however, the brothers had to rethink their structures. Not only had their numbers grown; the unifying influence of Francis was waning as well. The fourth, fifth and sixth chapters of the *Earlier Rule* suggests how Francis and the brothers resolved this by recourse, once again, to the gospel.[50] Practically speaking, the brothers perceived the need for ministers entrusted with many of the responsibilities exercised by Francis. The fourth chapter begins solemnly: "In the name of the Lord!" It continues with a description, as Dozzi described it in his study of the *Earlier Rule,* that is somewhat canon-

---

48. One could easily agree with Optatus van Asseldonk that the First Letter of Peter had a primary influence on the biblical thought of St. Francis: see "The Letters of Peter in the Writings of St. Francis," *Greyfriars Review* 11(1997): 243–55, and "Biblical Teachings in the Writings of St. Francis of Assisi," *Greyfriars Review* 3 (1989), 306–09.

49. ER 7.11 (I, 69). In his *Origins of the Franciscan Order,* Kajetan Esser writes of this phenomenon from two perspectives. Positively he writes of the life of the "Itinerant Preachers" that enabled the friars to live more closely the life of the gospel; negatively, he categorizes the "Absence of 'Conventual' Life" that weakened the bond of brotherhood. See Kajestan Esser, *Origins of the Franciscan Order,* translated by Aedan Daley and Irina Lynch (Chicago: Franciscan Herald Press, 1970), 54–58, 138–41.

50. See Dino Dozzi, *Il Vangelo,* 155–73.

ical in nature: "Let all the brothers who have been designated ministers and servants of the other brothers assign their brothers in the
provinces and places where they may be, and let them frequently
visit, admonish and encourage them spiritually." What cannot be
overlooked in this chapter is that the gospel is never far from their
inspiration: "Let the ministers and servants remember what the
Lord says: *I have not come to be served, but to serve* (Mt 20:28)." Moreover the gospel call to ministry and service of one another is, as
Dozzi points out, the core of the three chapters.

Chapter 4: "Let them behave among themselves according to
what the Lord says: *Do to others what you would have them do to you* (Mt
7:12); and 'do not do to others what you would not have them to
you.'"[51]

> Chapter 5: "Likewise, let all the brothers not have power or
> control in this instance, especially among themselves; for, as
> the Lord says in the Gospel: *The rulers of the Gentiles lord it
> over them and the great ones make their authority over them felt; it
> shall not be so among the brothers.* Let whoever *wishes to be the
> greater among them be* their *minister* (Mt 20:25–26) and *servant*
> (Mt 20:27). *Let whoever is the greater* among them *become the
> least* (Lk 22:26). Let no brother do or say anything evil to
> another; on the contrary, *through the charity of the Spirit, let
> them serve* and obey *one another* voluntarily (Gal 5:13). This is
> the true and holy obedience of our Lord Jesus Christ."[52]

Chapter 6: "Let no one be called '*prior,*' but let everyone in general
be called a lesser brother. Let one wash the feet of the other (Jn
13:14)."[53]

The intervening verses of these chapters are structural in nature,
that is, they are directed to one group or another, the ministers or
"the others." Nevertheless, these are the New Testament verses that
clearly indicate the gospel call incumbent on all.

Secondly, Francis's writings reveal how aware he was of the
discomfort brought to a fraternity by a brother who does not share
the same gospel idealism. Into many passages the reality of sin and

---

51. ER 4.4–5 (I, 66).
52. ER 5.9–15 (I, 67–68).
53. ER 6.3–4 (I, 68).

its aftereffects insert themselves. Yet Francis never tires encouraging his brothers, in light of the gospel, to reach out to the brother with a problem, to one who has sinned even repeatedly. He encourages the stronger to be compassionate, consoling, and merciful; at other times, he challenges the weaker to find hope in God's mercy and strength in God's word. No passage could express his sentiments more powerfully than his advice to an unknown minister:

> . . . I wish to know in this way that you love the Lord and me, His servant and yours: that there is not any brother in the world who has sinned — however much he could have sinned — who, after he has looked into your eyes, would ever depart without your mercy, if he is looking for mercy. And if he would sin a thousand times before your eyes, love him more than me so that you may draw him to the Lord; and always be merciful with brothers such as these.[54]

If we had no other passage, this alone would be sufficient to reveal the saint's gospel vision of fraternal life. Once again we find its very foundation the biblical concept of *misericordia* (mercy, or a heart sensitive to misery) and a word that Francis would have encountered any number of times each day as he prayed the psalms of the Divine Office.

In his critical edition of Francis's writings, Kajetan Esser surprisingly did not identify the biblical passage *feci misericordiam cum illis* (I showed mercy to them) in the saint's *Testament* 2. When reminiscing on his actions toward the leper, Francis quotes Luke's Gospel 10:37, the description of the Samaritan's actions to the man who fell in among robbers. The decisive moment in Francis's life seems to have resonated with Luke's articulation of Jesus' response to the question "Who is my neighbor?" The manifestation of *misericordia* (a heart sensitive to misery) was once again the pivotal concept. In Francis's experience, moreover, it was the decisive step of his conversion. Thus its emphasis in *The Letter to A Minister* suggests what the saint may well have seen as the foundational virtue of fraternal life. Thus the daily struggles of dealing with one who does not share the gospel idealism of his brothers demand

54. LtMin 9–11 (I, 97–98).

never-tiring expressions of *feci misericordia cum illis*. The fraternal
crucible of everyday life, then, presents continuing opportunities
for conversion, for the purification of the heart in which the gospel
virtue of God's mercy may be seen in all its clarity.

The Mission of the Gospel

One might argue about the priorities of the evangelical life envisioned by Francis. Accenting the interiorization of the word could
very easily lead to placing the contemplative, even eremitical
dimension, over the apostolic. Accentuating the fraternal dimension might readily be interpreted as being too inward-looking and
neglecting that of mission. The genius of Francis, however, was to
intuit that one naturally flows from the other: the word bringing to
new birth and revealing that Jesus is not only Son of God but a
brother. Centered in that Brother, fraternity is established and
strengthened but only that, evangelized, it can evangelize.[55]
This consciousness of being sent can clearly be seen in Francis's
Letter to the Entire Order:

> Listen, sons of the Lord and my brothers, (Acts 2:14) *pay*
> *attention to my words.* (Is 55:3) *Incline the ear* of your heart and
> obey the voice of the Son of God . . . (Ps 135:1) *Give praise* to
> Him *since He is good* (Tob 13:6) and *exalt* Him *by your deeds,*
> for He has sent you into the entire world for this reason that
> in word and deed you may give witness to His voice and
> bring everyone to know that there is (Tob 13:4) *no one who is*
> *all-powerful* except Him.[56]

How this mission unfolds is a profound expression of the evangelical spirituality of Francis. A brief glance at the fourteenth chapter
of the *Earlier Rule* shows how Francis described their day-to-day life
in terms of the missionary discourses of Luke and Matthew. The

---

55. The words of Paul VI are appropriate here as reflecting Francis's own experience.
The lives of Francis show how consultation of the Gospel was habitual when he
was confronted with a unique situation or questioning of initiatives to be taken.
Pope Paul VI, Apostolic Exhortation, *Evangelii Nuntiandi* 13 (Washington, D.C.:
United States Catholic Conference, 1976), 12.
56. LtOrd 5–9 (I, 116–17).

sixteenth chapter, the first of any religious rule to deal with foreign missions, does so in the context of living spiritually in two ways: through witness and through proclamation of the word. In the latter case, Francis intuits where such proclamation and nonbelievers may lead: to suffering and possible martyrdom.[57] Yet the twenty-second chapter with its underlying Johannine theology offers a profound evangelical insight into Francis's understanding of the call to mission.

A passage of the Last Supper Discourse of John's Gospel repeated three times throughout Francis's writings is John 17:8: "The words you gave to me, I gave to them; and they accepted them and truly know that I came from you and they believed that you sent me." In the context of the *Earlier Rule,* the passage appears with John 17:18: "As you sent me into the world, so I sent them into the world." The passages are undoubtedly at the heart of Francis's understanding of mission. In John's Gospel the unity of Jesus' words and those of the Father is expressly established, that is Jesus speaks of the words of God (cf. Jn 3:34; 8:47; 14:10). And it was with these words — spirit, life, energy, two-edged swords — given to Jesus by the Father that he was sent into the world. Jesus gave those words to his disciples with the mandate to go into the world, words that gave those who accepted and kept them (Jn 17:7–8) spirit and life (Jn 6:63) and eternal life (Jn 6:68).[58] To be sent is, according to John's theology, to be pulsing with vitality, energy and two-edged swords, that is, with simply the words of God; as Paul writes to Timothy: "there is no chaining the word of God!" As one biblical scholar expresses it:

> Everything starts with the revealed word, which, if accepted, unfolds in the depths of believers its mysterious but nonetheless experienced energies. In addition to enlightening the mind through a supernatural under-standing of the Christian mystery (1 Jn 4:2), these energies give rise to specific sentiments, those of God, which create a

---

57. In describing methods of evangelization in *Evangelii nuntiani,* Paul VI proposed the same approaches.
58. Among the many commentaries that illuminate this theology, that of Colin Brown may be helpful; see Colin Brown, "Word," *The New International Dictionary of the New Testament*, vol. III, edited by Colin Brown (Grand Rapids, MI: Zondervan Publishing House, 1973), 1081–1146.

> kind of connaturality with things divine (1 Jn 4:6b), so that
> believers are attracted to them (1 Jn 4:9b) and are spurred
> on to act in accordance with their demands.[59]

Thus, as Francis's *Letter to the Entire Order* indicates, mission
demands a commitment to interiorizing and preserving the words
of Jesus, the words of God, within the heart.

Concluding Thoughts

The debate over monastic or apostolic religious life did not
surface, as discussed at the beginning, until a few years later. The
issues were never as clear as those of the clerical/lay debate. Some
argued that it was a problem of language. The monastic and apostolic paradigms, they maintained, were both "evangelical," that is,
rooted in the traditional challenges of the gospels that have always
formed the foundations of religious life. As recently as 1995,
George A. Aschenbrenner, S.J., whose writings have contributed to
delineating the monastic and apostolic lifestyles,[60] responded to a
question concerning the evangelical form that, after reading all the
literature produced by Franciscans, he still saw no differences. He
may have had a point.

Franciscans continue to be driven by an active, apostolic lifestyle
and, as the cry of the poor and oppressed grows louder, they do so in
an increasingly praiseworthy manner. In order to stem the tide of
individualism, many Franciscan jurisdictions have been accentuating their call to respond to the needs of today's society by
appealing to the Franciscan charism of fraternity. As a result the
pressures exerted on individuals are enormous and, at times, contra-
dictory. Mission enervates fraternity; fraternity drains mission.
Frequently it becomes a choice of channeling energy and usually
apostolate wins. In the American culture, the struggle for the upper
hand is intensified in a work-centered, almost work-compulsive
society. In his *Of Time, Work and Leisure,* Sebastian de Grazia main-

---

59. Anselm Dalbesio, *Quello che abbiamo udito e veduto* (Bologna: Edizioni Dehoniane, 1990), 136.
60. George A. Aschenbrenner, "Active and Monastic: Two Apostolic Lifestyles," *Review for Religious* (1986): 653–88.

tains that while "many still cherish the myth of the liberating effects of technology — that by increasing efficiency, we create more time for leisure — men and especially women are currently devoting more time to work than ever before."[61] In this light, one might ask if corporately Franciscans are much different from other apostolic communities. One might ask if corporately religious have not become so active that the seed — the life, spirit energy, two edged-sword given throughout each day to us — falls by the wayside of daily life, or superficially on its rocky soil, or unwittingly entangled with the thorns of everyday cares and concerns of the apostolate.

In 1952 Ignatius Brady wrote an article in *Franciscan Studies* that he later considered seminal: "The History of Mental Prayer in the Order of Friars Minor."[62] While written in response to a question of historical interpretation prominent at the time, Brady contended that the active/contemplative struggle has had a history as long as the Order itself. "When Saint Francis set forth the Franciscan manner of working," he writes, "he at once stated *the* Franciscan problem and offered the key to its solution. The Friars must so labor that they do not extinguish the spirit of prayer and devotion." The spirit of prayer — and Brady emphasized mental prayer centered on the word — was so primary to the life of a Franciscan that everything was to contribute to it.[63]

Brady then proceeds to trace the history of mental prayer stressing the traditions of establishing in fraternities an environment nurturing prayer, of stressing a period of prayer with which the day began and another with which the day ended, and of emphasizing the belief that prayer was always *"la maestra principale, la madre e nutrice d'orni vera virtú"* (the principal teacher, the mother and nurturer of every true virtue).[64] In doing so, Brady notes the

61. Sebastian de Grazia, *Of Time, Work and Leisure* (New York: Random House, 1994).
62. Ignatius Brady, "The History of Mental Prayer in the Order of Friars Minor," *Franciscan Studies* 11 (1952): 317-45.
63. Francis placed this teaching in two different contexts. In the context of the call to manual work, he wrote in LR 5.2 (I, 102) of "the Spirit of holy prayer and devotion to which all temporal things must contribute." He repeated in an abbreviated form the same teaching in the context of teaching theology in his LtAnt 2 (I, 107).
64. Phrase taken from the first Capuchin Statutes of Albacina (1529); see Gherardo Del Colle, "Costituzioni d'Albacina e Rilievi Linguistico–Stilistici," *L'Italia Francescana* 53 (1978): 12.

argument proposed by many historians of his time — and our own — that Franciscans did not have any rule on mental prayer before the sixteenth century, and that it was then introduced by example and influence of the Jesuits. The contrary, Brady maintains, is true. Other historians maintain this position seeing the genius of the Franciscan tradition of beginning and ending the day with periods of mental prayer as not only the key to resolving the active-contemplative tension but of unlocking the enormous energies of mission.

Aschenbrenner may have unwittingly assisted Franciscans by being reluctant to admit to an evangelical paradigm of religious life. By challenging existing descriptions of its nature, he highlighted its elusive character or its fundamental incarnational tendency. In essence, all forms of religious life spring from the option to follow Christ and, as such, are evangelical. The difficulty in identifying these religious options as monastic, active apostolic, and evangelical paradigms may be, as in many other instances, the vocabulary. While the terms *monastic* and *active apostolic* are historically acceptable and more specific, the *evangelical* label is equally so but is more generic. It logically applies to all forms of consecrated life.

A more appropriate vocabulary might delineate the expressions of these paradigms.[65] The monastic paradigm, for example, accentuates a geographic or sociological option in which stability or rooted-ness and the cultivation of environment is important. Active apostolic stresses the ministerial option in which reading the signs of the times and responding to them for and with others are primary. The evangelical approach, however, emphasizes the human heart that interiorizes the word of God and underscores universality not distinctiveness. The transparent nature of this word-heart approach may well be what makes Francis of Assisi such a universally appealing and enduring saint. Ultimately the journey of *Francis of Assisi: Early Documents* teaches that the poverty embraced by the saint, taught by the founder, and heralded by the prophet led him to letting go of everything except God's word. "I have done what is mine;" he stated on his death bed, "may Christ teach you what is yours!"[66] Of the many lessons of the journey, that

---

65. The author is indebted to Joseph Chinnici for these reflections.
66. 2C 214 (II, 386), LMJ14.3 (II, 642).

of not clinging to history but to the dynamic of what inspired it, the word of God, is paramount.

The "Letter" of Fourteen Names

Reading "The Exhortation"

Margaret Carney

Since the appearance of the first volume in the new series of *Francis of Assisi: Early Documents* texts *The Saint*, a number of celebratory events have provided opportunities for experts to compare the contents of this series with the following volumes, that have been "standards" for the past twenty-five years. One of the benchmark texts for such comparison is, to my way of thinking, the "Earlier Exhortation to the Brothers and Sisters of Penance." (Throughout this article this text will be referenced simply as *The Exhortation*.) This text has been known most commonly in the English-speaking world as the "First Letter to all the Faithful" and was not included when the Franciscan Herald Press first published the *Omnibus of Sources* in 1973.[1] Three years later, Kajetan Esser's critical edition of the writings of Francis included this text.[2] Esser's positive evaluation of both its authenticity and contents ushered in a period of enthusiastic engagement in analysis of this record of the early movement.

Its first appearance in a volume accessible to the English-speaking public was delayed until 1982 with the Paulist Press

---

1. Marion Habig, ed., *St. Francis of Assisi: Writings and Early Biographies* [*English Omnibus of the Sources for the Life of St. Francis*] (Chicago: Franciscan Herald Press, 1973).
2. Kajetan Esser, ed., *Die Opuscula des Hl. Franziskus von Assisi* (Grottaferrata: Collegii S. Bonaventurae ad Claras Aquas, 1976).

edition *Francis and Clare: The Complete Works*.[3] If we take the inaugu-
ration of the academic program at the Franciscan Institute in 1972
as yet another benchmark, we can see that even the first "generation" of today's professionally educated Franciscan readers did not
have this important text at their disposal. Thus, the first studies of
The Exhortation published in Europe made little impact in the
English-speaking world given its absence in the *Omnibus*, which was
the primary vehicle for dissemination of Francis's writings for at
least six years.

If printed volumes did not place the text in hand quickly, two
important events in modern Franciscan history did. In 1978 Paul
VI approved a new Rule for the Secular Franciscan Order and in
1982 John Paul II approved the Third Order Regular's new rule.[4]
With both branches of the third "house" of the Franciscan Order
intent upon redacting a rule that was faithful to historical anteced-
ents, the availability of this text and early studies of its content was
of crucial importance. From the viewpoint of those who were
engaged in both of these rule revision projects, the new understanding of the nature and importance of *The Exhortation* provided a
new stimulus to renewal of the ancient tradition of "brothers and
sisters of penance" in the Franciscan order. In other words, the first
appearance of this "writing" came at an intersection of monumental
change for thousands of Franciscan men and women and became a
foundation for that change. It stands at the beginning of both
pontifically approved rule texts to express a textual and spiritual
connection with the earliest Franciscan penitents. For this reason
some appreciation of the way in which it has been studied and some
attempt to categorize the varieties of interpretation now available
seem timely indeed. (The Third Order Regular celebrated the twentieth anniversary of its Rule and Life in 2002. In 2003 the Secular
Franciscan Order marked the twentyfifth-anniversary of the
"Pauline" Rule.)

---

3. Regis Armstrong and Ignatius Brady, eds., *Francis and Clare: The Complete Works*
(New York: Paulist Press, 1982).
4. The text for the Secular Franciscan Order Rule can be found in *Acta apostolicae sedis*
70 (1978): 454–55. The text for the Third Order Regular Rule is in Acta
apostolicae sedis 75 (1983), 544. Study editions are available from the national
offices of each entity.

I will proceed to examine four points: 1) the establishment of the text and subsequent publication; 2) problems associated with dating and naming the text; 3) interpretations of the spiritual and historical content; 4) prospects for future study.

Establishing the Text

Paul Sabatier published *The Exhortation* in 1900 after his discovery of the single surviving manuscript in codex 225 of the Bibliotheca Guarnacci in Volterra.[5] (Thus many early commentators used the designation "the Volterra letter." This title also helped to distinguish it from the other longer version of the text called *The Later Admonition and Exhortation to the Brothers and Sisters of Penance* in FA:ED and the *Second Version of the Letter to the Faithful* in the Paulist Press edition). Two thorny problems asserted themselves at once and have been with us ever since: dating and naming this work. It is not my intent to settle these arguments but to offer a summary of the current state of scholarship. Suffice it to say that *ab initio* there has been disagreement as to which of these texts is the earliest composition and which the later. Secondly—and this is a point to which we will return—the plethora of proposed titles for this short document makes it difficult to maintain clarity for both reader and writer.

But to return to Sabatier, he not only published the manuscript, he wrote glowingly of its extraordinary vision of Christian life. Sabatier's praise might have been just enough to convince those offended by the great Protestant's interpretations of Francis's program that contrary opinions must be registered. In any event, in spite of positive acceptance by Goetz, this document was not included in publications of the opuscula in 1904. Not until Esser and the Quaracchi editors assembled the texts for a new critical edition did another look at The Exhortation bring it to prominence. Esser, in an article first published in *Collectanea Francescana* in 1975 and published again in the *Analecta TOR*, validated Sabatier's views on the importance of the content with his own comments on its

---

5. For a very helpful summary of recent scholarship and fundamental points of reference, see Enrico Menestò, "A Re-reading of Francis of Assisi's Letter to the Faithful," *Greyfriars Review* 14.2 (2000): 97–110.

theological depth.[6] He also stated: "It is quite clear therefore that we have before us a written instruction directed toward persons who have joined the penance movement of the later Middle Ages, a movement to which Francis and his brotherhood were deeply attached and obligated."[7] He holds in favor of the position that this text is, indeed, an early draft — a *recensio prior* — of the longer text found in the Assisi codex 338 and in forty-seven other manuscripts. Following the critical edition of the writings, published in 1976, the new editions issued in various languages included two versions of this message to the early penitents or lay adherents of the Franciscan movement.

Esser's position was the "gold standard" of interpretation at that point, so it is small wonder that the work on both third order rules took his views into account and incorporated *The Exhortation* with the assumption that it represented the earliest witness of an official relationship between Franciscan the penitents. With the benefit of hindsight we can affirm that the emergence of Esser's work was nothing short of a providential confirmation of aspirations of many Third Order Regular scholars and students. In the wake of the counciliar call to renewal of identity based on a proper charism, Third Order Regular members had been frustrated by the ambivalence or ignorance that greeted their questions about their specific origins and spiritual patrimony. A 1974 gathering of superiors of this branch of the Order addressed the desire to use whatever scholarship was at hand to formulate better responses to the question of the place of the "third" order within the juridical, historical and theological frameworks being elaborated for renewal and refounding.[8] The rediscovery of this ancient text, now affirmed as a body of explicit directives from Francis to his earliest lay followers, appeared as manna on the parched land of tertiary needs and hopes.

The *Analecta TOR* under the editorship of Raphaele Pazzelli appropriated this material with enthusiasm and alacrity. As Third

---

6. Kajetan Esser, "A Forerunner of the 'Epistola ad Fideles' of St. Francis of Assisi (Cod. 255 of the Biblioteca Guarnacci of Volterra)," *Analecta TOR* 14.129 (1978): 11–47.
7. Esser, "Forerunner," 38.
8. Documentation of the proceedings of the Madrid meeting can be found in *Analecta TOR* 13.123 (1974).

Order federations throughout Western Europe and the Americas met the challenge of study in service of renewal, the work of Esser propagated by Pazzelli (and teams working on the new rules) disseminated Esser's views beyond scholarly circles very rapidly. It might not be an exaggeration to state that there has probably never been a more rapid evolution of a scholarly question's pastoral importance in Franciscan circles. Ignatius Brady stated that Esser first wrote his opinion on this text in 1974.[9] In less than a decade this "Volterra letter" was inscribed as a font of indelible importance in two papally approved rules followed by thousands of professed Franciscans. One can only hope that future generations will continue to make such concrete connections between scholarly work and the quotidian concerns of the Franciscan orders with as much conviction and enthusiasm.

Naming and Dating

The topic of dating this particular document is complex. Not only is there disagreement about the precise date for *The Exhortation*, there is a considerable opinion that it is the late version or summation of the longer document typically called the second version of *The Letter to the Faithful* or the *Later Admonition and Exhortation*. In short—what has been called the "first" letter since 1976 is now regarded by David Flood as certainly a later short summation of that "letter"—so it is, in fact, the "second." The reader will sympathize if I do not attempt a solution for that difficulty within this article. My real concern is the title.

The question of what to call these documents is equally vexing. The appendix that lists the titles from Sabatier to Armstrong-Hellmann-Short demonstrates at a glance the complexity of the problem. A few words to "connect the dots" may be helpful here.

Esser's edition put the proper Latin titles into relatively wide circulation. Thus the literal translation of the Paulist edition of the writings simply translated the "Epistola ad fideles" into "The Letter to the Faithful." Esser had, however, noted the dilemma concerning

---

9. See Ignatius Brady's "Introductory Note" in *Analecta TOR* 129 (1978): 11.

the title.[10] When Pazzelli examined the Volterra codex himself he discovered that Esser, working from a copy of the manuscript, did not have an important clue. The words *"Haec sunt verba vitae et salutis"* (These are the words of life and salvation) are in red ink! Esser and others thought they were the conclusion of the *Admonitions*, which are placed before this material in the codex. Now it was evident why the Quaracchi group missed the clear rubrical indication that these words were indeed a title. Thus, the choice of the title "Epistola . . . " was their insertion/solution to the question of how best to name this material. Pazzelli's discovery clarifies the rationale for Sabatier's preference for *"verba vitae et salutis."* This, the ancient form of title, was subsequently embraced by Pazzelli. This wording also is alluded to in the earliest manuscripts of the new Third Order Regular rule text. Nonetheless, the desire to find more manageable titles continued with the result that we now can survey fourteen attempts at a title spanning the years from Sabatier to the New City Press volumes.

While the choice of the New City editorial team can be validated by reference to several studies in the past decade, the difficulty of substituting two lengthy new designations ("Earlier Exhortation to the Brothers and Sisters of Penance" and "Later Admonition and Exhortation to the Brothers and Sisters of Penance") for two slightly shorter and much more familiar ones (*The First Version of the Letter to the Faithful / The Second Version of the Letter to the Faithful*) will be daunting for those promoting a new nomenclature.

Interpretation of the Content

If title and dating issues continue to engage the scholarly circle, how many issues concerning The Exortation's content and intended audience need our attention? The two questions are inextricably linked. Those who have made notable contributions to this part of our study include: Casolini, Lehmann, Flood, Freeman, Temperini, Pazzelli, Menesto, and Stewart — to offer a select

---

10. A thorough examination of the arguments concerning the title up to 1987 will be found in Pazzelli's "The Title of the First Letter to the Faithful," *Analecta TOR* 19.142 (1987): 231–48.

sampling. It is fair to note that in addition to articles in scholarly journals, a number of fine works intended for formative purposes have been published both by *The Cord* and by the Franciscan Federation of the Brothers and Sisters of the Third Order Regular of the USA. In this category writers such as Nancy Celaschi, OSF, Bernard Tickerhoof, TOR, Kathleen Moffatt, OSF and the late Thaddeus Horgan, SA have served their constituents with an abundance of helpful historical, linguistic and pastoral tools for assimilation of the penitential tradition.

Theological Interpretations: Pazzelli and Lehmann

In this category, Raffaele Pazzelli took up where Esser left off and continued to write on the theological depth contained within *The Exhortation*. While he has been equally at home with more technical concerns, Pazzelli who served as *peritus* to the TOR Rule project, has always been eager to emphasize the scope of the penitential program of the early Franciscans. In the tenth and eleventh chapters of his work, *St. Francis and the Third Order*, he explores the biblical and sacramental themes of the "letters."[11] Adherence to the church, the place of eucharist and priesthood, the state of penance as a journey to God, the characteristic virtues of the penitent, the relationship of penance/*metanoia* to the identity of the Third Order—all are themes that he underscores with his well-documented exploration of the texts. Add to this his survey of the rise of the Order of Penance in ecclesial tradition and we see that Pazzelli has consistently argued for a strong identification of *The Exhortation* with the equivalent of a "rule" for a clearly recognizable "sub-set" within the Franciscan fraternities of the first decades.

A more recent study by Capuchin Leonhard Lehmann takes great pains to outline similarities and divergences between the two versions of the text.[12] With precise attention to every linguistic nuance, he insists upon the profound spiritual content with its

---

11. Raffaele Pazzelli, *St. Francis and the Third Order* (Chicago: Franciscan Herald Press, 1989).
12. Leonhard Lehmann, "Exultation and Exhortation to Penance: A Study of the Form and Content of the First Version of the Letter to the Faithful," *Greyfriars Review* 4.2 (1990): 1–33.

contrast of the joy of the true penitent contrasted with the bitter experience of those who do not "do penance." Lehmann sees this work as "a contemplative prayer of praise and rejoicing."[13] This rejoicing is, however, balanced by the warning to those who remain in moral blindness. He stresses the active, urgent nature of the appeal to "doing" penance through good works. The practices of penance lead to an experience of filial relationship to God. The frequent juxtaposition of verbs *faciunt* (they do, make) and *sunt* (they are) express this mutual influence. Lehmann focuses on the Johannine content of the text. He proposes a new name: "Exultation and Exhortation to Penance." He holds it to be addressed to a group of followers of Francis, but also intended for a wider audience, a sermon transformed into a letter.

Social and Historical Interpretations: Flood and Chinnici

David Flood brings his considerable acumen to bear upon these questions with dramatic results.[14] However, convinced that the Volterra manuscript actually presents a later redaction of the original, his focus is on the longer *Exhortation*. I include some indication of his interpretation here just the same in view of the important alternative path he cuts out for attempting to reconstruct an adequate picture of the relationship between Francis and these early lay collaborators. In a little known study entitled, *Work for Everyone: Francis of Assisi and the Ethic of Service*, Flood proposed a reading that sees these documents as evidence of the economic agreements that forged the nascent Franciscan communities. To a fresh new translation of the later *Exhortation*, which he names "The Message," he adds a lengthy study. Its themes are the world of work, of labor, of economic necessity and of mutual respect and care arising from a reading of gospel imperatives by the hard-working Assisians. A single citation from *Work for Everyone* will serve to make the point:

---

13. Lehmann, "Exultation and Exhortation to Penance," 8.
14. David Flood, *Work for Everyone: Francis of Assisi and the Ethic of Service* (Quezon City, Philippines: FIA Contact Publications, 1997). This work is related to an earlier series of essays published in *Haversack* from 1979–1980. Details in the bibliography.

The new Penitents need the means of their survival and of
their human progress; and they need the sense of security,
that sense of security, which the brothers swore they found
in one another. Moreover, as movement people, insofar as
they enter into the spirit of the great adventure, they will
begin putting their means with ever greater assurance at the
service of the good cause. We see that in people today.
Many couples of means do not hesitate to use their
resources for the cause they believe in. In a parallel to Francis' terms, they invest in the broad action of a movement
and their lives expand accordingly. Francis encourages his
audience to continue the disciplines and the pieties of
Christian culture. In effect, he recuperates as much as he
can from the cultural substratum of medieval life. . . . The
point is that he is not simply its creature but first of all its
enhancer.[15]

Finally, Joseph P. Chinnici, OFM, in a turn-of-the-century lecture
on the practices of a Trinitarian life, used *The Exhortation* as a focal
point for describing the recovered vision of penitential practice for
our time.[16] With the text in hand, he invited his audience to see in
its content the paradigmatic model for engagement with the questions of contemporary culture. He finds in the text evidence that "in
this way of life, God-imaged practices and institutional embodi-
ments address the fundamental desires and needs of a people to
belong, to love and be loved, to be significant, to share, to create and
make. What is held out is hardly a society of 'loose connections'
without social capital, relational definition, common mission or
structured disciplines. . . . Rather this is a society that chooses to
proclaim God as a common good precisely because Goodness has
revealed itself within human experience as adoptive generating."[17]

---

15. Flood, *Work for Everyone*, 76.
16. Joseph Chinnici, "Negotiating the Social Gaps: Practicing a Trinitarian Experience
    in the Tradition of the Evangelical Life," *The Cord* 51.3 (2001): 138-52.
17. Chinnici, "Negotiating the Social Gaps," 148.

Postscript

We benefit from continuing growth of our grasp of the anthropological environment of the text. That growth in understanding can suggest that our way of reading it may owe far too much to the subtle conditioning of our image and experience of the contemporary relationship of friars to fraternities of secular Franciscans. We persist in imagining this to be the ancient version of the pastoral role of the friar "spiritual assistant" to the lay "tertiaries" in need of pastoral care and theological instruction, and, to that extent, we may be missing an important new reading of both social source and Franciscan scripture.

During a conference at the annual International Medieval Congress at Western Michigan University by Dr. Timothy Johnson in 2001, I was struck by his remarks on Francis as the "interpreter" of a medieval textual community. Following his lead, I began to work with Flood's representation of the early penitents as groups of workers and artisans gathered to reflect upon their Christian vocation.[18] For years, I lectured on this text formed by the explicit and implicit assumptions that accompany the notion of a "letter." The image and constructs that such a title suggest include the notion of an expert and an audience, of a leader and followers, of an organization in which the educated instruct the ignorant. The notion of the content comprising a sermon later recorded in letter form seemed self-evident. In fact, the practice we all know in our own time of friars serving as spiritual guides to groups of Franciscan "third order" members was implicitly influencing my image of what this particular "letter" represented.

Taking my cue from the conversation with Dr. Johnson and from some of the literature emerging in Europe concerning the early Franciscan movement, I began to reformulate my images and interpretations. The new "talking points" of my lecture now read as follows.

The penitents of the first Franciscan generations ponder a text, but it is not a letter from Francis; it is the letter of the gospel, the

---

18. This exercise in re-imagining the genesis of the document found a starting point in Flood and Johnson, but owes much to the other commentators mentioned here and in the bibliography.

scripture, with Francis as guide or recorder. They speak of the questions that life thrusts upon them: How shall I gain eternal life? How can I see/experience God? What is my destiny? Am I damned by reason of my secular calling and marginal social and ecclesial standing? The texts that respond to their questions emerge and find a place in their communal meditation. The texts are recorded and the words that recall their happy discoveries or their sobering conscientization are recorded as well. The result is this record of a community of penitents working out the Christian solution for existential problems. (For any person with experience of a Latin American *comunidade de base* the analogy is clear and inviting.)

Understood in this way, the continuing *de facto* debate over titles creates significant problems. As long as we are looking at a "letter" written by a highly visible charismatic leader to a largely nameless multitude, we keep reinforcing a kind of stereotypical image of even the earliest penitents. All of the other title versions that make this a "letter," "exhortation," "admonition," "epistle," *to* the penitents or other Christians, reinforce the prevailing image.

What is It?

These titles indicate a quasi-clericalized Francis addressing his less educated lay followers from a position of ecclesiastical responsibility for the care of their souls. The implications of the original position of Sabatier and the more recent echoes in Pazzelli and Flood fail to get our attention. Their "titles" — actually, their use of the material the manuscript provides — allows for a reading that places Francis within the circle of the community speaking its new truth. This image rising from the convergence of new insights about the text and about the textual communities of the late Middle Ages, needs time to mature. Would it be too rash to suggest that we erase all of the titles for an experimental period? Might we then read with fresh eyes the record of these earliest and undifferentiated strata of the evolution of Franciscan evangelical life?

Future Prospects

Should zealous students of Franciscan sources be willing to advance our understanding of *The Exhortation*, several kinds of work are available. Third Order friar, Peter Runje has offered a tantalizing example of following the path of the textual transmission to see what turns up.[19] In his study of an ancient Croation manuscript containing a glagolitic translation, he models a kind of research that might do much to advance our appreciation of the spread of writings addressed to those who followed the tertiary path. If we hypothesize that translations into language systems beyond the Romance languages indicate a wide appreciation of these texts, finding other early examples of such translation should be promoted.

Obviously, I have avoided taking a side in the question of the date of *The Exhortation* or its rank as first or second. It is equally obvious that I continue to hold to the position that it is the first version not a later summation. This may be stubborn habit, concern for the integrity of the two new Rule texts, or simply the inability to find my way through the maze of arguments for and against each position to a point of absolute certainty. However, the question is with us and will continue to be with us. Our commentaries and lectures must invite our audiences into an attitude of willingness to place current assertions in a path open to serious revision in the future.

The hermeneutical task that this document imposes will continue to provide new and demanding interpretations. We can already argue the danger of being satisfied with a single interpretive schema, whether that of a Lehmann or that of a Flood. Given the relatively recent publication of *The Exhortation*, we have many decades ahead in which to test our theories in the abstract and in the concrete. In the period following the Madrid TOR conference, Roland Faley and others worked to provide a strong foundation in biblical exegesis for the meaning of a call to "those who do penance." Since then, few Franciscan commentators have taken the

---

19. Peter Runje, "Dio 'Pisma Vjernicima I.' sv. *Franje u srednjovjekovnom hrvatskom prijevodu u Ivancicevu zborniku [Pars primae epistulae S. Francisci ad fideles lingua glagolitica* in *codice mediaevali]* Ivancicev Zbornik," *Kacic* 25 (1993): 437-48.

biblical-liturgical analysis of these particular texts forward with the
kind of thorough analysis that Robert Karris brought to his study of
the *Admonitions*, to give a single example.[20] The future uses of *The
Exhortations* would be well served by such thorough critique.

Conclusion

Finally, the milieu that gave rise to this fundamental experience
of the early Franciscans is gradually emerging from the shadows and
from the preoccupation of the last century with establishing the
history and spirituality of the First and Second Orders. Perhaps the
twenty-first century will witness an unfolding of the lay character
that stands at the root of Franciscan awareness. Perhaps in that
process this document (these documents?) will ultimately be read
alongside such key texts as the Rule of 1221, the *Admonitions* and,
the Rule of Clare as a repository of the most important indicators of
Franciscan authenticity for those engaged in its modern incarna-
tions.

Select Bibliography

D'Alatri, Mariano. *Lettera di san Francesco ai cristiani impegnati*. Rome: Istituto
    Storico dei Cappucini, 1978.
van Asseldonk, Optatus. "La lettera ai fedeli." *Vita Minorum* 52 (1981):
    153–62.
_____. "Non sapienti secondo la carne, ma semplici, umili e puri (2 *Lettera ai
    fedeli*, 45–60)" 157–70. In *Lo spirito da la vita: Chiara, Francesco e I Penitenti.
    Dimensioni Spirituali* 13, Rome: *Laurentianum*, 1994.
Aveling, Harry. "Reflection: A Letter from St. Francis (EdFidI)." *The Cord* 38
    (1988): 257–61.
Blasucci, Antonio. *Una Forma di vita cristiana nel mondo secondo S. Francesco in
    Ritorno di S. Francisco*. Rome: CIMP, 1978.
_____. *Frate Francesco. A tutti gli abitanti della terra (Epistola ad fideles II)*. S.
    Maria degli Angeli-Assisi: Edizioni Porziuncola, 1976. Also "Epistula as.
    Francisci Asisinatis ad fideles." *Latinitas* 25 (1977): 256–59.

---

20. Robert Karris, *The Admonitions of St. Francis: Sources and Meaning* (St. Bonaventure,
    NY: Franciscan Institute, 1999), ix-xi.

Candela, Elena. "*L'alter Christus* nella *Epistola ad fideles* di Francesco d'Assisi" 957–72. In *Sangue e antropologia nel medioevo. Atti del VIII settimana della Pia Unione Preziosissimo Sangue. Roma 25–30, November 1991*. Vol. II. Edited by F. Vattoni. Rome, 1993.

Casolini, Fausta. "Un ipotesi reguardante il 'Memoriale propositi' dal 1221 e a 'lettera ai fideli.'" *Frate Francesco* 46 (1979): 237–39.

Conti, Martino. "Il genere letterario della lettera di san Francesco a tutti i fedeli. Una lettera per la pace." *Vita Minorum* 58 (1986): 29–38.

Doerger, Berard. "Brother Francis Sends Greetings: A Study of the Letters of St. Francis." *The Cord* 35 (1985): 228–40.

Del Fabbro, P. Leoppoldo. *San Francesco d'Assisi, Lettera a tutti I fedeli e ai reggitori di popoli. 2ᵃ e 3ᵃ parte del Testamento*. Franciscana 3. Commento di Vicenza. L.I.E.F., 1992.

Esser, Kajetan. "La lettera di San Francesco ai fedeli" 65–78. In *L'Ordine della penitenza di san Francesco d'Assisi nel secolo XIII. Atti del Convegno di studi francescani. Assisi, 1972*. Edited by Octavian Schmucki. Rome: Convegno di studi francescani, 1973. [*Collectanea Franciscana*, XLIII, 1973].

Desbonnets, Théophile. "La lettre à tous les fidèles de François d'Assise." In *I frati Minori e il Terzo Ordine: Problemi e discussioni storiografiche. Atti del XXIII Convegno di Studi del Centro di studi sulla spiritualità medievale*. Todi: Accademia Tudertina, 1985. 53–76.

Flood, David. "The Commonitorium." *Haversack* 3.1 (1979–80). [Since this commentary is divided into six segments in vol. III I list the locations here for the reader's use: Commonitorium 1.1 (December 1979), Commonitorium 2.2 (December 1979), Commonitorium 3.3 (February 1980), Commonitorium 4.4 (April, 1980), Commonitorium 5.5 (June, 1980), Commonitorium 6.6 (August 1980).

_____. *Francis of Assisi and the Franciscan Movement*. Quezon City, Philippines: FIA Contact Publications, 1989.

_____. *Work for Everyone*. Quezon City: FIA Contact Publications, 1997.

_____. *Franciscans and Work*. Unpublished ms. Franciscan Institute, 2001.

Freeman, Gerard Pieter. "Gelukkig wie in Jesus' voetspoor gaat. Een historisch kommentaar op de twee redakties van de Brief aan de Gelovingen von Francisjus van Assisi." Diss. Utrecht, Katholieke Theologische Hogeschool, 1981.

_____. "Hoestralend is de Heilige Geest? Bij de vertaling van 2BrGel 55." *Franciscaans Leven* 71 (1988): 225–27.

Horgan, Thaddeus. "The First Letter to All the Faithful." *The Cord* 35 (1985): 303–10.

Lauriola, Giovanni. "La personalità di Francesco d'Assisi nelle sue lettere." *Frate Francesco* 49 (1982): 163–79.

_____. "Il pensiero di Francesco d'Assisi nelle 'lettere.'" *Italia francescana* 57 (1982): 541–60.

Lehmann, Leonhard. "Der Mensch franziskus im Licht seiner Briefe." *Wissenschaft und Weisheit* 46 (1983): 108–38.

_____. "Exultation and Exhortation to Penance: A Study of the Form and Content of the First Version of the Letter to the Faithful." *Greyfriars Review* 4.3 (1990): 1–33; original in *Laurentianum* 29 (1988): 564–608. See also,

Metodi di lettura delle fonti francescane. In *Collana: Dimensiioni Spirituali 9*. Edited by E. Covi and F. Raurell. Rome: Editrice Collegio S. Lorenao da Brindisi, 1988.

_____. "Der Brief des hl. Franziskus an die Völker Aufbau und missionarische Angliegen." *Laurentianum* 25 (1984): 287–324.

Lopez, Sebastian. "Mas con el ejemplo que con las palabras. Siendo rico, eligio la pobreza (2Cta F, 5)." *Selecciones Francescanesimo* 8 (1979): 321–34.

Matanic, A.G. "San Francesco d'Assisi scrive a tutti i cristiani." *Frate Francescano* 50 (1983): 19–28.

Mateo, Guillén and Maria Pilar. "La inhabitación trinitaria en Francisco de Asís, según la carta a los fieles: 'Los que hacen penitencia'" 60–101. In *La habitación trinitaria: experiencia del amor*. Rome: Pontificium Athenaeum "Atonianum" *Institutum Franciscanum Spiritualitatis*, 1993.

Pastor-Oliver, B. "Un precurso de la 'carta a los fieles' de San Francisco de Asis (Codice 225 de la Biblioteca Guarnacci de Volterra) Comparación con otros textos precedents." *Analecta TOR* 14 (1980): 751–68.

Pazzelli, Raffaele. "Il titolo della 'Prima recensiione della lettera ai fedeli:' Precisaziioni sul Codice 225 di Volterra (cod. VO)." *Analaecta TOR* 19.142 (1987): 233–40. ["The Title of the 'Recensio Prior of the Letter to the Faithful:' Clarifications Regarding Codex 225 of Volterra (cod.VO)," *Greyfriars Review* 4.3 (1990): 1–6].

_____. "Le somiglianze di idée e di fraseologia fra le 'lettera ai fedeli' e la 'Rogola non Bollata:' come ipotesi di datazione." *Analaecta TOR* 21.146 (1989): 213–34.

Runje, Peter. "Dio 'Pisma Vjernicima I.' sv. Franje u srednjovjekovnom hrvatskom prijevodu u *Ivancicevu zborniku [Pars primae epistulae S. Francisci ad fideles lingua glagolitica* in *codice mediaevali]* Ivancicev Zbornik." *Kacic* 25 (1993): 437–48.

Stewart, Robert. De illis qui faciunt penitentiam. *The Rule of the Secular Franciscan Order: Origins, Development Interpretation*. In *Bibliotheca Seraphico-Cappucina 39*. Rome: Istituto Storico dei Cappuccini, 1991.

Sabatier, Paul. "Fratris Francisci Bartholi de Assisio Tractatus de indulgentia S. Mariae de Portiuncula, nunc primum integer edidit P. Sabatier" 132–35. In *Collection d'études et de documents sur l'histoire religieuse et littéraire du Moyen âge*. Vol. II. Paris: Libraire Fischbacher, 1900.

Temprini, Lino, ed. *Frate Francesco a tutti i suoi fedeli*. Rome: Franciscanum, 1996. [Contains reproduction in color of Volterra ms.]

Tickerhoof, Bernard. "Francis' Volterra Letter: A Gospel Spirituality." *The Cord* 29 (1979): 164–75.

Saint Francis's Doxological Mysticism in Light of His Prayers

Jay M. Hammond

Saint Francis of Assisi has probably had more written about him than any other medieval religious figure.[1] It is indisputable that later hagiography portrays him as a mystic, even *the* mystic *par excellence*. More recently Ewert Cousins, largely supporting his argument with Bonaventure's theology, even boldly states, "There is reason to claim that Francis' visionary mysticism had more influence in shaping the history of Christian spirituality than any other mystical experience in history."[2] Considering the prominent place allotted to Francis in the history of Western Christian mysticism it is odd that only a handful of studies interpret his mysticism in light of his own writings instead of refracted through the lens of stories about him. Methodological approach is crucial because the mystical element that emerges from his own writings contrasts considerably with the various depictions narrated by the hagiographical traditions. Thus, an integral facet of reinterpreting Saint Francis's significance for the

---

1. The superb collection *Francis of Assisi: Early Documents*, vols. I–III (New York: New City Press, 1999–2001) testifies to this fact. All citations utilize the abbreviations in these volumes and simply refer to them via volume and page number: Test (I, 124–27).
2. Ewert Cousins, "Francis of Assisi: Nature, Poverty, and the Humanity of Christ," in *Mystics of the Book*, edited by R.A. Herrera (New York: Peter Lang, 1993), 203. Elsewhere Cousins argues that Francis inaugurates a new form of mysticism which he calls "mysticism of the historical event," but his interpretation is again largely based on the mystical theology of Saint Bonaventure, not the writings of Francis ["Francis of Assisi: Christian Mysticism at the Crossroads," in *Mysticism and Religious Traditions*, edited by Stephen Katz (Oxford: Oxford University Press, 1983), 163–90].

twenty-first century will be a better understanding of how his writings can be labeled mystical.

Several studies in the last twenty years have already begun by asking whether Francis was a mystic,[3] and countless others simply assume he was. Two studies are of particular relevance. Octavian Schmucki examines several elements and themes which he identifies as mystical including: Trinitarian and Christological indwelling, radical passivity, divine goodness and love, Eucharistic devotion, Christ's sonship, the image and likeness of God, spiritual nuptials, evangelical discipleship, and a theocentric view of nature leading "to a vital, cosmic sense of unity with the being and life of nature."[4] In response to Schmucki's study, Bernard McGinn comments:

> There is a difference between expressing fundamental theological truths that underlie mysticism and a teaching that sets out a program of mystical transformation, whether expressed in exegetical, theoretical, or biographical terms. From this perspective, it does not seem that the majority of Francis's writings are explicitly mystical. There may, however, be a few exceptions to this, especially among the saint's prayers.[5]

---

3. In chronological order: Octavian Schmucki, "Fundamental Characteristics of the Franciscan 'Form of Life,'" *Greyfriars Review* 5 (1991/German 1979): 325–66; Norbert Nguyên-Van-Khanh, *The Teacher of His Heart: Jesus Christ in the Thought and Writings of St. Francis* (St. Bonaventure, NY: Franciscan Institute, 1994/Italian 1984), 4–7; Kurt Ruh, *Geschichte der abendländische Mystik. Band II, Frauenmystik und Franziskaniche Mystik der Fruhzeit* (Munich: Beck, 1993), 380–98; Thaddée Matura, *Francis of Assisi: The Message in His Writings* (St. Bonaventure, NY: Franciscan Institute, 1997/French 1996), 31, 86–88, 178–85; Bernard McGinn, "Was St. Francis a Mystic?" in *Doors of Understanding: Conversations on Global Spirituality in Honor of Ewert Cousins*, edited by Stephen Chase (Quincy, IL: Franciscan Press, 1997), 145–74; and Paul Lachance, "Mysticism and Social Transformation According to the Franciscan Way," in *Mysticism and Social Transformation*, edited by Janet Ruffing (New York: Syracuse University Press, 2001), 55–75. For an older study that offers a valuable overview and analysis of Francis's mysticism see Éphrem Longpré, "Frères mineurs: I. Saint François d'Assise," in *Dictionnaire de Spiritualité* 5, 1292–1303.
4. Octavian Schmucki, "The Mysticism of St. Francis in Light of His Writings," *Greyfriars Review* 3 (1989): 241–66, quotation from 263.
5. Bernard McGinn, *The Flowering of Mysticism* (New York: Crossroad Publishing, 1998), 41–64, quotation from 54. Earlier McGinn comments, ". . . a perusal of Francis's own writings gives sparse evidence of emphasis on the mystical element in Christianity . . . it is difficult to claim that his writings can, in general, be called mystical literature, despite the efforts of some to make them so" (50–51); later he reiterates, "All of this is ample evidence for the richness of the theology of *Il*

However, McGinn does not illustrate why or how Francis's prayers can be considered mystical. The only prayer he considers with any depth is *The Canticle of the Creatures*, which he says expresses a "single harmonious theophany of God" that represents "a distinctive form of theophanic nature mysticism."[6]

Even though both scholars focus on Francis's writings, these two studies approach Francis's mysticism from two different perspectives. Schmucki employs a broader, more open understanding of mysticism and therefore more easily interprets Francis's writings as mystical.[7] McGinn is more cautious and applies a narrower criteria for mysticism: "a teaching that sets out a program of mystical transformation, whether expressed in exegetical, theoretical, or biographical terms." But according to his own criteria, such an assertion does not necessarily substantiate that some of Francis's prayers, especially the *Canticle*, are *per se* mystical.[8] So even though McGinn acknowledges some of Francis's prayers as mystical, his study lacks an *applied* hermeneutical framework by which the prayers can be interpreted as mystical. Although both Schmucki and McGinn help clarify the issue at hand, neither directly demon-

---

    Poverello, but not, I submit, for explicit and developed mystical teaching" (53); and footnote 117 states, "My claim is that we cannot penetrate to what Francis chose not to speak of, but that we can show that what he did express and what was said about him became the basis for new forms of mystical expression" (346).

6. McGinn, *Flowering*, 55 and 56. He elaborates: "Francis presents a specifically Christian nature mysticism in which God's presence is experienced as luminously real and immediate in the cosmos as a whole and in each of its elements insofar as they reflect some aspect of the divine fullness."

7. Schmucki states, "Mysticism is the immediate experience of a supernatural sharing in the life of the triune God, though it is psychologically conditioned and therefore not independent of one's temperament and cultural values" ("The Mysticism of St. Francis," 246).

8. Given the expansive scope of McGinn's massive history of Western Christian mysticism, it is understandable that he could not dedicate the space needed to tease out the nuances of his argument. He simply demurs to Matura's judgment (*Flowering*, 345, footnote 117): "Although Francis is rightly regarded as one of the greatest of saints, he is never thought of as a mystic or theologian. But, as the Fathers of the Church understood the terms, a *mystic* is someone who discovers and penetrates into the mystery of God and His works, while a *theologian* discerns and contemplates the depths of visible and invisible reality. In the patristic sense, then, Francis was both a mystic and theologian" (Matura, *Francis of Assisi*, 31). Even though I am critical of McGinn's reservations concerning Francis's mysticism, I am indebted to his research in the area of mysticism. As my own research demonstrates, I have adopted his criteria and guidelines for examining the mystical elements in Francis's writings.

strates *how* Francis programmatically sets forth an explicit and
developed teaching that leads to mystical transformation.

I argue Francis's prayers[9] constitute an explicit form of
doxological mysticism that conveys his mystical consciousness of
God while expressing a consistent teaching of mystical transformation. It is precisely in the act of praising God that Francis responds
to his encounter with God's direct presence thereby leading to a
transformation of consciousness. And since he chose to preserve his
prayers, he wanted to share his practice of praising God with others
thereby constituting a disseminated teaching.[10] To demonstrate
this, I will examine four of Francis's prayers: *The Prayer before the
Crucifix* (1205/06), Chapter 23 of the *Earlier Rule* (1220), *The Praises
of God* (1224), and *The Canticle of the Creatures* (1225–26).

Furthermore, by employing the metaphor of a circle, I will also
illustrate that Francis mediates his doxological mysticism through
Christ.[11] First, *The Prayer before the Crucifix* metaphorically positions

---

9. Francis's corpus contains approximately twenty prayers. Some are independent,
some exist within larger works, and there are inevitably others not mentioned
here scattered throughout his writings. The prayers include: PrCr (I, 40), 2LtF 61–62
(I, 49–50), ER 17.17–19 (I, 76), ER 21.2–9 (I, 78), ER 23.1–11 (I, 81–86), PrsG
(I, 109), CtC (I, 113–14), CtExh (I, 115), LtOrd 26–29 (I, 118), LtOrd 50–52 (I,
120–21), ExhP (I, 138), OfP (I, 139–57), OfP antiphon (I, 141), OfP closing
prayer (I, 141), PrOF (I, 158–60), PH (I, 161–62), SalBVM (I,163), and SalV (I,
164–65). The editors of FA:ED did not assign an abbreviation to *The Praises to be
Said at All Hours* so I utilize the abbreviation PH in the footnotes. For the general
elements of Francis's prayer see Leonhard Lehmann, *Francesco: Maestro di Preghiera*
(Rome: Istituto Storico dei Cappuccini, 1993), 21–40.

10. In two places Francis offers blessing for those who copy, disseminate, preserve and
study his writings: 2LtF 88 (I, 51) and 1LtCl 15 (I, 53). Francis also repeatedly
stresses that people should teach by example: 1LtF 10 (I, 42), 2LtF 53 (I, 49), ER
4.6 (I, 66–67), ER 11.6 (I, 72), ER 17.3 (I, 75), LtOrd 8–9 (I, 117), Adm 7.4 (I,
132), Adm 9.2 (I, 132), Adm 20.1–3 (I, 135). And in the Test (I, 124–27) Francis
begins with five personal examples (1–23) by which the four issues in part two
should be addressed (24–33) so that the brothers "might observe the Rule we have
promised in a more Catholic way" (34). And AC 84 (II, 186) reports that Francis
taught the brothers the CtC so they could "go through the world preaching and
praising God." The evidence suggests that Francis desired his "teaching" to be
disseminated to others so they could observe them in order to come into closer
relationship with God.

11. For an excellent study of Christ in Francis's own writings see Nguyên-Van-Khanh,
The Teaching of His Heart; for a study of the relationship between Christ and Francis
in the later hagiographical tradition see Giovanni Iammarrone, "La Sequela di
Cristo nelle fonti francescane," *Miscellanea Francescana* 82 (1981): 417–61. We
must not forget that Francis's Christology always functions within a Trinitarian
dynamic. It is more accurate to say that his writings are theocentric in a Trinitarian
sense than they are Christocentric. Moreover, he never speculates on the mystery

Francis on the circumference of a circle looking in at the center who is Christ. Second, Chapter 23 of the *Earlier Rule* encapsulates his summative description of the journey toward the center by following in the footsteps of Jesus Christ.[12] Third, *The Praises of God* figuratively locates him at the center of the circle shortly after receiving the stigmata. Fourth, *The Canticle of the Creatures* culminates with Francis symbolically standing in the circle's center gazing out at the wondrous circumference of all of God's creation through the eyes of Christ. In effect, Francis has come full circle both literally and figuratively. Literally, from his conversion to his debilitating illness, he begins and ends his quest of following Christ at San Damiano. In this journey, he has figuratively progressed toward closer union with God through Christ who "is the perfect doxology, the perfect reflection of God's glory."[13] Thus, in contrast to many of the mystics in the Christian tradition who end with apophatic imagery, Francis's doxological approach is *hyper-*cataphatic.

---

of the Trinity, rather it functions as his interpretive framework through which he understands salvation history. Francis's writings simply relate to God as Trinity. 1LtF 6–13 (I, 42) and 2LtF 48–53 (I, 48–49) present clear examples of how he interweaves the Trinity, Christ and the Spirit. LtOrd 50–52 (I, 120–21) and ER 23 (I, 81-86) also encapsulate his Trinitarian hermeneutic. For an overview of the place of the Trinity in Francis's thought see Matura, *Francis of Assisi*, 53-88. For a study on the nature and role of the Father see Thaddée Matura, "'My Holy Father!' God as Father in the Writings of St. Francis," *Greyfriars Review* 1.1 (1987): 105-33; for Christ see Nguyên-Van Khanh, "*The Teacher of His Heart*," 59-89; and for the Spirit see Optatus Van Asseldonk, "The Spirit of the Lord and Its Holy Activity in the Writings of St. Francis," *Greyfriars Review* 5 (1991): 105-58.

12. Five times Francis mentions following in the footprints of Jesus Christ. This image was fundamental to his understanding of living a life as a penitent. Its importance can be measured by the fact that Francis opens his ER with it. Thus, the life he proposed was "to follow the teaching and footprints of our Lord Jesus Christ" ER 1.1 (I, 64); also see 2LtF 13 (I, 46), Adm 22.2 (I, 79), LtOrd 51 (I, 121), LtL 3 (I, 122-23).

13. Arlo Duba, "Doxology," in *The New Dictionary of Sacramental Worship*, edited by Peter Fink (Collegevill, MN: Liturgical Press, 1990), 366.

Some terminological clarification is in order. First, doxological simply means "an utterance which expresses praise to God."[14] Scriptural,[15] sacramental,[16] and liturgical[17] elements pervade Francis's prayers and they all intertwine to form the basis from which his doxological mysticism springs forth. Although his prayers describe God with a multitude of terms, he consistently employs six terms to stress how one should pray to God by giving all praise, glory, thanks, honor, blessing and good to God.[18] These six are the leading characteristics of his doxology. Specifically, he employs the term *praise* (*laudo*) seventy-four times in his writings and reserves it for God alone. Only God, who is the source of all good, is worthy of praise. The refrain from *The Praises to be Said at All Hours* encapsulates Francis's basic attitude of praise: "Let us praise and glorify Him

---

14. Duba, "Doxology," 365.
15. Scripture is omnipresent throughout Francis's writings and studies on his use of scripture are substantial. See Matura, *Francis of Assisi*, 15-21; Nguyên-Van-Khanh, *The Teacher of His Heart*, 187-215; Théophile Desbonnets, "The Franciscan Reading of the Scriptures," 45, and Anton Rotzetter, "Mysticism and Literal Observance of the Gospel in Francis of Assisi," 56-64, in *Francis of Assisi Today*, edited by Christian Duquoc and Casiano Floristán (New York: Seabury Press, 1981).
16. Often when Francis writes about the Eucharist he also speaks of God's Word(s) in the same breath. Of the eleven places he mentions the Eucharist, seven likewise refer to scripture within the context of the sacramental presence, see: Adm 1.9 (I, 128), 2LtF 34–35 (I, 47–48), 1LtCl 1–12 (I, 52–53), 1LtCus 2–8 (I, 56–57), LtOrd 12–37 (I, 117–19), and Test 10–12 (I, 125). This indicates that he perceived the living sacramental presence of both the Eucharist and scripture in almost identical terms. For the times he speaks of the Eucharist without mentioning scripture, see: ER 20.5 (I, 78), 1LtF 3 (I, 45), LtR 6 (I, 58), and Adm 26 (I, 136). Also see Matura, *Francis of Assisi*, 67–75, 121–26; Nguyên-Van-Khanh, *The Teacher of His Heart*, 153–86; Raoul Manselli, *St. Francis of Assisi* (Chicago: Franciscan Herald Press, 1988), 290–97; and Bernard Cornet, "Le 'De Reverentia Corporis Domini,' exhortation et lettre de saint François," *Etudes Franciscaines* 6 (1995): 65–91, 7 (1996): 28–58, 155–71, 8 (1997): 35–53.
17. Francis emphasizes the importance of the Office in five places: ER 3.10 (I, 65–66), LR 3.1–4 (I, 101), LtOrd 41–43 (I, 119–20), RH 3–6 (I, 61), and Test 18 especially 29–33 (I, 125–26). For an analysis of the important place of the Office in Francis's prayer see Octavian Schmucki, "Divine Praise and Meditation according to the Teaching and Example of St. Francis of Assisi," *Greyfriars Review* 4.1 (1990): 23–40.
18. Although there are other terms Francis employs (holy, respect, fear, adore, love, believe, serve, magnify, exalt; at least eighty-six qualities in all) to describe how one should pray to God, he consistently combines variations of these six terms in at least ten places: 2LtF 61 (I, 49–50), 1LtCus 7 (I, 57), LtR 7 (I, 59), ER 17.18 (I, 76), ER 21.2 (I, 78), ER 23.11 (I, 85–86), CtC 1, 14 (I, 113–14), ExhP 1–15 (I, 138), OfP closing prayer (I, 141), PH 1–11 (I, 161–62).

forever."[19] Francis accepts all things as free gifts from an utterly good God, and he freely returns everything to God through praise. Poverty and praise sum up his basic attitude before God and so the essence of his doxological mysticism is the joyous and kenotic affirmation: *All is Gift! Praise God!*[20]

Second, to avoid getting bogged down in the current debates on mysticism, I turn to McGinn's heuristic description of the term: "the mystical element in Christianity is that part of its belief and practices that concerns the preparation for, the consciousness of, and the reaction to what can be described as the immediate or direct presence of God."[21] Moreover, I further qualify the meaning with the comments McGinn ascribes to Francis's writings, "a teaching that sets out a program of mystical transformation,"[22] but I identify Francis's prayers as doxological rather than "exegetical, theoretical, or biographical."[23] It is within a doxological framework that I will illustrate how Francis's prayers represent a doxological mysticism. Thus the goal is to demonstrate how Francis's practice of praising God expresses his consciousness of and response to God's direct presence resulting in a program of mystical transformation.

---

19. PH 1–10 (I, 161). Francis recited this undated prayer at least eight times daily in preparation for saying the Office. See footnotes 17, 131 and 133 for a further explanation of Francis's practice of reciting the Office. Also see Lehmann, *Francesco: Maestro di Preghiera*, 99–121.

20. In the deepest sense this is the true meaning of Franciscan poverty. All freely comes from God, so to cling to anything is to restrict God's gifts. To be poor is to be open to God and to return everything to God who is the original source.

21. McGinn, *The Foundations of Mysticism*, xvii. This description is actually the last of three guidelines he outlines, namely: 1) mysticism is always part of a wider religious tradition, and 2) mysticism is always a process involving all life's aspects (xviii–xx); also see his later summaries and clarifications on the same issues in *The Growth of Mysticism*, x–xi, *The Flowering of Mysticism*, xi–xiii, and "Quo Vadis? Reflections on the Current Study of Mysticism," *Christian Spirituality Bulletin* 6.1 (1998), 13–21.

22. McGinn, *The Flowering of Mysticism*, 53–54.

23. Elsewhere McGinn clarifies his position: "The fundamental characteristic of a mystical text, as I view the matter, rests in the way in which it invites and instructs the reader toward a transformation of consciousness in God, whether this is done on the basis of a more or less autobiographical account, through exegesis of the mystical sense of scripture, or in *some other form*. Mystical texts are fundamentally invitations toward a new framework that transforms all the activities of consciousness" ("Quo Vadis?" 18). Thus, I propose doxology as "some other form" that invites and instructs the recipient in a particular practice leading to the opportunity for a mystical transformation of consciousness.

Illustrating *how* Francis teaches an explicit doxological program leading to mystical transformation is elusive because there is a real gap between what we can know about his mysticism and what he explicitly states about his experiences of God. Nowhere in his writings does Francis provide a direct account of his own visions, ecstasies or mystical experiences.[24] In *Admonition* twenty-one, he warns against such a practice, stating that one's behavior, rather than one's words, should reveal God's gifts, and *Admonition* twenty-eight states, "Blessed is the servant who safeguards the secrets of the Lord in his heart."[25] Thus, was Francis simply silent about his experiences of God? I think not. But since we are barred from direct access to his mystical experiences, we are left to examine the evidence by judging their effects upon him. After all, this is really the only standard ever offered by Jesus: "You will know them by their fruits" (Mt 7:16).

Yet, to discern Francis's doxological mysticism through its effects as evidenced in his prayers is a delicate matter. My approach is threefold.[26] First, since texts always have con-texts, Francis's prayers must be situated in their appropriate historical settings because their doxological content can not be properly understood without examining when, why, and how they were written. Thus, later sources will be examined to help furnish the contexts of his prayers. Second, a comparison of the contexts and Francis's response to them via the contents of his prayers allow their effects to emerge into greater clarity. Third, identifying the effects, which

---

24. In fact, only the *Testament* provides any autobiographical details about Francis's spiritual journey; see Test 1–23 (I, 124). Therein Francis claims "the Most High Himself revealed to me that I should live according to the pattern of the Holy Gospel" (14; also see 39). However, this declaration does not provide any description of the event.

25. Adm 21.1–2 (I, 135), Adm 28.3 (I, 137).

26. My presupposition is that historical events embed Francis's prayers, and a contextual reading of his prayers allows for a recovery of Francis's own description of key historical events wherein he encountered God. McGinn's comments regarding mystical texts are worth repeating: "Those who define mysticism in terms of a certain type of experience of God often seem to forget that there can be no direct access to experience for the historian. Experience as such is not a part of the historical record. The only thing directly available to the historian or historical theologian is the evidence, largely in the form of written records . . ." (*The Foundations of Mysticism*, xiv). Since Francis only left written records, and a surprising amount for one who considered himself *simplex et idiota* [LtOrd 39 (I, 119)], it is to these that the researcher must turn to discern his contribution to mysticism because the abundance of Franciscan iconography implies secondary theological interpretation.

are embedded in the prayers, signal Francis's consciousness of God's presence.

Francis's prayers convey his encounter with God, and he shares them not only to inform, but also to transform the consciousness of others by eliciting like praise from them, which in turn, leads to an opportunity for encountering God's presence. In this sense, Francis's prayers offer a consistent teaching of transformation that can be termed doxological mysticism. Although his prayers do not present explicit information *about* mysticism, they do convey an expressed teaching that mystical transformation occurs *through* and *in* the act of praising God.[27] To read Francis's prayers in such a way is to discover that what first may appear tacit is actually a profoundly simple and simply profound form of doxological mysticism.

The Prayer before the Crucifix (1205/06)[28]

While this prayer is not *per se* doxological nor mystical, I include it for four reasons: it is the earliest of Francis's prayers, it does contain inceptive doxological elements, it conveys Francis's encounter with God during his initial conversion, and it illustrates how he mediates his prayer through Christ.

The prayer's exact context remains hidden in the shadows of history.[29] Yet its context is not completely lost. After being disillu-

---

27. Of course language mediates Francis's experience, and even though experience *qua* experience remains inaccessible to the observer, language attempts to convey the meaning(s) of experience to others. Thus, mystical texts always present "encoded experience(s)" which are charged with multiple meanings. So even though mystical "experience" is always interpreted, mediated, and communicated through, in, and by language, experience can and does precede conscious thought. In other words, there can be an encounter/experience without language but no language without experience. It is to this "immediate" or "direct" encounter that we attempt to penetrate via Francis's prayers which employ language to convey his consciousness of the event.

28. FA:ED I, 40 (*Fontes* 167; Esser, *Opuscula*, 354-62); also see Lehmann, *Francesco: Maestro di Preghiera*, 41-60.

29. The prayer was probably "polished" by others as the editors of FA:ED suggest: "the prayer was embellished and lost some of its simplicity" (I, 40). But even though the prayer has an "editorial history," its content still "remained fundamentally the same" and summarizes Francis's yearnings during his conversion (Lehmann, *Francesco: Maestro di Preghiera*, 48). Also see Regis Armstrong, *St. Francis of Assisi: Writings for a Gospel Life* (New York: Crossroad, 1994), 34. Lehmann also argues that the prayer is a clear example of Francis's vernacular writings (*Francesco:*

sioned by his imprisonment in Perugia and lengthy illness
(1202–04), Francis was restless. Later sources place this prayer on
Francis's lips as he entered the deteriorating church of San
Damiano and knelt before the crucifix (1205).[30] For example, *The
Legend of the Three Companions* conveys that the Spirit led Francis
into the church,[31] where he received a reply to his petition, "Lord
that I may carry out Your holy and true command." All the stories
concur that the crucifix responded, "Francis, don't you see that my
house is being destroyed? Go, then, and rebuild it for me."[32] Christ
gives Francis a command to follow him for the rest of his life, and
Francis simply answers, "I will do so gladly Lord." Whatever the
historical veracity of this event, the prayer indicates that Francis
was searching to discern God's will. Regis Armstrong emphasizes
this point by broadening the prayer's context, suggesting that it
may be from an extended period when Francis initially struggled to
know God's will for him.[33] During this spiritual struggle Francis
probably recited this prayer repeatedly as he sought consolation
from God.[34] There is nothing to indicate otherwise.

Regardless, the prayer represents Francis's desire for conversion
sometime between 1205 and 1206. During this time there was a
great deal of activity as Francis struggled to discern God's will.
Some of the events narrated in later stories include:[35] his dream on

Maestro di Preghiera, 43). The *Fontes* and Esser's *Opuscula* both contain Latin and
Italian versions.

30. See FA:ED II, 76, footnote a. For analysis of the crucifix see Marc Picard, *The Icon of
the Christ of San Damiano* (Assisi: Casa Editrice Francescana, 1989); for
information on the church of San Damiano see Marino Bigaroni, "San
Damiano-Assisi: The First Church of Saint Francis," *Franciscan Studies* 47 (1986):
45–97.

31. L3C 13 (II, 76).

32. This quotation is from L3C but all the other references are in substantial
agreement even though they employ variant phraseology. However, the two earlier
accounts 1C 8–9 (I, 188–89) and LJS 6 (I, 373) do not narrate the story about the
crucifix speaking to Francis when he enters San Damiano.

33. Armstrong, *St. Francis of Assisi*, 31.

34. Lehmann, *Francesco: Maestro di Preghiera*, 41.

35. Interestingly, the stories about Francis in the *Prophet*, which covers 1277 to 1365,
omit *any* reference to Francis's conversion. In effect, the texts present him as the
perfect saint, one who does not struggle to discern God's will; rather, he knows
God's will and fights the odds and obstacles that prevent him from attaining his
goal. Such an interpretation precludes any interior conversion by assigning all
impediments to external factors. Francis is thereby portrayed in a much more
"objective" manner by removing the "subjective" struggles of his conversion.

the way to Apulia in the spring of 1205,[36] his living with and service to lepers and outcasts of society later that summer,[37] his experience before the crucifix at San Damiano[38] along with his conflict with his father in the fall,[39] and his renunciation of the world before Bishop Guido in the spring of 1206.[40] By the summer of 1206 Francis began to repair San Damiano so he wrote this prayer before that date. These events illustrate that Francis's initial conversion was a process.[41] Undoubtedly this time was marked by intense emotion, confusion and spiritual awakening to God's presence. Thomas of Celano captures this tension: "He prayed with all his heart that the eternal and true God guide his way and teach him to do His will. He endured great suffering in his soul, and he was not able to rest until he accomplished in action what he had conceived in his heart."[42]

---

36. 1C 5 (I, 185–86), LJS 3 (I, 371–72), AP 5–7 (II, 36), L3C 5–6 (II, 70–71), 2C 6 (II, 245–46), LMj 1.3 (II, 533).

37. While 1C 17 (I, 195) and LJS 12 (I, 376–77) present Francis's association with lepers as a movement of humility *after* stripping naked before the bishop, L3C 11–12 (II, 74–75) reports he moved in with lepers *before* publicly renouncing his social status before the bishop. Thomas shifts his chronology in 2C 9 (II, 248) by placing Francis's encounter with a single leper and then houses of lepers *before* the incident with the bishop. Bonaventure follows the chronology of 2C in LMj 1.5–6 (II, 533–34) and now presents the event as an encounter with Christ crucified; also see LMj 2.6 (II, 539), LMn 1.4 (II, 686), 4Srm (II, 750). While the later sources consistently mention other events, in Test 1-3 (I, 124) Francis only reports the encounter with the lepers when describing his conversion. His choice is instructive (as is the purpose of the *Testament*) for only his actions with the lepers fulfill Jesus' command, "love one another as I have loved you" (Jn 15:12). In effect, Francis points to the "first fruits" of his conversion to instruct his brothers in the way of following Christ. He does not expect the brothers to reproduce all his "conversion events," but he does expect them to follow Jesus' commandment which necessarily leads to conversion. Also see AC 9 (II, 123).

38. L3C 13 (II, 76), 2C 10 (II, 249), LMj 2.1 and 2.7 (II, 536, 540), LMn 1.5 (II, 686); also see 4Srm (II, 760), Jacopo de Voragine's *Golden Legend* 5 (II, 792), and the anonymous *A Life of Francis* 5 (III, 841).

39. 1C 10–12 (I, 190–92), LJS 7–8 (I, 373–74), AP 8–9 (II, 37), L3C 16–17 (II, 78–79), 2C 12 (II, 251), LMj 2.2 (II, 537).

40. 1C 14–15 (I, 193–94), LJS 9 (I, 375), AP 8 (II, 37), L3C 19–20 (II, 79–80), 2C 12 (II, 251), LMj 2.4 (II, 538).

41. See Pierre Brunette, *Francis of Assisi and His Conversions* (Quincy, IL: Franciscan Press, 1997). The idea of process touches on McGinn's second characteristic of mysticism, "mysticism is always a process or a way of life" (*Foundations*, xvi). Although it escapes the focus of the present paper, I can only comment in passing that an authentic and lasting conversion opens to and is probably a result of a new consciousness of God's presence. In short, mystical encounters and conversions are inextricably intertwined.

42. 1C 6 (I, 187).

So in the midst of his restless search for conversion, *how* does
Francis respond? He responds by turning to the "Most High,
glorious God" in humble prayer. Three points from this earliest
prayer are significant. First, inceptive doxological elements are
present in the opening praise of God who is unqualifiedly "Most
High." Francis uses the term "Most High" (*altissimo/summe*)
thirty-five times and reserves it only for God generally, God the
Father, Jesus Christ, or once for wisdom given by God.[43] Over half,
twenty-one, occur in Francis's prayers. Before the Most High
Francis humbly asks for enlightenment. Such an attitude is basic to
Francis doxology as it is expressed in his later writings and forms the
core to the mystical dimension of his prayers. Experience taught
Francis to simply call God the "Most High" from whom all goodness flows. He later elaborates in his daily prayer: "All-powerful,
most holy, most high, supreme God: all good, supreme good, totally
good, You Who alone are good, may we give You all praise, all glory,
all thanks, all honor, all blessing, and all good."[44]

Second, this short prayer has three simple parts containing two
invocations and two petitions.[45] The first invocation, "Most High,
glorious God" is immediately followed by the first petition,
"enlighten the darkness of my heart." Francis asks for the light of
the "Most High" to penetrate the darkness of his heart.[46] Such is the

---

43. God/Trinity: PrCr (I, 40), ER 17.17–18 (I, 76), twice in ER 23.11 (I, 85–86), PrsG
    3 (I, 109), CtC 1, 2, 4, 11 (I, 113–14), LtOrd 1 (I, 116), Test 14 (I, 125), Adm 7.4
    (I, 132), Adm 8.3 (I, 132), Adm 28.2 (I, 137), OfP part 4, compline 6 (I, 154), PH
    11 (I, 162); Father: 2LtF 4 (I, 46), PrsG 2 (I, 109), LtOrd 4 (I, 116), LtOrd 50 (I,
    121), Test 40 (I, 127), OfP antiphon 2 (I, 141), OfP part 1, prime 3 (I, 143), OfP
    part 1, vespers 2 (I, 147), OfP part 5, vespers 2, 4, 8 (I, 156); Christ: 1LtCl 3 (I,
    52), 2LtCl 3 (I, 54), LtOrd 14–15 (I, 117), Test 10 (I, 125), OfP part 5, vespers 4
    (I, 156); wisdom: Adm 5.6 (I, 131).
44. PH 11 (I, 162).
45. Lehmann, *Francesco: Maestro di Preghiera*, 48–49. The three parts consist of: 1)
    "Most . . . heart," 2) "enlighten . . . knowledge," and 3) "Lord . . . command."
46. Awareness of the heart's disposition is a preeminent concern for Francis
    throughout his writings. Fifty times he mentions the heart (excluding the
    Worchester Cathedral Fragments). His teaching on the heart is thoroughly
    biblical: nine times he alludes to a pure or clean heart [Mt 5:8 in 2LtF 14 and 19 (I,
    46), ER 22.26 and 22.29 (I, 80), LR 10.9 (I, 105), LtOrd 42 (I, 120), three times in
    Adm 16 (I, 134)]; five times he refers to loving God with all one's heart [Dt 6:5, Mt
    22:39, Mk 12:30, Lk 10:25 in 1LtF (I, 41), 2LtF 18 (I, 46), ER 23.8 (I, 84), LtOrd
    7 (I, 117), PrOF 5 (I, 159)]; five times he asserts that sin flows from one's heart
    [Mt 15:18–19, Mk 7:21–23 in 1LtF 12 (I, 43), 2LtF 37 and 69 (I, 48, 50), ER
    22.7–8 (I, 79)]; six times he mentions sowing/hearing God's Word in one's heart

basic insight of Francis's conversion, so easily known in theory but so hard to appropriate in praxis. To know *what* to desire, is an intellectual assent to which he had already committed himself, but *how* to fulfill his desire is more a matter of the heart. Joining the two is the struggle of his conversion and of every conversion. Thus, he simply asks for transformation by praying for the theological virtues to inform his heart.[47] Yet, aware of his own spiritual poverty, he is sure that only the "Most High" can give *true* faith, *certain* hope, and *perfect* charity. Francis turns from his own "darkness" and relies totally upon God's gifts. Only with God's gifts can he correctly use his senses and knowledge to fulfill God's will. Here the prayer ends with the second invocation to the "Lord," and the second petition, "that I may carry out Your holy and true command." The prayer's simplicity should not obscure its two poles: invocation where he asks and intention where he acts. And both hinge on God's gifts of faith, hope, and charity. Francis begins by seeking God's will (enlighten) and he ends by doing God's will (command). Indeed, this is a prayer for conversion. Its effect moves Francis from simply knowing to actively doing God's will. Such an encounter marks a conversion of Francis's consciousness because it resulted in a *wholehearted* embrace of Christ.

Third, only by considering the immediate context of where Francis utters this prayer before the crucifix of San Damiano, does a Christological dimension emerge. The prayer's specific context before the cross calls for a recognition of the mediating, even sacramental function the crucifix plays. It is *through, by,* and *in* the mediation of the cross that Francis offers his prayer to God. And so, it is *through, by* and *in* Christ's cross that he seeks "true faith, certain

---

and/or the devil's intention to snatch it away [Mt 13:19, Lk 8:12 twice in ER 22.13, once in 22.17, and three times in 22.19–20 (I, 79), LtOrd 6 (I, 116)]; two other times he quotes scripture as it relates to the heart [Lk 21:34–35, Lk 18:1 in ER 9.14 and 22.29 (I, 71, 80)]; and he quotes the psalms ten times with eight occurring in the OfP [Ps 62:9 in LtOrd 28 (I, 118); Ps 4:3 in Adm 1.14 (I, 129); and in the OfP, Ps 62:9 (I, 118), 69:21 (I, 142), twice from 57:8 (I, 143), 22:15 (I, 146), 20:5 (I, 152), 13:2 and 13:6 (I, 154)]. Moreover, he juxtaposes the heart with the body in three places [1LtF 10, 12–14 (I, 42–43), 2LtF 14, 53 (I, 46, 49), ER 22.5–8 (I, 79)].

47. Francis refers to the theological virtues in only one other place, PrsG 5 (I, 109). Interestingly, he only mentions the theological virtues within the context of the crucifixion: 1) the San Damiano crucifix and 2) the stigmata.

hope, and perfect charity, sense, and knowledge," and only *with* the cross can Francis carry out God's command. Consequently, this prayer for conversion indicates *how* Francis understood God's relationship to him, namely, the humility of the cross reveals the "Most High," and the light of this mystery brings the darkness of his heart into focus.[48]

Like Christ crucified, Francis, at the outset of his conversion, abandons everything to the Father's will, which implies a death to one's own self. This is graphically illustrated by the fact that this prayer is the last time Francis utilizes the first-person singular until, twenty years later, he writes *The Canticle of the Creatures* and employs the first-person singular possessive pronoun *mi* (my).[49] As will be shown, the *Canticle* is Francis's vision of the new creation wherein he receives a *new* personal identity. To seek God's will is to be open to the possibility of radical conversion, the very reorientation of one's identity, even to the point of death by embracing the transformative mystery of Christ's cross. Even though the prayer does not explicitly mention the crucifixion, its context indicates this mystery as a seminal aspect of Francis's mysticism.

Thus, Christ crucified is the *medium* through whom Francis offers his prayer, and Christ crucified is likewise the *medium* or center of Francis's entire spiritual journey. It is to Christ crucified that Francis fixes his heart's desire and it is with Christ crucified that he abandons everything and sets out to follow and fulfill the Lord's commands. Here we can begin to envision the metaphor of the circle mentioned in the introduction. Francis is figuratively on the circle's circumference looking in at the center who is Christ upon whom he now centers his entire life.

In a context of existential unease and restlessness, the *Prayer before the Crucifix* stands out as a simple prayer for conversion. But on

---

48. Lehmann, *Francesco: Maestro di Preghiera*, 53.
49. Francis also utilizes the first-person singular in the CtExh 4 (I, 115), but, as the title indicates, this writing may be interpreted more as a exhortation to the sisters rather than a prayer. Overall, excluding direct quotations from scripture (110 times), Francis employs the first-person singular "I" in pronoun or verb form 101 times in his writings, and excluding quotations from scripture (again 110 times), he employs the first-person singular possessive "my" 49 times. Francis's prayers usually employ the second person plural "we/us" or third-person singular indicative.

a deeper level it points toward the "mystical transformation" of Francis's consciousness as he encounters the presence of the "Most High" in the humility of the cross. Conversion leads Francis to seek a new identity lovingly shaped by God's will. Such a "mystical" encounter reoriented Francis's identity and redirected his life. These effects largely define Francis's subsequent journey toward God, a journey he explicates further in Chapter 23 of the *Earlier Rule*.

Chapter 23 of the Earlier Rule (1220)[50]

The *Earlier Rule* is Francis's longest writing and Chapter 23, with the exception of *The Office of the Passion*, is his longest prayer.[51] The prayer's position in the *Earlier Rule* and its length indicate its importance to Francis. But why does he insert such a long prayer to conclude a legal document?[52] David Flood argues that Chapter 23 "concerns the life of the friars around 1220,"[53] and even though he warns that "the concrete circumstances which gave rise to this song remain unknown to us,"[54] its general context can be hypothetically reconstructed.[55]

---

50. FA:ED I, 81–86 (*Fontes*, 209–11; Esser, *Opuscula*, 399–401); also see Leonhard Lehmann, "*Gratias agimus tibi*: Structure and Content of Chapter 23 of the *Regula non bullata*," *Laurentianum* 23 (1982): 312–75; reproduced as "*We Thank You*: The Structure and Content of Chapter 23 of the Earlier Rule," *Greyfriars Review* 5.1 (1991): 1–54.
51. Since the OfP mostly consists of a compilation of the Psalms, Chapter 23 can arguably be Francis's longest "original" prayer. Given the length of Chapter 23, it is interesting that the entire prayer only contains eleven sentences, two of which (2 and 10) are quite short.
52. Lehmann considers this question in "*Gratias agimus tibi*," 347–51.
53. Flood, *The Birth of a Movement*, 48–51, quotation from 48. This work is derived and developed from Flood's earlier study, *Die Regula non bullata der Minderbrüder* (Werl: Dietrich-Coelde-Verlag, 1967), 133–35.
54. Flood, *The Birth of a Movement*, 51.
55. I base my reconstruction on evidence presented by Miccoli in "Francis of Assisi's Christian Proposal," *Greyfriars Review* 3.2 (1989): 153–61; Manselli, *St. Francis*, 222–32; Arnaldo Fortini, *Francis of Assisi* (New York: Crossroad, 1981), 453–56; John Moorman, *A History of the Franciscan Order* (Oxford: Clarendon Press, 1968), 46–61; Edith Pásztòr, "St. Francis, Cardinal Hugolino, and the 'Franciscan Question,'" *Greyfriars Review* 1 (1987): 1–29; James Powell, "The Papacy and the Early Franciscans," *Franciscan Studies* 36 (1976): 248–62, especially 255–59; Malcolm Lambert, *Franciscan Poverty: The Doctrine of the Absolute Poverty of Christ and the Apostles in the Franciscan Order 1210–1323* (London: SPCK, 1961), 1–30, 68–72; Kajetan Esser, *Origins of the Franciscan Order* (Chicago: Franciscan Herald

After learning of the difficulties and changes facing the brother-hood during his year-long absence in the Holy Land,[56] Francis returned to Italy, and in the turmoil of preparing the final draft of the *Earlier Rule*,[57] he composed Chapter 23 as an addendum to emphasize his understanding of the gospel life he proposed.[58] The level of discord at this time can be measured by two facts: Francis's resignation as Minister General in September of 1220,[59] and the

Press, 1970), 137–85; and Kajetan Esser, "*Sancta Mater Ecclesia Romana*: Die Kirchenfrömmigkeit des hl. Franziskus von Assisi," *Wissenschaft und Weisheit* 24 (1961): 1–26.

56. See *Chronica fratris Iordani* 11–15, edited by Pierre Beguin (Louvain: CETEDOC, 1990); translated by Placid Herman in *XIIIth Century Chronicles* (Chicago: Franciscan Herald Press, 1961), 26–30. Also see Moorman, *History*, 50–52.

57. Concerning the redrafting of the Rule, AC 102 (II, 206–07) reports that Francis vented: "The brother ministers think they can deceive God and me. Indeed, that all the brothers may know that they are bound to observe the perfection of the holy gospel, I want it written at the beginning and at the end of the Rule that the brothers are bound to observe the holy gospel of our Lord Jesus Christ." If Francis fought for this, then his wish seems to be embodied in the LR 1.1 which begins "to observe the holy gospel of Our Lord Jesus Christ" and ends 12.4 "we may observe poverty, humility and the holy gospel of our Lord Jesus Christ as we have firmly promised." Also see 2C 62 (II, 288), KSF 19 (III, 704), Manselli, *St. Francis of Assisi*, 256–72, and Powell, "The Papacy and the Early Franciscans," 255–59.

58. There is internal cohesion between Chapters 22 and 23. Whereas 22 represents Francis's expectations of the brothers in the form of a "testament" prior to his departure to Egypt in 1219 and the prospect of martyrdom, 23 signals Francis's realization that his expectations are not being actualized. Thus, upon his return and the project of rewriting the Rule, Francis inserts Chapter 23 as a concluding *forma vitae* for his brothers, a life to be formed by praise; see David Flood, *Die Regula non bullata der Minderbrüder, Franziskanische Forschungen, Heft* 19 (Werl: Dietrich-Coelde-Verlag, 1967), 133–36. In contrast, Kajetan Esser does not arrive at the same conclusion arguing that Chapter 22 is a summary of gospel discipleship for instructing the brothers, *Textkritische Untersuchungen zur Regula non bullata der Minderbrüder, Spicilegium Bonaventurianum* 9 (Grottaferrata: Editiones Collegii S. Bonaventurae ad Claras Aquas, 1974). Also see Lehmann, "*Gratias agimus tibi*," 348–49.

59. AC 11 (II, 125–26) reports Francis resigned with the simple statement "From now on I am dead to you." There are a number of possible explanations for his resignation: 1) the reality of his failing health; 2) the incomparability of his growing power with his desire for a life of simplicity; 3) the opportunity to teach his fellow brothers, by way of example, about humility and obedience; 4) the fact that the order simply became too large for Francis to govern; and/or 5) the disillusionment over the growing rift between his primitive gospel ideal and the direction of the brotherhood toward conformity with more traditional structures and contrivances (Manselli, *St. Francis*, 230–32; Fortini, *Francis of Assisi*, 453–56; and Moorman, *History*, 51). It would be prudent to consider all these aspects as playing a part in this trying time of Francis's life, but Francis's firm averment "I am dead to you" strongly suggests that his decision was not entirely amicable. As a result of his resignation, Francis assigned Peter Catanii, his earlier travel companion in the Holy Land, to replace him, and asked Pope Honorius III to name Cardinal Hugolino the protector of the brotherhood. After Peter's death in March 1221, Elias is named vicar, and in March 1227 Hugolino becomes pope Gregory IX.

rejection of the *Earlier Rule* in the spring of 1221.[60] Regardless of why he resigned and the Rule rejected, it is an irrefutable fact that there was a painful crisis resulting from the tension between the original form of life envisioned by Francis and opposing viewpoints and developments in the brotherhood.[61] The problem of codifying the Rule brought rivaling parties, both within and outside the order, face to face in a struggle to control the order's development and direction. Raoul Manselli terms this time as "a gigantic and tragic clash."[62] Thus, when Thaddée Matura calls this prayer Francis's *Credo*,[63] it is within this context of crisis that Chapter 23 should be read as a concise synthesis of Francis's understanding of the gospel life he proposed for himself and the brothers, an understanding that was being questioned, challenged, and altered.[64]

---

60. It is clear that there was a week-long intense discussion of the ER at the General Chapter held at the Portiuncula in May 1220 (ChrJG 15–17; in Herman, *XIIIth Century*, 30–34), but the historical reasons for its rejection are unclear. There are several possible explanations: 1) those writing the Rule were not satisfied with it because it did not convey what was intended; 2) the brothers who were to receive the Rule were not satisfied with it because they did not agree with the vision proposed; and/or 3) the ecclesiastical authorities were not satisfied with it because it lacked clear juridical norms acceptable to the curia. Again, it is prudent to consider all these possibilities, but all of them, either individually or collectively, speak to the fact that the rejection itself signals disagreement over the nature and form of the Rule, and therefore, to the struggle for a normative interpretation of the Franciscan ideal. See, Manselli, *St. Francis*, 256–72; Moorman, *History*, 51–52; Powell, "The Papacy and the Early Franciscans," 258–59; and Esser, *Origins*, 151–85.

61. See Esser, *Origins*, 184; Lambert, *Franciscan Poverty*, 68–72; Moorman, *History*, 46–61; McGinn, *Flowering*, 49–50; and Miccoli, "Francis's Christian Proposal," 153–61.

62. Manselli, *St. Francis of Assisi*, 198. McGinn is less dramatic. He describes the situation as "a painful tension [that] developed between Francis's original vision of apostolic spontaneity and the necessity for organization, rationalization, and full ecclesiastical approbation" (*Flowering*, 49).

63. Matura, *Francis of Assisi*, 33. He writes, "This section of the *Rule* must have been very dear to Francis because he lingered so long over it and used it as a glorious finale to the plan of the gospel life which he proposed to his brothers." Matura only considers ER 23.1–6. My comments incorporate all of Chapter 23. Others also envision Chapter 23 as Francis's *Credo*: Armstrong, *St Francis of Assisi*, 101; Lehmann, "*Gratias agimus tibi*," 314; Kajetan Esser and Englebert Grau, *Love's Reply* (Chicago: Franciscan Herald Press, 1963), 3; and Flood, *Die Regula non bullata*, 134.

64. For an alternative interpretation see "*Gratias agimus tibi*," 341–51 where Lehmann argues that the context is not the negative challenges but the positive situation of the growing order that now sought to minister to a "universal audience." For a similar argument see Flood, *The Birth of a Movement*, 50. My brief historical reconstruction critically questions Lehmann's and Flood's claim that Chapter 23 emerges "positively" from the order's "rapid growth" and the "universal audience"

If this historical sketch is valid, then Chapter 23 provides access
to Francis's own understanding of God's presence as he faced the
flux in the life of the brothers around 1220. The prayer provides a
critical framework for discerning *what* effects God's presence had
upon Francis's consciousness and *how* he communicated his
consciousness to others. In short, Francis conceived penance as
joyful praise with peace as the ultimate goal.

So *how* does Francis respond? He responds with a doxological
laude that serves as a *forma vitae*.[65] In a setting of strife he calls his
brothers to action by praising God, and their thankful praise *is* their
reconciling penance. So as the brothers and others argued over the
Rule, Francis attempts to remind everyone of the original intention,
purpose, and ultimate goal of living the Rule: *All is Gift! Praise God!*
If the *Earlier Rule* represents the means to living the gospel life, then
Chapter 23 renders its end, namely, giving all praise and all
thanksgiving to God. By doing this, Francis desires to move the
brothers from divisive arguments to harmonious praise.

While the prayer's content forms a *Credo*, its function is
distinctly doxological. Part I (1–6) is an invocation directly
thanking God, while part II (7–11) is an evocation inspiring
everyone to join in thankful praise for God's overflowing gracious-
ness and goodness.[66] The first presents God's action, the second
represents a call to action addressed to all humans. Four points,
corresponding with the prayer's basic structure,[67] highlight this
doxological function and bring Francis's mysticism into clearer
focus.

---

to whom the brothers could now reach with their preaching. Alternatively, I too
situate the prayer within the order's rapid expansion, but consider the audience
primarily to be the Lesser Brothers themselves who are interpreting, living and
arguing over the Rule in ways that did not correlate with Francis's own
understanding of the Rule. Thus, the prayer resulted from what Francis judged to
be "negative" developments within the order, and he responded to them by calling
his brothers to conversion through prayer. Only then should the brothers preach
to others. On the order's rapid growth see Esser, *Origins*, 37–40.

65. Lehmann, "*Gratias agimus tibi*," 349.
66. For a similar explanation see Lehmann, "*Gratias agimus tibi*," 321–23.
67. The prayer has two parts, each subdivided into two sections: part I, section 1
    contains sentences 1–4, and section 2 includes sentences 5–6; part II, section 1
    involves sentences 7–8, and section 2 consists of sentences 9–11. See Lehmann,
    "*Gratias agimus tibi*," 321–26, and Flood, *Birth of a Movement*, 49.

First, the prayer's all encompassing theme is thanksgiving. Seven times the prayer repeats variations of "We thank you" (*gratias agimus tibi*).[68] Specifically, sentences 1–5 open by alternating between positive thanks offered to God and negative actions that alienate humans from God. Throughout, Francis's doxology engages the dynamic dialogue of salvation history:

Sentence 1: (+) We thank You:
    1) for yourself
    2) for creating everything
    3) for making humans

Sentence 2: (–) Through our own fault we fell

Sentences 3–4: (+) We thank You:
    1) for our creation through your Son
       and his Incarnation
    2) for our redemption through
       his cross, blood and death
    3) for our salvation through his
       return and judgment of:[69]
          (–) the wicked
          (+) the blessed

Sentence 5: (–) We, wretches and sinners, are not worthy
       to pronounce Your name.

---

68. *Gratias agimus tibi* occurs in sentences 1–5, *tibi gratias* in 6 and *gratias agamus* in 11. A more literal translation for *gratias agimus tibi* is "we give you thanks" and better captures that the prayer is a *gratiarum actio*.

69. The direct quotation of Jesus' words from Mt 25:34 that ends the first section of the prayer's first part intensifies the concept of the final judgment where the wicked and the blessed will be separated according to the measure of their penance. Parallels are found in 1LtF 1.1, 2.1 (I, 41, 43), 2LtF 25, 63 (I, 47, 50) and ER 21.7–8 (I, 78). In Chapter 23 Francis presents stark contrasts: 1) the wicked who do not perform penance are sent into "eternal fire," while 2) the "blessed of my Father" who adore and serve God in penance "receive the kingdom prepared for you from the beginning of the world." The final judgment is a mainstay of Francis's eschatology. Shortly before his death, he returns to this theme in strophe 13 of the CtC (I, 114) where he again sets forth a sharp division between the blessed and the damned. For an analysis of Francis's eschatology see Kajetan Esser, "*Homo alterius saeculi*: Endzeitliche Heilswirklichkeit im Leben des hl. Franziskus," *Wissenschaft und Weisheit* 20 (1957): 180–97.

Sentence 5: (+) We humbly ask
    1) our Lord Jesus Christ
    2) and the Holy Spirit
    to give You thanks for everything.

Gratitude binds the entire prayer together. This underscores thankful praise as the programmatic element of Francis's doxological mysticism. Praise explicates *how* he understood the essential dynamic of responding to the salvific gifts of God's presence in Christ and the Spirit, which in turn, indicate the attitude and action that is to characterize the gospel life.

Second, there is logical organization between the three cascading orders (5: divine, 6: heavenly, and 7: earthly), and the prayer's basic division between God's action (1–6) and the exhortation to prayerful action by humans (7–11). This organization overlaps the cascading orders (5–7) with the prayer's basic division that represents the dialogue between God (1–6) and humans (7–11). A dialogue ruptured by sin (2), but reconciled by Christ (3–5). Throughout, Francis is clear that salvation depends on mediated communication with the Father.

Three times Francis humbly asks and begs others to praise God the Father.[70] These supplications correspond with: 1) the divine order (5), where Francis humbly asks God's self-gifts of Jesus Christ and the Holy Spirit, God's Word (Jn 1:1) and Breath (Jn 20:22), to utter his doxology to the Father because humans "are not worthy to pronounce Your name;" 2) the heavenly order (6), where the first litany, in response to God's love, humbly begs the heavenly host to thank unceasingly the Father, Son and Spirit for everything; and 3) the earthly order (7), where the second litany joins the lesser brothers with everyone on earth who "humbly ask and beg those who wish to serve the Lord God" by persevering "in the true faith and in penance . . ." These three orders involve everything that exists and every relationship. All salvation history is caught up in Francis's thankful doxology. Francis excludes nothing from the

---

70. The three petitions of sentences 5–7 form linguistic parallelisms. Sentence 5: "we humbly ask" (*suppliciter exoramus*); sentence 6: "we humbly beg" (*humiliter deprecamur*); and sentence 7: "we humbly ask and beg" (*humiliter rogamus et supplicamus*). See Lehmann, "*Gratias agimus tibi*," 329.

glorious dialogue of praise. This sweeping vision holds Francis in God's universal presence.

Yet, the three cascading orders overlap with the prayer's basic division corresponding with the two long back to back litanies inviting all to share in praising God.[71] The numbers in these two litanies are significant. Sentence 6, which ends part one, contains a litany of thirty saints, angels and heavenly powers comprising the heavenly church triumphant. Sentence 7, which begins part two, lists a litany of forty groups or orders existing within the earthly church militant. Altogether Francis invokes seventy "other voices" to join the lesser brothers in praising and thanking God for *everything*. The number seventy signifies Francis's desire to offer perfect praise in thanksgiving for the Father's perfect gifts, namely, Jesus Christ and the Holy Spirit through, in and by which the dialogue of salvation history unfolds. The effects are significant. Francis summons and joins *everyone* in thankfully praising God for *everything*, with the implication that the union of the heavenly and the earthly churches becomes real through doxology. Francis teaches that both the heavens and the earth join in the sacred dialogue of salvation history by giving doxological praise to God who is the loving source of every gift.

Equally significant to the number seventy is the place of the lesser brothers within both litanies. The English translation obscures the fact that the lesser brothers are in the last place within the second long litany.[72] At the very center of the prayer (7), Francis presents the lesser brothers as humbly accepting the last place behind everyone else in heaven and on earth. Thus, the lesser brothers are "useless servants" (Lk 17:10) who desire to serve God with faith and penitence. It is with this desire, emphasized by the

---

71. The double affirmation "Amen. Alleluia!" that separates the two litanies at the end of sentence 6 directly emphasizes the prayer's basic division. See Lehmann, "*Gratias agimus tibi*," 331–32.

72. It is also noteworthy that the second litany begins with *Domino Deo* and ends with the lesser brothers. In short, God is first, and the lesser brothers are last. See Lehmann, "*Gratias agimus tibi*," 337.

inclusive summons of the second person plural throughout,[73] that Francis gently and subtly invites his brothers to overcome their differences through, in and by praising God. Their praise is to serve God by literally serving everyone who goes before them, from "our Lord Jesus Christ" to "all peoples everywhere on earth."

Third, but *how* is a penitent, led by Jesus Christ, the Spirit, and the heavenly church (part I), to remain in "true faith" and return, via penance, to the loving presence of God the Father? Francis's instruction is straightforward (part II, section 2). He teaches that true faith and penance converge in praise: faith and penance is the root, thanksgiving and praise is the fruit. Faith and penance are the basic demands, and yet the only true demands, that Francis places upon the lesser brothers. Francis calls his brothers to action whereby their penance becomes real performance through and in their praise. And it is this "joyful playing before the Lord"[74] that the brothers are to preach, not only in word, but especially by example. Francis's exhortation to his brothers is simple, do your penance by praising God.

The particulars of *why* Francis calls his brothers to praise God are also clear.[75] He begins "let us all love the Lord God" with everything we are because God "did and does everything good for us" even though we are "ungrateful." The language of salvation is one of gift: God gives entirely, and so a penitent Francis exhorts everyone to give themselves entirely. The union of the two is love. Sentence nine speaks to this reciprocal self-giving. God's fecund goodness made a particularly deep impression upon Francis. Eight times he acknowledges all good as belonging to God alone,[76] and six times he

---

73. Matura comments: "Francis's plural 'we' is like a thread that runs through the whole fabric of his prayer. Strangely, this 'we' concerns the present (which is normal) as well as the past. It is *we* who have been created, been placed in paradise and fallen. It is *we* who have been freed from the slavery of sin. It is for *us* that the kingdom was prepared 'from the beginning of the world,' that kingdom which we have lost but whose gates remain open to us" (38–39). In light of what has been done for us, Francis teaches his brothers that "we" should respond with thankful praise. For a closer linguistic analysis of the "we-form" see Lehmann, "*Gratias agimus tibi*," 330-31.
74. Flood, *Die Regula non bullata*, 135; also see Lehmann, "*Gratias agimus tibi*," 341.
75. Lehmann, "*Gratias agimus tibi*," 363-65.
76. 2LtF 61 (I, 49), CtC 1 (I, 113), LtOrd 8 (I, 117), Adm 7.4 (I, 132), Adm 17.1 (I, 134), Adm 18.2 (I, 134), ExhP 10 (I, 138), and the closing prayer of OfP (I, 141) which Francis would have repeated at least eight times a day.

praises God by repeating the word "good" (*bonum*) in rapid succession, as he does here in Chapter 23:

> Therefore,
> let us desire nothing else,
> let us want nothing else,
> let nothing else please us and cause us delight
> except our Creator, Redeemer and Savior,
> the only true God,
> Who is the fullness of good,
> all good, every good, the true and supreme good,
> Who alone is good.[77]

Francis experiences God's presence precisely in God's goodness.[78] Gratitude for God's goodness inspires Francis's doxology. Of the over fifty attributes Francis assigns to God in Chapter 23, the goodness of God as gracious Creator, Redeemer, and Savior is central.[79] This triad in sentence nine links the prayer's second part (human response) with its first part (God's action). Francis simply glimpses all as gift from an audaciously good God. In contrast, alone, isolated from God, he taught that "we may know with certainty that nothing belongs to us except our vices and sins."[80] Francis echoes a similar opinion in this prayer when he tersely states at the outset, "Through our own fault we fell."[81] It is only through and in Jesus Christ that the alienation from God can be reconciled. Such reconciliation inspires Francis to summon his brothers to a penitential and grateful attitude before God's gifts (part one), and to a greater consciousness of God's presence by submitting entirely to God through humble, heartfelt doxology (part two). To do so is to follow

---

77. ER 23.9 (I, 85). Four other times Francis presents a similar litany, see: ER 17.17-18 (I, 76), PrsG 3 (I, 109), PrOF 2 (I, 158), PH 11 (I, 162). The fifth source is from the fragment of the Worcester Cathedral, 1Frg 54 (I, 90).
78. Luke18:19 (Mt 19:17; Mk 10:18) "No one is good but God alone" was central in Francis's understanding of God and it is closely related to his understanding of poverty: "Sell all that you own and distribute the money to the poor, and you will have treasure in heaven; then come, follow me" [Lk 18:22 in ER 1.2 (I, 64)].
79. For an explanation of the Christological dimensions to this Trinitarian formula see Nguyên-Van Khanh, *The Teacher of His Heart*, 59–89. Also see Lehmann, *"Gratias agimus tibi,"* 336–37.
80. ER 17.7 (I, 75). Also see Matura, *Francis of Assisi*, 98–106 and 132–34.
81. ER 23.2 (I, 82).

Jesus, the Father's perfect doxology "Who always satisfies [the Father] in everything."[82]

Fourth, just as the prayer opens with an alternation between God's action and sinful humanity (1–5), it also ends with an oscillating movement between positive and negative exhortations that call humans to action by praising God (8–11). Thus, it calls everyone to love God with contrasting dimensions of responding to God:[83]

Sentence 8: (+) Let us love God with *everything* we are
and have even though we are
(–) "miserable and wretched, rotten and foul, ungrateful and evil ones."

Sentence 9: (–) Therefore, let us desire *nothing*
(+) except our Creator, Redeemer and Savior . . .

Sentence 10: (–) Therefore, let *nothing* hinder . . .
(this short sentence supplies extra emphasis)

Sentence 11: (+) Let us *always* and *everywhere* give thanks to the Father, Son and Holy Spirit our belief, hope and love.
(–) Seven negative or ineffable characteristics of the Trinity.
(+) Ten positive characteristics of the Trinity.

In effect, the second part of the prayer's basic division also alludes to the dynamic dialogue that is salvation history by teaching humans, or the brothers specifically, how to be conscious of God's presence through the act of praise. In sum, Francis insists that to be a penitent is to praise God, and this praise requires both positive and negative responses.

Chapter 23 encapsulates Francis's summative description of salvation history and his summons to all to participate in that history by following in the footsteps of Jesus Christ. The prayer also illustrates the place of Christ in Francis's doxological mysticism.

---

82. ER 23.5 (I, 83).
83. Lehmann offers a similar explanation in "*Gratias agimus tibi*," 326 and 363–70.

Francis turns to Christ as the way to the Father because without Christ, the dialogue of salvation history would be muted since humans "are not worthy to pronounce Your name." This Christological dimension of salvation history alludes to the metaphor of the circle. Moving from the circumference of his conversion, Francis here continues the journey toward the center of salvation history itself, to the mystery of the Father sending Jesus Christ. The *Earlier Rule* is Francis's roadmap for the journey. And if it represents the means to living the gospel life, then this prayer renders its end by giving all praise and all thanksgiving to God. By doing this, Francis reminded everyone of the very heart of Rule's goal: "to observe the holy gospel of our Lord Jesus Christ." However, history testifies to the fact that his summons to thank and praise God in Chapter 23 did not allay the problems confronting the growing fraternity and its rapid transformation into a canonical order. This dilemma stages the drama of Francis's final years.

The Praises of God (1224)[84]

The immediate context of this prayer signals the mystical climax of Francis's life. Throughout the Franciscan tradition and beyond, the stigmata has been presented as *the* defining event of Francis's life, as the definitive "proof" that he was a mystic *par excellence*, and as the divine seal of his form of gospel life inspiring the orders he founded.[85] While there is inevitably much theological truth to these claims, such declarations and explanations still remain secondary interpretations and reports. Only *The Praises of God* provide a portal to exploring what Francis wished to convey about the event.[86]

---

84. FA:ED I, 109 (*Fontes*, 45; Esser, *Opuscula*, 134–42); also see Lehmann, *Francesco: Maestro di Preghiera*, 247–78. The Latin title reads *Laudes Dei altissimi*, "Praises of the Most High God."

85. For references to the stigmata in the hagiographical tradition see the index, FA:ED IV, 127.

86. FA:ED I, 108. I base my analysis on the Lapsanski and Esser edition of the PrsG. For a contextual interpretation of the stigmata see Miccoli, "Francis's Christian Proposal," 160. For two contrasting interpretations of the stigmata see Octavian Schmucki, *The Stigmata of St. Francis of Assisi: A Critical Investigation in the Light of the Thirteenth-Century Sources* (St. Bonaventure: The Franciscan Institute, 1991); and Chiara Frugoni, *Francesco e l'invenzione delle stimmate: Una storia per parole e immagini fino a Bonaventura e Giotto* (Turin: Einaudi, 1993); also see, André Vauchez, "The Stigmata of St. Francis and Its Medieval Detractors," *Greyfriars Review* 13.1

While I assume the basic fact that *something* happened to Francis during his extended retreat at La Verna,[87] I contend that it is most prudent to look at his own veiled report of the event when discerning the meaning of his "seraphic" encounter with God.[88] Although the stigmata's context as well as the prayer's doxological content justifies identifying the *Praises* as "the writing of Francis the mystic,"[89] we must examine *how* the context and content support the text as mystical. Specifically, how do they affect Francis?

Brother Leo of Assisi provides the immediate historical context in the *Chartula*. He reports that Francis wrote *The Praises of God* while on retreat at LaVerna in the fall of 1224 after the vision of the seraph and reception of the stigmata.[90] Leo records that Francis wrote the prayer "in his own hand, thanking God for the kindness bestowed on him."[91] Other sources provide further historical information about Leo's desire to have a writing from Francis to help him overcome an unidentified "serious temptation" he was suffering at this time.[92] During this same period, Francis was also suffering an unidentified "serious temptation" that lasted for more than two

(1999): 61–89; and for a good summary of the current issues surrounding the stigmata see McGinn, *Flowering*, 59–64.

87. Francis's retreat was a forty day fast lasting from the feast of the Assumption (August 15) to the feast of Saint Michael the Archangel (September 29). Tradition reports that he received the stigmata on September 14, the feast of the exaltation of the cross, but an exact date is elusive.

88. For Frugoni's argument about the relation of the seraph to the PrsG see *Francesco e l'invenzione delle stimmate*, 139–48, especially 147 and 154 where she argues that Francis opens and closes the PrsG with implicit references to Isaiah 6 even though neither Esser's *Opuscula* nor the *Fontes* identify Isaiah as a source. The FA:ED follows the biblical references from the Psalms identified in the *Fontes*. While I am unconvinced that the PrsG reflects an implicit reference to the seraph in Isaiah 6, the PH, which Francis recited at least eight times daily, begins with "Holy, holy, holy Lord God Almighty" a direct reference to Isaiah 6:3. The PrsG and the PH share Francis's emphasis on praising God, and the PH shows that he praised God along with the seraphim.

89. Armstrong, *St. Francis of Assisi*, 203.

90. J.A. Wayne Hellmann convincingly argues that Brother Leo probably added his explanation on the *Parchment* or *Chartula* sometime after 1229, but does not provide a terminal date: see "The Seraph in Thomas of Celano's *Vita Prima*," in *That Others May Know and Love*, edited by Michael Cusato and Edward Coughlin (St. Bonaventure, NY: Franciscan Institute, 1997), 24–27; for a thorough analysis of the *Chartula* see Duane Lapsanski, "The Autographs on the 'Chartula' of St. Francis of Assisi," *Archivium Franciscanum Historicum* 67 (1974): 18–37.

91. FA:ED I, 108; Lapsanski, "The Autographs," 35.

92. 2C 49 (II, 280), LMj 11.9 (II, 618), LMn 4.6 (II, 701), Jacopo de Voragine's *Golden Legend* 41 (II, 801). The sources report that Leo's temptation was "of the spirit not the flesh," but do not provide any more details.

years (1222–1224?) causing him to *withdraw* from the company of the brothers.[93] What were these "serious temptations" that so upset these two close companions? To seek an answer, the historical context needs to be expanded beyond the *Chartula*.

Later sources give spotty evidence outlining the conflicts with which Francis wrestled, but the evidence usually does not directly situate the events within the drama of institutionalizing the order during Francis's the last two years.[94] In short, Francis was (along with his close companions like Leo) caught between being faithful to his vision of the gospel life and obedience to Rome which was (aligned with like-minded brothers) translating his gospel vision into more commonly accepted norms within the church.[95]

The tension is vividly described in Francis's outburst against following an existing monastic rule at the Chapter of Mats in 1222,[96] his remonstrative dismantling of a house next to the Portiuncula,[97] his stern response to the brothers regarding the Rule he was writing at Fonte Colombo in 1223,[98] the episode from an

---

93. AC 63 (II, 165–66), 2C 115 (II, 324), BPr 3.12 (III, 43), 2MP 99 (III, 346). The sources state that Francis's temptation was "of the spirit" and tormented him "inside and out, in body and spirit" but they do not identify the cause of the temptation. However, it was so severe that "he sometimes withdrew from the close company of the brothers."

94. However, a study that does examine Francis's last years in relation to the institutionalization of the order is Achim Wesohann's, "Simplicitas als Franziskanisches Ideal und der Prozess der Instutionalisierung des Minoritenordens," in *Die Bettelorden im Aufbau*, edited by Gert Melville and Jörg Oberste (Münster: Lit, 1999), 107–67; also see Moorman, *History*, 53–61.

95. Miccoli, "Francis's Christian Proposal," 153-61. On the question of Francis's understanding of obedience and division see Duncan Nimmo, *Reform and Division in the Franciscan Order* (Rome: Instituto Storico dei Cappuccini, 1995), 34-46. We should remember that it was Francis who first asked the Roman curia and Cardinal Hugolino to assist him with the growing order and its problems. However, bits of historical evidence indicate that Francis was not entirely satisfied with the direction of the help he received.

96. AC 18 (II, 132-33), WSF 4 (III, 124-25), 2MP 68 (III, 313-14), HTrb 45-95 (III, 402-04), KnSF 24 (III, 709-10). Miccoli, "Francis's Christian Proposal," 155-56. The Chapter of Mats is likely one of the Chapters of Pentecost held at the Portiuncula [AP 37 (II, 51), L3C 57 (100-03)]; see Rosalind Brooke, *Early Franciscan Government: Elias to Bonaventure* (Cambridge: Cambridge University Press, 1959), 287, and Moorman, *History*, 54.

97. 2C 57 (II, 285), 2MP 7 (III, 260-61). The sources do not provide a date for this event. Also see 2C 58 (II, 286) where it narrates that Francis kicked all the brothers out of a "house of the brothers" located in Bologna; 2MP 6 (III, 259-60), HTrb 158 (III, 406-07).

98. AC 17 (II, 131-32), WSF 3 (III, 123), 2MP introduction (III, 253-54), HTrb 369-447 (III, 416-20), KSF 27b (III, 713). Fortini supplies the date of 1223

undated Chapter at the Portiuncula (probably 1221–1223) which recounts that some of the brothers did not want Francis to rule over them because he was a simple and uneducated prelate,[99] his clarifications concerning the Rule, especially poverty,[100] and his angry quip: "Who are these people? They have snatched out of my hands my religion and that of the brothers. If I go to the general chapter, then I'll show them what is my will!"[101] Other intermittent indications in the sources also allude to the drama of Francis's last years,[102] and his undated *On True and Perfect Joy* where he is repeatedly told to "Go away" also speaks to this period of his estrangement from the direction of the order.[103] In such a context, Giovanni Miccoli surmises:

> [Francis's] grave temptation, then, would have been to rebel — to reaffirm his original ideals in terms directly opposed to the line of development Rome and the ministers were imposing on the order. This interpretation, risky though it

(*Francis of Assisi*, 523).

99. AC 109 (II, 217), 2C 145 (II, 340-41), 1MP 38 (III, 247), 2MP 64 (III, 307-08). The story is presented as a "teaching moment" used by Francis to illustrate being a true Lesser Brother. However, Francis's point most probably has real historical roots.

100. AC 101-106 (II, 101-105) has been called *Intentio Regulae*, "The Intention of the Rule" (FA:ED II, 114, 204 footnote b). Later writings like the 1-2MP, HTrb, TL and the KSF make extensive use of the *Intentio Regulae*. Interestingly, the "official" biographies of Thomas of Celano's 2C and Bonaventure's LMj and LMn excise these potentially controversial episodes. 2C does retain two very brief allusions to the *Intentio Regulae*, but the episodes have been drastically toned down: AC 102 in 2C 62 (II, 288) and AC 104 in 2C 195 (II, 372).

101. AC 44 (II, 146), 2C 188 (I, 367), 2MP 41 (III, 288).

102. Thomas of Celano has Francis predicting future problems in the order [1C 28 (I, 206)], rebuking those brothers who seek positions of authority [1C 104 (I, 273-74)], and foretelling of those who will forsake the Rule because of "the scandals that are to come" [1C 108 (I, 276)]. The AC also has Francis's foretelling of the brothers' bad reputation [AC 2 (II, 118-19)], and how, disappointed by their bad example, he tries to give the order back to the Lord [AC 112 (II, 219)]. 2C has a slightly different account and reports that Francis actually *withdrew* from the brothers' company because of their deeds and his foretelling of the brothers' bad reputation [2C 157 (II, 348-49)]. All these stories reappear in later writings: 2MP 70 (III, 315-16), HTrb 220 (III, 389-90), KSF 34b (III, 723).

103. TPJ 10-13 (I, 166-67). Other phrases like "You are simple and stupid" and "we don't need you" echo opposing viewpoints against Francis rising within the order. Again, while Francis presents the TPJ as a "teaching moment" to instruct the brothers, it surely emerged from historical circumstances. See André Jansen, "The Story of True Joy: An Autobiographical Reading," *Greyfriars Review* 5 (1991): 367-87, and Manselli, *St. Francis of Assisi*, 242-45. Also see DBF 7 (III, 449-50) and LFl 8 (III, 579-81).

may be, seems to me unavoidable. The real alternative to conflict and rebellion is the cross, the condition of the authentic following of Christ.[104]

Such was the stigmata's historical context. The order became Francis's cross,[105] and this existential crisis had two poles: "serious temptation" and the mystery of the seraph/stigmata.[106] Thus, by following the crucified Christ Francis received the grace to come to peace with his conscience, with his brothers, with his church, and with God who gave him the order.

So if the stigmata represent the concrete solution to Francis's "serious temptation" to rebel against or simply leave the brotherhood he started, then *how* does he respond to both? He responds to life's trials, culminating in the mystical embrace of Christ's cross, by bursting forth in unconditional and uninterrupted praise of God. LaVerna was Francis's Gethsemane, and by giving everything to God, God gave everything to Francis. In his kenotic self-emptying Francis encountered God's *awe*some, *awe*ful presence, and before

---

104. Miccoli, "Francis's Christian Proposal," 160. The gravity of the issue is highlighted by the fact that the bull *Solet annuere*, which confirmed the Rule of 1223, ends by stating that any brother who left the order would be excommunicated (*Bullarium Franciscanum*, vol. 1, 15-19, threat of excommunication, 19). Thus Francis's and Leo's "temptation" risked excommunication, and so it was indeed "serious."

105. Francis's encounter with God must not be separated from his gospel-life of penance, humility, service, charity, poverty and obedience, nor from those adverse events that directly challenged their authenticity as Francis wanted to live them to the letter without gloss [Test 35-39 (I, 127)]. Francis's agony at LaVerna is reported in AC 118 (II, 227): "If the brothers knew how many trials the demons cause me, there would not be one of them who would not have great piety and compassion for me." Also see 1MP 21 (III, 232), 2MP 99 (III, 346).

106. Joining Hellmann, Frugoni and McGinn, I suggest that the seraph is a theological construct, originally separate from the stigmata, that provides an interpretive framework for understanding the stigmata [Hellmann, "The Seraph in Thomas of Celano's *Vita Prima*," 27–4; Frugoni, *Francesco e l'invenzione delle stimmate*, 137–82, especially 155ff, including the iconography of the seraph/stigmata on 168ff; and McGinn, *Flowering*, 61–63]. Thus, the seraph imagery represents: 1) a sign of the mystery of the Father's love manifested in the incarnation and culminating in the crucifixion, 2) a symbol of the transformation achieved through purifying love (Isaiah 6:6–8), which is combined into 3) an allegorical and pedagogical explanation of the stigmata via the seraph's six wings and burning body. Even though Hellmann argues that Thomas of Celano was the first to connect the seraph imagery with the stigmata within the hagiographical tradition, I do not preclude the possibility that the seraph imagery itself goes back to Francis and his experience at LaVerna. AC 118 (II, 226–27) even mentions the seraph without any reference to the stigmata. For information on the seraph as a pedagogical tool see FA:ED I, 282, footnote c, and Hellmann, "The Seraph," 32–39.

such a presence he can only glorify and give praise to God's wondrous gifts: *All is gift! Praise God!* Three elements help reveal the prayer's doxological mysticism.

First, if this prayer is our only opportunity to glimpse and possibly discern Francis's own veiled description of the stigmata, then one fact is perfectly clear, his description erupts with uncontrollable excitement. Francis does not contain himself because his self-renouncing, self-emptying embrace of Jesus' cross is the decisive moment of transformation where the anguish of his "serious temptation" gives way to joyous praise. In effect, Francis does not "look back" to question what happened, he simply "runs forward" thanking and praising his "Lord, God and Savior" for *everything*. By dying to self Francis was freed and he simply responds "Thank God!"

The prayer's doxology consists of three simple parts that can be subdivided into six line numbers and thirty-three strophes.[107] In response to God's presence, Francis directly addresses his praise to God with the repetition of the second person singular "You are" (*tu es*) thirty-one times.[108] Such intimacy signals the most striking characteristic of the prayer's immediacy and emphasizes that it is written as a direct doxology to God. In effect, Francis spoke *to* God not about God, thereby translating his mystical encounter into pure praise.

Second, the prayer highlights God's greatness and goodness as "living and true," and again names the Triune God as "the good, all good, the highest good" from whom one receives everything.[109] God's gifts alone provide "riches to sufficiency," and gentle protection leading to "eternal life." Within the cadence of *tu es* Francis stumbles to adequately describe God's presence by employing no less than forty terms to describe the "wonderful things" God does,

---

107. Lehmann, *Francesco: Maestro di Preghiera*, 257–60. The three parts include: 1) the opening strophes 1–8 addressed to God the Father, 2) strophes 9–32 which list twenty-four attributes, and 3) strophe 33 which closes with the triple naming of Lord, God, Savior. The FA:ED follows the line numbering proposed by Esser, *Opuscula*, 42, *Gli scritti S. Francesco*, 170–71, and accepted by the *Fontes*, 45.
108. Strophe 6 only contains *tu*, but is a direct address to the "holy Father, king of heaven and earth." Strophe 33 ends by breaking the repetition.
109. See footnote 77.

the prayer's only relative clause.[110] His ecstatic stammering trips over itself, repeating the words good, love/charity three times, and the words holy, great, beauty, meekness, and hope each twice. Overall, Francis wraps the entire prayer within the double affirmation that God is wonderful *(mirabilia/admirabilis)*. Exasperated by the limitations of language, Francis strains the limits of language to name what he experientially knows by identifying the effects of God's presence in his life. The mystical encounter does not lead him to apophatic silence; rather, he erupts into a *hyper*-cataphatic doxology. Such a simple and direct approach employs language to convey the spontaneous consolation of encountering God's wondrous presence, a consolation that heals his "serious temptation."

Third, returning to the *Chartula* and interpreting the parchment "in context" suggests a subtle but significant connection between the *Praises of God* on one side and the *Blessing to Brother Leo* on the other.[111] Francis did not begin his life as a penitent alone, so if he was "seriously tempted" to leave the fraternity (either quietly or in open revolt), he probably would not have departed alone. And so Leo, his closest companion who accompanied him to LaVerna, also had a "serious temptation" to leave the growing fraternity along with all its complexities.[112] The "serious temptation" they both likely shared speaks to the debate over the nature of the *Chartula* and the relationship of the two sides.[113] On one side, Francis responds to his own serious temptation by directly addressing God

110. Lehmann, *Francesco: Maestro di Preghiera*, 261. The terms Francis employs are central for understanding his image of God and for interpreting his consciousness of God's presence. Also see Matura, *Francis of Assisi*, 54.
111. Discerning the "meaning" of these texts must include the fact that they were intentionally bound together. Thus, the PrsG informs the BlL and *vice versa*. To interpret the texts independently is to remove them from their proper historical and textual contexts.
112. This group probably also included Angelo, Masseo, Rufino and a few others who had accompanied Francis to LaVerna, see ChrTE 13 in *XIIIth Century Chronicles* (Chicago: Franciscan Herald Press, 1961).
113. Lapsanski, "The Autographs," 18–37; Esser, *Gli scritti*, 162–76; Lehmann, *Francesco: Maestro di Preghiera*, 279–95; Stephen van Dijk, "Saint Francis's Blessing of Brother Leo," *Archivum Franciscanum Historicum* 47 (1954): 199–201; Attilio Bartoli Langeli, "Gli scritti da Francesco: L'autografo di un '*illiteratus*,'" in *Frate Francisco di Assisi* (Spoleto: Atti dei Convegni della Società internazionale di studi francescani e del Centro, 1994), 101–59, and his later critical edition, *Gli Autografi di Frate Francesco e di Frate Leone*, in *Corpus Christianorum: Autographa Medii Aeui*, vol. 5 (Turnhout: Brepols Publishers, 2000).

with the *Praises* thereby receiving peace, a direct result of his "seraphic" embrace of the cross. On the other, he responds to Leo's serious temptation and request with the *Blessing* (Nm 6:24–27)[114] by simply asking the Lord to bless Leo and give him peace. The historical context of "serious temptation" unites the prayers of the *Chartula* together, and their effects are powerful and momentous: neither Francis nor Leo leave the order. By clinging to the cross Francis simultaneously "lets go" of the order. What was previously a serious temptation is transformed into a renewed consciousness of God's "wondrous" presence. Francis's doxology again expresses the effects of his mystical transformation.

Although the prayer's content indicates that Francis addressed it to the Father and to the Trinity, the prayer's context again indicates that he uttered his praise to the Lord God through Christ's mediation, specifically through Christ crucified. Here we can imagine *The Praises of God* figuratively locating Francis at the center of the circle shortly after receiving the stigmata. At LaVerna Francis undergoes a radical transformation that registers a profound effect upon his consciousness. Centered in Christ, Francis praises God with uninhibited abandon. Like his initial conversion, Francis locates his struggles, spiritual and physical, on the cross.[115] Nothing he suffered overshadowed Jesus' redemptive suffering. Daily Francis centered his prayers on Christ's passion and he ends his *Office of the Passion* with the simple prayer: "Take up your bodies and carry his holy cross and follow his most holy commands even to the end."[116] And at the end of his life he recalled the simple liturgical prayer he had taught his brothers: "We adore you, Lord Jesus Christ and we bless you because by your holy cross you redeemed the world."[117] Francis's journey in the footsteps of Christ brought him to the

114. For analysis of the BlL as a prayer see Lehmann, *Francesco: Maestro di Preghiera*, 279–92.
115. For a study of the crucifixion in Francis's thinking and the later hagiographical tradition see: Octavian Schmucki, "The Passion of Christ in the Life of St. Francis of Assisi: A Comparative Study of the Sources in the Light of the Devotion to the Passion Practiced in his Time," *Greyfriars Review* 4 (1990): 1–101.
116. OfP part 5, vespers 13 (I, 157), repeated in OfP part 1, vespers 8 (I, 147). In effect, Christ's cross encapsulates Francis's entire office, making the cross a major image in his prayer.
117. Test 5 (I, 124–25). See Lehmann, *Francesco: Maestro di Preghiera*, 61–78.

cross.[118] However, the death of the cross opens to the new life of the resurrection. In the stigmata Francis confronted death, but in *The Canticle of the Creatures* he envisions the life of the new creation.

The Canticle of the Creatures (1225–26)[119]

With the *Canticle* we arrive at Francis's most celebrated masterpiece.[120] The *Canticle* encapsulates his deeply sacramental vision of reality and proclaims his wondrous image of God's glory, power, and goodness. Francis wrote the poem in his native Umbrian dialect while convalescing at San Damiano for over fifty days early in 1225,[121] six to nine months after receiving the stigmata.[122] It provides a culminating insight into Francis's doxological mysticism. The *Canticle* represents Francis's vision of the new creation where God's own self-expression throughout all creation transfigures all creation into a harmonious doxology of God's presence: *All is God's self-gift: Praise God!*

The *Canticle* is a deceptively simple poem that can be read on many different levels. Its organization has five basic parts[123] forming a harmonious balance that follows a precise numerical scheme:[124] 1) stanzas 1–2 are theological, introducing a tension

118. 2LtF 6–13 (I, 46), Adm 5.8 (I, 131), Adm 6.1 (I, 131).
119. FA:ED I, 113–14 (*Fontes*, 39–41; Esser, *Opuscula*, 122–33); also see Lehmann, *Francesco: Maestro di Preghiera*, 325–59. The traditional title to this work is *Cantico di frate Sole*, "The Canticle of Brother Sun." I extend the *Canticle*'s date to 1226 because Francis added stanzas 12–13 in late 1226.
120. The literature on the *Canticle* is massive. Regis Armstrong counts over five hundred articles and more than twenty books in the twentieth century [*Francis and Clare: The Complete Works* (New York: Paulist Press, 1982), 37]. For selections see Bibliography following this essay.
121. AC 83 (II, 185).
122. The *Canticle*'s context indicates that even after the mystical experience of LaVerna and its profound consolation, Francis was not exempt from the desolation of renewed spiritual tribulations and doubts. Such a repertoire speaks to the nature of Christian discipleship.
123. McGinn, *Flowering*, 54–55 and Schmucki, "The Mysticism of St. Francis," 261; for an alternative structure see Leclerc, *The Canticle of Creatures*, 19–23, and Lehmann, *Francesco: Maestro di Preghiera*, 336–40.
124. Pozzi, "Canticle of Brother Sun," 19–20. My interpretation differs slightly from Pozzi's "very rigid scheme" which ignores certain attributes ("blessing" in stanza 2 or "serve" in stanza 14) to make them into tricolons, and stretches the text to allow the number two to constantly appear in the paired stanzas of the last two verses (10–13).

between the praise of God and an apophatic qualification directed at humans[125] marked by seven attributes reserved for God alone: most high, all powerful, good, praises, glory, honor, blessing; 2) stanzas 3–9 are cosmological, dividing the praise of God between the firmament of the sun, moon, stars (3–5), with three attributes assigned to each, and the terrestrial four elements of air, water, fire, earth (6–9), with four attributes assigned to each; 3) stanzas 10–11 are anthropological, celebrating pardon and peace, the fruits of God's love; 4) stanzas 12–13 are eschatological, relating to the universality of death and the promise of eternal life; and 5) stanza 14 is probably a refrain to be sung after each verse.[126]

The *Assisi Compilation* provides the *Canticle*'s historical background.[127] It conveys that, while almost blind, Francis greatly suffered physical afflictions,[128] and the torment of living in a mouse-infested house. In this state of anguish he was "moved by pity for himself" and asked the Lord to help him bear his illness patiently. In response, Francis "was told in spirit" that he would receive a "great and precious treasure" for all his sufferings. The inner dialogue ends with a promise: "be glad and rejoice in your illness and troubles, because as of now, you are as secure as if you were already in my kingdom." The next morning, Francis gave thanks to the Trinity for "such a great grace and blessing" in promising him the kingdom and decided to write the *Canticle*:

125. CtC 2 (I, 113) reads "No human is worthy to mention Your name." Francis also mentions the same apophatic restriction in ER 23.5 (I, 82): ". . . all of us, wretches and sinners, are not worthy to pronounce Your name."
126. FA:ED I, 113. The AC reports that the *Canticle* was composed in three parts at different times: AC 83 describes verses 1–9, AC 84 verses 10–11, and AC 7 verses 12–14. As mentioned, verse 14 is probably a refrain written sometime shortly after verses 1–9.
127. AC 7 (II, 120), 66 (II, 169), 83–84 (II, 184–88), 88 (II, 192), and 99–100 (II, 202–04). Also see 2C 213 (II, 384–85). The stories from the AC are reproduced in 2MP 100–01 (III, 346–50) and 118–23 (III, 366–71). 1C 81 (I, 251) offers an earlier allusion to the *Canticle* but offers no historical information. Also see LMj 8.6 (II, 590).
128. For a description of Francis's illness at this time see Octavian Schmucki, "The Illness of Francis During the Last Years of His Life," *Greyfriars Review* 13.1 (1999), 21–59; for a description of his health before 1224 see Octavian Schmucki, "The Illness of St. Francis of Assisi before His Stigmatization," *Greyfriars Review* 4.3 (1990): 31–61.

Therefore for His praise, for our consolation and for the edification of our neighbor, I want to write a new *Praise of the Lord* for his creatures, which we use every day, and without which we cannot live. Through them the human race greatly offends the Creator, and every day we are ungrateful for such great graces, because we do not praise, as we should, our Creator and the Giver of all good.[129]

The praise of God, consolation of the spirit, and the edification of neighbor define the *Canticle's* threefold purpose. Once again the existential effect on Francis is profound. He is converted from angst to joy, and the result of the event is a spontaneous doxology.[130]

Even though the *Assisi Compilation* reports that the *Canticle* arose spontaneously, it did not originate in a vacuum. It has roots in Francis's earlier prayers, especially *The Praises to be Said at All Hours* that he prayed at least eight times a day as a prelude to the Divine Office;[131] he also ended each hour with a shorter prayer.[132] Such prayerful repetition must have profoundly influenced his image of God and likely forms the immediate backdrop to the *Canticle*.[133]

---

129. AC 83 (II, 185–86).
130. AC 83 (II, 186) reports the spontaneous nature or the *Canticle's* composition, "Sitting down, he began to meditate and then said."
131. The introductory and closing directives to the OfP mention that Francis began each hour with the PH (I, 139, 157); for the text itself see FA:ED 161. The LR mentions eight hours (Matins, Lauds, Prime, Terce, Sext, None, Vespers, Compline) while Francis's OfP presents only seven, with Lauds being consistently absent (probably a result of combining Matins with Lauds at daybreak, not an uncommon practice). In any event, Francis prefaced each hour of the Office with an *Our Father*, a *Glory Be* and the PH. For an analysis of the place of the PH in Francis's prayer see Schmucki, "Divine Praise and Meditation," 42–46, and Lehmann, *Francesco: Maestro di Preghiera*, 99–121.
132. OfP closing prayer (I, 141): "Let us bless the Lord God living and true! Let us always render Him praise, glory, honor, blessing and every good. Amen. Amen. So be it. So be it."
133. Scholars also identify other "external" influences: Pozzi identifies the *Benedicite* of the Three Young Men found in Daniel 3:52–90 as the primary source and excludes Psalm 148 ("Canticle of Brother Sun," 3–7); in contrast, Sorrell argues for the primary influence of both the *Benedicite* and Psalm 148 (*St. Francis of Assisi*, 102–05) as well as other possible secondary sources: Psalms 19, 66, 99 (99), the eleventh century Advent hymn *Jubilemus omnes* (105), and troubadour lyrics familiar to Francis (106–08). Yet, the best evidence comes from the instructions to Francis's own breviary, which Brother Leo reports Francis had from 1223 onwards. It reveals that Francis said Lauds at sunrise with Psalm 148 repeated every morning with the *Benedicite* and Psalm 99 joined on every Sunday and feast day [Stephen van Dijk, "The Breviary of Saint Francis," *Franciscan Studies* 9

Francis's own statement "I want to write a new *Praise of the Lord*" confirms it,[134] and the similar phraseology shared by the two prayers corroborates it.[135] Thus, the *Canticle* sprang forth from the rich liturgical rhythm of the *Praises* and Office.

So when Francis is promised the kingdom, he utilizes memorized prayers to compose a new *Praise of the Lord* that is *The Canticle of the Creatures*. But why if he is promised the heavenly kingdom does he praise physical reality? Four points will help illustrate *how* the *Canticle* represents, not only "a distinctive form of theophanic nature mysticism" in general, but a specific form of doxological mysticism that envisions the promise of a new creation.

First, if the *Assisi Compilation*'s report about Francis being promised the kingdom is reliable, then the *Canticle* should be interpreted within an eschatological framework. In this context, Francis sings the praise of the new creation.[136] The three celestial objects of sun, moon, stars and the four elements of wind, water, fire, earth are all transfigured in a panoramic hymn of praise and become signs of the

---

(1949): 13–40; Gius Abate, "Il primitivo Breviario francescano (1224–27)," *Miscellanea Francescana* 60 (1960): 47–240; Bartoli Langeli, *Gli Autografi di Frate Francesco*, 82–89; and Sorrell, *St. Francis of Assisi*, 99]. Since Francis's devotional Office did not supplant the Divine Office as prescribed in the LR, he would have said the Office eight times daily. Thus, the PH, Psalm 148, and the *Benedicite* were burned into Francis's mind.

134. AC 83 (II, 186). The reference to a "new *Praise of the Lord*" could also refer back to *The Praises of God* that would connect the *Canticle* with Francis's earlier experience with God at LaVerna. However, the shared phraseology between the CtC and the PH suggests a stronger connection.

135. The similar phraseology is threefold: 1) The phrase "praise, glory, honor and blessing" only occurs in these opening (twice) and closing prayers to the Office (I, 141, 161) in a prayer within the 2LtF (I, 49–50), and in the first verse of the CtC (I, 113); 2) the wording "Most High, all-powerful, good" in any combination only occurs in the ending prayer of the PH and the first line of the CtC; and 3) the present, subjunctive, active (*laudemus/superexaltemus*) of the PH's refrain "And let us praise and glorify Him forever" (Rv 4:8) shares a close linguistic proximity to the perfect, subjunctive, passive (*laudato si/laudatus sis*) of the *Canticle*'s repetition of "Praised be You." All these prayers seem to be linked thematically since each calls for unconditional praise of God with 2LtF, CtC and PH inciting all creation to praise God. Nearly all the images in 2LtF 61–62 are also found in the PH with a repetition of Rv 5:13 in both.

136. The images employed within the eschatological framework of the AC 83 (II, 185) share thematic parallels with the images presented in the CtC. Just as the AC describes Francis's internal dialogue about the treasure he will receive for his sufferings with images of the earth transformed into pure gold, rocks into precious stones, and water into perfume, the CtC describes transformed creation with similar imagery.

new creation. But, what do the selection of the seven objects convey about the new creation?

The symbolism of the number seven is obvious. It recalls the first creation narrative in Genesis thereby affirming that God creates all things, creation is ordered, and above all, creation is good.[137] To capture this, the *Canticle* employs the most inclusive symbols possible: the three orbs of the heavens and the four elements of earth to arrive at seven, the number of perfection. On the one hand, the sun, moon and stars represent everything that was known to exist in the heavenly firmament. All the seasons, night and day, as well as astrology depended on these celestial orbs. Thus, the rhythm of these celestial objects "creates" time itself. On the other, the four elements symbolically represent everything that exists on earth. Every solid (earth), liquid (water) and vapor (wind) and their transformation from one to another through the agency of heat (fire) represents the complex interconnectedness of creation. Thus, the harmony of these four elements "creates" all physical space. In effect, Francis's vision of the new creation involves all time and all space which ultimately point to God their eternal and infinite Creator. This imagery symbolically conveys Francis's new understanding of both God and creation as inextricably intertwined in a grand interconnected reality on every level of existence. Francis's imagery excludes nothing. The stanzas added later provide concrete examples of what the new creation entails: peace on earth and eternal life in heaven. The *Canticle*'s all-inclusive doxology transforms every relationship into a mystical vision of the new creation.[138]

Second, this eschatological interpretation gains support by considering the passive subjunctive construction of the *Pater noster*, "holy be your name, your kingdom come, your will be done on earth

---

137. It also likely alludes to John 1:1 and the belief that creation is through the Word, and therefore, the affirmation that the new creation will likewise be through the Word's redemption.
138. Duba, "Doxology," 369. The "universality of praise" in Chapter 23 of the *Earlier Rule* which Francis tried to convey with his two lengthy litanies is now complete by employing simpler, more inclusive imagery; see above footnote 71 and related text. Also note the parallel between the number 70 in the two litanies and the number 7 in the cosmic elements.

as in heaven."[139] As Giovanni Pozzi points out, "the third petition of the Our Father is linguistically identical to the expression 'praised be' used by Francis."[140] So while *The Praises to be Said at All Hours* may be an immediate source for the *Canticle* generally, the *Our Father*, which Francis said before the *Praises* during the Office,[141] is the immediate source for the passive construction specifically. Moreover, the fact that this line of the *Our Father* immediately precedes the eschatological hope of the kingdom elucidates why Francis sings the praises of creation in response to the promise of the kingdom, literally: "on earth as it is in heaven." Such a reading identifies the *Canticle* as an eschatological celebration of the new creation!

Third, the key to the *Canticle* is the iterative phrase *Laudato si, mi signore, per* that occurs eight times,[142] and provides the laude's structural and rhythmic backbone. The unique combination of the passive subjunctive "Praised be You" (*Laudato si*) with the complex meaning of the preposition *per* leads to the central question of who is giving praise in the *Canticle*? The answer centers on the interpretation of the preposition *per*. Four explanations have been offered, each with supporters and detractors:[143] 1) *Per* as causal, meaning

---

139. The *Our Father* was central to Francis's prayer life as well as that of the brothers. He recited the prayer at least eight times a day (I, 139, 157), but if he followed the directives for the lay brothers in the LR 3.3 then he recited the prayer at least seventy-six times a day (I, 101). The ER 3.10 had the lay brothers reciting the prayer eighty-six times a day (I, 66). Moreover, Francis wrote a prayerful commentary of the *Our Father* that "is perhaps the only instance in which we find an example of how Francis responded to his brothers' request to teach them how to pray" (I, 158); also see 2LtF 21 (I, 47), Test 18 (I, 125), 1C 45 (I, 222), LJS 27 (I, 388), LMj 4.3 (II, 551), and Lehmann, *Francesco: Maestro di Preghiera*, 189–224. In addition to the *Our Father*, it seems that Francis also directly taught the brothers at least four other prayers, see: ER 17.17 (I, 76), ER 21.2–9 (I, 78), Test 4–5 (I, 124–25), and in light of AC 83 (II, 186), the CtC (I, 113–14).

140. Pozzi, "Canticle of Brother Sun," 12. While the linguistic function of the two verbs is identical, their conjugation does differ slightly: "Holy be" (*sanctificetur*) is third person, present, subjunctive, passive while "praised be" (*laudato si/laudatus sis*) is second person, perfect, subjunctive, passive. The shift from the third to second person supports Pozzi's claim "that the one giving praise is the very God who is being praised" (12); see footnote 145.

141. See the introductory and closing directives of the OfP (I, 139, 157).

142. Stanza three begins with the preposition "with" (*cun*) and the following stanzas follow with the preposition "through" (*per*).

143. See Coy, "The Problem of 'Per' in the *Cantico di Frate Sole*," 1–2, who covers the interpretations of several variant readings; also see Pozzi, "Canticle of Brother Sun," 16–18; Sorrell, *St. Francis and Nature*, 115–24; Cousins, "Francis and

"for" where Francis exhorts humanity to give God praise for God's creatures;[144] 2) *per* as agency, meaning "by" where creatures themselves give praise to God; 3) *per* as instrumentality, meaning "by means of" where humans praise God by means of creatures; and 4) *per* as mediation, meaning "through" where God is the very agent of praise to whom all creation begins and ends.[145] In short, creation itself manifests God's self-communicative praise. Given the grammatical complexity of the *Canticle*, it seems that all four meanings of *per* (for, by, by means of, through) are valid and call for a "polyvalent" reading that struggles to express the nexus of relationships shared among God-Humans-Creation.[146] Thus, the *Canticle* operates on several levels signifying distinct but interconnected relationships involving both praise and thanksgiving. Such genius should not be underestimated,[147] because the report of Francis's own explanation for the prayer indicates that he understood the prayer on more than one level.[148]

Although a polyvalent reading of *per* is warranted by external and internal evidence, the translation of "through," with the implica-

---

Bonaventure," 85–88; Brown, "Appendix VIII: The Canticle of Brother Sun," 442–43; Schmucki, "The Mysticism of St. Francis," 260; Lehmann, *Francesco: Maestro di Preghiera*, 337; and FA:ED 114, footnote a.

144. This is the traditional interpretation and finds support in AC 83 which states "I want to write a new *Praise of the Lord* for (*de* meaning *propter*) his creatures." Other possible translations include, "on account of," or "because of."

145. The FA:ED opts for translating *per* as "through," which supports a mystical interpretation whereby all creatures reflect God's "objective glory" that is the source, exemplar, and end of all doxology. Thus all creation exists as symbols of the Creator, and their very existence *is* God's praise. This interpretation finds support in 1C 80–81 (I, 250–51) and LMj 9.1 (II, 596–97). For the notion of God's self praise see footnote 140 and related text.

146. See Cunningham, *Saint Francis of Assisi*, 53; Cousins, "Francis of Assisi and Bonaventure," 88; and Coy, "The Problem of 'Per' in the *Cantico di Frate Sole*, 1.

147. I disagree with Sorrell's judgment, "Yet, it is difficult to believe that Francis would consciously have inserted such an ambiguity into a poem of clearly spontaneous origin" (*St. Francis and Nature*, 116). Rather, Francis's heightened consciousness glimpses a cosmic nexus of praise with the polyvalent term *per*. Such intention does not introduce "ambiguity" into the *Canticle*, rather, it represents Francis's mystical insight into what bonds all reality together: praise and thanksgiving. My position concurs with Pozzi, "[Francis] must have wanted to express an idea for which the available rules seemed to him inadequate, at least regarding the use of the preposition" ("Canticle of Brother Sun," 17).

148. AC 83 (II, 186) records Francis as explaining, ". . . for [God's] praise, for our consolation and for the edification of our neighbor . . . " From the outset Francis conceived the praise within the *Canticle* from several perspectives simultaneously. The *Canticle*'s praise subsists in communal and participatory relationships.

tion that God is the very agent of praise, gains support when linked with the passive subjunctive "Praised be" (*Laudato si*). The important relation between *laudato si* and the *Our Father* was mentioned above, but there is deeper meaning to this unique construction that takes on special significance when combined with the preposition *per*. Given the apophatic restriction in strophe two,[149] the mediating function of *per*, and the repetitive use of *laudato si* as a "theological passive" referring to God, Giovanni Pozzi convincingly argues that "the one giving praise is the very God who is being praised."[150] In the deepest sense only God's self-communication can give authentic praise to the ineffable mystery of the divine reality freely extended to creation by God's creative act. God's self-expressive praise of God *through* creatures exemplifies the central and climactic insight of Francis's doxological mysticism. Such an insight glimpses the ineffable beauty of God's self-communicative presence transforming everything in the new creation into participatory praise of God.

For Francis, the only proper response to God's self-communication as praise is to join in by praising. This dialectic between God's self-praise and the human's response *through* participatory praise is present in the transition between the passive subjunctive *laudato si* (3, 5–10, 12) and the active indicative *laudate* which ends the prayer (14).[151] Further, if the closing stanza serves as the refrain, then the doxological dialectic between Creator and created permeates the entire *Canticle*. Such a dialectic strongly suggests that Francis understood mystical union to be in the very act of doxology itself. In effect, God and creation become one through praise!

The effects of this mystical union upon Francis's consciousness are graphically expressed by his use of the first person possessive

149. See footnote 125 and Pozzi, "Canticle of Brother Sun, 14–15.
150. Pozzi, "Canticle of Brother Sun," 12–14; also see Coy, "The Problem of 'Per' in the *Cantico di Frate Sole*," 6–8 and McGinn, *Flowering*, 55.
151. *Laudato si* begins the praise with God's self-expressive calling forth, and Francis, along "with (*cun*) all your creatures," answers back with *laudate*. The rhythmic dialectic resembles a cosmic mantra of praise: God exhales, all creation inhales, whereby all reality becomes one harmonious doxology. Such grammatical complexity, including the preposition *per*, illustrates the amazing sophistication of Francis's mysticism, especially for one who considered himself "an ignorant, uneducated person" [LtOrd 39 (I, 119)]; see Octavian Schmucki, "St. Francis's Level of Education," *Greyfriars Review* 10 (1996): 153–71.

"my Lord" (*mi signore*), and in his change of language to his native Italian. On the one hand, Francis again, for the first time in twenty years, employs the first person in his prayer,[152] and its very position in the grammatical construction of *Laudato si, mi signore, per* is suggestive. Between God's self-communicative praise echoing through creation, is a personal identification that directly joins Francis's praise to God's. With this doxological act, Francis partici-pates in the reconciliation of the new creation resulting in his humble reception of a *new* personal identity. He now identifies himself by mystically joining God's own praise "with (*cun*) all your creatures."[153] In effect, by joining God's self-expressive praise, Francis becomes a con-creator of the new creation; a profound mysticism has profound consequences. On the other hand, if language gives rise to thought, then Francis's shift in language signi-fies a new consciousness of God that spills over into his new vision of reality.[154] Although he may have written the *Canticle* in the vernacular to more easily disseminate it,[155] this practical consider-ation does not preclude the simple fact that he may have shifted language because he wanted to express his new understanding in his own terms. In effect, both the use of the personal pronoun *mi* and the vernacular shift signifies a profound personal transformation.

Fourth, Francis's new identity within the new creation is vividly expressed by the use of the titles Brother and Sister throughout the

---

152. The only other time Francis used a first-person singular pronoun in his prayers was in *The Prayer before the Crucifix*; see footnote 49 and related text.
153. The preposition *cun* in CtC 3 (I, 113) provides a valuable insight into Francis's relationship to the praise being offered in the *Canticle*. If God is the agent of praise who is also the only one worthy of praise, then the preposition "with" signifies that Francis identifies himself as participating in God's own act of praising. Moreover, since *cun* precedes the following seven instances of *per*, this shared act of praise is most likely extended throughout the *Canticle*, suggesting that Francis receives his true identity *through* the act of praising God in all things.
154. I do not wish to suggest that verbal or written language is, *per se*, the only or even primary media of individual consciousness or cultural milieus. As Margaret Miles illustrates, images are equally influential and powerful in constructing human consciousness, see: *Image as Insight: Visual Understanding in Western Christianity and Secular Culture* (Boston: Bracon Press, 1985). However, Francis left writings not images.
155. AC 83 (II, 186); McGinn, *Flowering*, 347, footnote 135; Sorrell, *St. Francis*, 114–15. Dominic Monti examines the vernacular nature of Francis's thinking in "Francis as a Vernacular Theologian?," in *The Franciscan Intellectual Tradition*, edited by Elise Saggau (St. Bonaventure, NY: Franciscan Institute, 2002).

Canticle.[156] By joining God's self-expressive praise, Francis joins God's family. This is not mere sentimental imagery. Rather, three coupled siblings, surrounded by parents, order all creation into a reconciled cosmic family:

> *Sir* Brother Sun
>> Sister Moon
>>> Brother Wind
>> Sister Water
> Brother Fire
Sister *Mother* Earth

All created things are brothers and sisters because they all originate from the same loving Father, and so with this imagery Francis celebrates "the universal fatherhood of God."[157] Later in stanza 12 Francis introduces Sister Bodily Death thereby breaking the parallelism. However, Francis implies the parallel because he is the Brother who has been promised the eternal life of the Father's kingdom. So Sister Death sings with Brother Francis and together they join in God's self-expressive love, and *through* the act of participatory praise, they reconcile with each other.[158] If this interpretation holds, then the addition of the eschatological stanzas about the universality of death and the promise of eternal life closes the *Canticle* at the same place where it initially arose, God's promise of the kingdom. In effect, God's self-communicative praise crowns the new creation with a cosmic communion of peace, harmony, and reconciliation.

If the *Canticle* represents creation as God's self-expressive doxology, then why is Christ, the perfect expression of God, not explicitly mentioned in the prayer? There are two elements that provide inferential evidence of Christ's pervasive albeit implicit

156. See Lehmann, *Francesco: Maestro di Preghiera*, 340–41; Pozzi, "Canticle of Brother Sun, 18–19; Leclerc, *The Canticle of Creatures*, 10–15; Sorrell, *St. Francis of Assisi and Nature*, 127–30; and Nairn, "St. Francis of Assisi's *Canticle of Creatures*," 205–06, 209.
157. Leclerc, *The Canticle of Creatures*, 11.
158. This interpretation gains support from AC 7 (II, 121) that conveys Francis wrote the stanza in response to his approaching death. Also see AC 100 (II, 204) where Francis welcomes sister death, and 1C 109 (I, 277) that mentions that Francis added the stanza as he rejoiced over his approaching death.

presence. First, just as in Chapter 23 of the *Earlier Rule*, Francis places an apophatic restriction at the outset: "no human is worthy to mention your name." In the earlier prayer it is Christ who mediates between creation and the Father, and the same dynamic is implicit in the *Canticle*.[159] It is Christ who enables Francis to join in God's praise. Thus, Francis's own participatory praise utters God's self-expression who is Christ. Since all creation is through the Word, the new creation is also through the Word.

Second, the identification of the created elements as brothers and sisters also points to Christ. Earlier in the *Second Letter to the Faithful* Francis wrote:

> We are brothers, moreover, when we do the will of His Father who is in heaven . . . O how holy and how loving, gratifying, humbling, peace-giving, sweet, worthy of love, and above all things desirable it is to have such a Brother and such a Son: our Lord Jesus Christ![160]

The *Canticle* extrapolates Francis's familial identification with Christ to all of creation.[161] It is through Christ, God's Son, that all creation relates to the Father. And so, the "enfraterization" [162] of creation is ultimately rooted in the divine Sonship of Jesus Christ who is the invisible center of creation's interconnection. By identifying himself as the little brother, literally a *lesser* brother to the Son of God, Francis set out "to follow His footprints," and with the *Canticle*, Francis encounters God's vestiges or "footprints" throughout all creation. Thus, with a grand doxological theophany he renders all creatures as visible signs of God's invisible presence, and invites all creation to join in the participatory praise of God worshiping God through everything.

---

159. Pozzi, "The Canticle of Brother Sun," 13–14.
160. 2LtF 49–56 (I, 48–49); also see 1LtF 7–13 (I, 41–42). Referring to this passage, Schmucki comments, "Nowhere else do we find the mystical life of the saint presented more clearly" ("The Mysticism of St. Francis," 254). The word brother (*frater*) occurs 306 times in Francis's writings [Jean-François Godet and Georges Mailleux, *Opuscula sancti Francisci. Scripta sanctae Clarae: concordance, index, listes de fréquence, tables comparatives* (Louvain: CETEDOC, 1976), 118–22], and usually refers to his brothers specifically or to other human beings. The only other place Francis utilizes the personification of "sister" is in SalV (I, 164–65).
161. Schmucki, "The Mysticism of St. Francis," 263.
162. Sorrell, *St. Francis of Assisi*, 127–29; also see McGinn, *Flowering*, 54–55.

Stepping back from the sheer beauty of the *Canticle*'s vision, we can figuratively locate Francis at the circle's center gazing back out at the wondrous circumference of God's majestic creation. Twenty years after hearing the voice of Christ at San Damiano, Francis, nearing death, returns to the place of his conversion. Just as he embarked on his journey by praying before the crucifix without uttering Jesus' name, he now gazes upon the harmonious splendor of God's "new" creation without again expressing Jesus' name. By standing in the center, the center seems to disappear because Francis, altogether penetrated by Christ, now looks out at the circle's circumference *through* Christ, and delighted by the beauty he sees, he responds by praising God *through* Christ. In a very real sense, the medium is the message. The medium is Christ and the message is that all the created elements are brothers and sisters who share the same origin from God and thus ultimately the same fundamental vocation: to give praise to God who is a mystery of Triune love. Francis calls all creation to share in this loving communion of God's self-praise. Such is the climatic insight of Francis's doxological mysticism.

Conclusion

Do the selected prayers support the claim that Francis was a mystic? The evidence is threefold: 1) each of the prayers convey the effects of God's presence upon Francis's consciousness; 2) the prayers' contexts dramatically highlight these effects; and 3) the prayers' unique form of *hyper*-linguistic doxology signify Francis's response to God's presence and embody his mystical transformation.

First, Francis does speak about his mystical encounters of God, but we must respect *how* he chose to convey his consciousness of those events. Throughout his life he responded to troubling events by praising God. His struggle for conversion in 1205/06, his summons to the brothers regarding the Rule's ultimate purpose in 1220, his two-year serious temptation culminating in the stigmata in 1224, and his physical tribulations and concerns about death in 1225-26, all indicate that Francis's prayers emerged from upsetting existential moments in his spiritual journey. During these times of difficulty he always turned to God and offered unreserved praise for God's overflowing goodness.

Abstraction was alien to Francis's mystical insights. Rather, his doxological mysticism is performative. The act of praise is the effect of Francis's encounter with God, and the doxology itself conveys Francis's mystical transformation. Throughout his life, his doxological prayers transformed times of desolation into moments of consolation. Francis's doxology does not so much inform the mind about reality but transform the spirit's appreciation of God's self-expressive presence in everything. Francis prepared for, was conscious of, and reacted to God's immediate presence through, in, by and with the act of kenotic praise: *All is Gift! Praise God!*

Second, this paper has argued that the study of mysticism should always wed mystical content with its historical context. This is true of the study of mysticism in general, and is even more necessary when examining Francis's writings because the content alone offers inconclusive results. A mysticism in isolation is an abstraction because it separates the goal from the process and the encounter from the person. Such an act boxes the mystical into neatly defined categories that often ignore or distort the sapping struggles and enlivening joys entangled in the sacred quest for God. In contrast, all authentic Christian mysticism must fuse content with context. To alienate the content from the context, or *vice versa*, is to rip the mystical encounter or experience from the environment from which it came. Regardless of good intentions, such inadvertent carelessness renders the mystical event an abstraction, reduces mysticism to rarified events outside everyday reality, and robs the event of its original and authentic meaning.

If mysticism is the product of particular contexts, then it is the contexts that give rise to particular articulations of mystical content. Mysticism does not take a person outside of reality, rather, it plunges into reality (Francis's contexts), and emerges from that concrete reality (Francis's prayers). To divide the two is unrealistic and inadequate. To separate the two is to seek or interpret only the mystical goal or the product of mystical union, while ignoring the process that attains the end result. Such a division is a bogus dichotomy that leads to naive interpretations and/or false understandings. In sum, the Incarnation, which insists upon the union of the human with the divine, is the model for interpreting all *Christian* mysticism. To interpret mysticism otherwise is to risk interpreting it "out of context" or reducing it to "empty content."

Third, Francis emphasizes God's ineffability in only five places,[163] but this is not to say that his writings easily conceptualize, verbalize or describe God's presence. Even though he was restricted to the medium of language to convey his experiences of God, he employs doxology to overcome the limitations of language.[164] Instead of ending in the silence of God's ineffability, he presses the limits of language as he cries out in praise of God. He paradoxically desires to transcend the threshold of his consciousness and all its linguistic limitations with doxology, and through doxology experience a transformative encounter with God's presence. In effect, doxologies can serve a *hyper*-linguistic function: "Doxologies in worship seek to give expression to the inexpressible. They seek to break the boundaries of the limitations of words."[165]

This doxological strategy is one of the most unique and spirited aspects of Francis's prayers, and his approach has a double effect upon his mysticism. In one way, the doxology is a result of Francis's own direct encounter with God's presence; in another, it can also be preparatory because it aims at evoking a similar state of consciousness in others by participating in the act of praise. In this sense, the doxological strategy is circular; an encounter with God gives rise to praise that then can function as a program for further transformation. In, through, by and with this circular process, doxology employs language as it attempts to leave the fetters of language behind as it leaps forward into the unfathomable and incomprehensible mystery of God. Hence, the goal of doxology always calls a person forth into a numinous encounter with God's presence where all categories, all mediation falls short. It is within these "intermediate spaces" between something and nothing, the known and the unknown, at the very fringe of language, that a "direct" mystical encounter with God can and does transform consciousness. In such

---

163. Especially ER 23.5 (I, 82), ER 23.11 (I, 86), CtC 2 (I, 113), Adm 5 (I, 128), and only in passing in PrOF 7 (I, 159).

164. For example, in ER 23.11 (I, 86) he ends by juxtaposing seven negative expressions recognizing God's transcendent ineffability with ten positive expressions affirming God's immediate accessibility.

165. Duba, "Doxology," 367.

spaces we can encounter the numinous, and in responding to its mystery "We become doxology."[166] This intended transformation is the heart of Francis's doxological mysticism. In sum, to "Praise and bless my Lord and give Him thanks and serve Him with great humility"[167] is to live the gospel life of following in the footsteps of Jesus Christ, God's perfect doxology.

Select Bibliography
on *The Canticle of the Creatures*

Bajetto, F. "Un trentennio di studi (1941-1973) sul Cantico di Frate Sole: Bibliografia ragionata." *L'Italia Francescana* 49 (1974): 5-62.

Benedetto, Luigi Foscolo. *Il Cantico di Frate Sole.* Florence: G. C. Sansoni, 1941.

Branca, Vittore. "Il Cantico di Frate Sole." *Archivium Franciscanum Historicum* (1949): 1-87.

Brown, Raphael. "Appendix VIII: The Canticle of Brother Sun." 441-58. In *Saint Francis of Assisi.* Edited by Omar Englebert. Chicago: Franciscan Herald Press, 1965.

Casella, Mario. "Il Cantico delle creature." *Studi Medievali* 16 (1943-50): 102-131.

Cousins, Ewert. "Francis and Bonaventure: Mysticism and Theological Interpretation." 81-88. In *The Other Side of God.* Edited by Peter Berger. New York: Archor, 1981.

Coy, Susanna. "The Problem of 'Per' in the Cantico di Frate Sole." *Modern Language Notes* 91 (1976): 1-11.

Cunningham, Lawrence. *Saint Francis of Assisi.* 51-59. Boston: Twayne Publishers, 1976.

Doyle, Eric. "The Canticle of Brother Sun." *New Blackfriars* 55 (1974): 392-402.

_____. *St. Francis and the Song of Brotherhood.* New York: Seabury Press, 1981.

Esser, Kajetan. *Die Opuscula Des Hl. Franziskus von Assisi: Neue textkritische Edition.* 122-33. Grottaferrata: Editiones Collegii S. Bonaventurae ad Claras Aquas, 1976.

Getto, Giovanni. *Francesco d'Assisi e il Cantico di Frate Sole.* Turin: Università di Torino, 1956.

Leclerc, Eloi. *The Canticle of Creatures: Symbols of Union.* Chicago: Franciscan Herald Press, 1978.

---

166. Duba, "Doxology," 369.
167. CtC 14 (I, 114).

Lehmann, Leonhard. *Tiefe und Weite: Der universale Grundzug in den Gebeten des Franziskus von Assisi*. 297-324. Werl: Dietrich-Coelde-Verlag, 1984.

_____. *Francesco: Maestro di Preghiera*. 325-59. Rome: Istituto Storico dei Cappuccini, 1993.

Nairn, Thomas. "St. Francis of Assisi's Canticle of Creatures as an Exercise of the Moral Imagination." 202-13. In *Finding Voice to Give God Praise*. Edited by Kathleen Hughes. Collegeville, MN: Liturgical Press, 1998.

Oxilia, Adolfo. *Il Cantico di frate Sole*. Florence: Nardini, 1984.

Pagliaro, Antonio. "Il Cantico di Frate Sole." 201-226. In *Saggi di critica semantica*. Edited by Antonio Pagliaro. Florence: G. d'Anna, 1953.

Paolazzi, Carlo. *Il Cantico di Frate Sole*. Genova: Marietti, 1992.

Platzeck, Erhard-Wolfram. *Das Sonnenlied Des Heiligen Franziskus von Assisi*. Werl: Dietrich-Coelde-Verlag, 1984.

Pozzi, Giovanni. "Dittico per S. Francesco." *Revue Suisse des Littératures Romanes* 1 (1981): 9-26.

_____. "The Canticle of Brother Sun: From Grammar to Prayer." *Greyfriars Review* 4 (1992): 1-21.

Sabatelli, Giacomo. "Studi recenti sul Cantico di Frate Sole." *Archivium Franciscanum Historicum* 51 (1958): 3-24.

Schmucki, Octavian. "The Mysticism of St. Francis in Light of His Writings." *Greyfriars Review* 3 (1989): 259-63.

Sorrell, Roger. *St. Francis of Assisi and Nature*. 98-137. New York: Oxford University Press, 1988.

Francis, the "New" Saint in the Tradition of Christian Hagiography

Thomas of Celano's Life of Saint Francis

William J. Short

In one of many delightful conversations about the project of publishing this new translation of early documents about Francis, my fellow-editors, Regis Armstrong O.F.M. Cap., and Wayne Hellmann, O.F.M. Conv., called my attention to the way in which Francis is described as a new kind of saint in the earliest hagiographical texts of our tradition. The observation rings true on several levels. Two years after his death, Francis was declared a saint in a solemn papal canonization. This was a relatively new procedure for saint-making, increasing the authority of the Roman Pontiff in the creation of new saints for the church. When Thomas of Celano began writing about Francis, he was one of the first hagiographers to work within this new framework for canonizations. Besides this, he also needed to demonstrate to his audience that the newly canonized saint from Assisi was, in fact, a saint: the audience needed to recognize what they considered signs of sanctity in the person whose feast they were to celebrate each October 4. For this reason the new saint had to conform in some way to earlier models of sanctity as these were presented in classic texts of the hagiographical tradition. To add the final, and perhaps most important, challenge Thomas wanted to show that Francis also represented a new kind of holiness, breaking with, surpassing or transcending the tradition.

In this essay I wish to explore these several challenges. A glance at
the finale of the canonization ceremony will illustrate Thomas's
consistent emphasis on what is "new" about this event. Glancing
back, we will see how he endeavors to implement the new norms for
canonization in his emphasis on virtues over miracles in the *Life of
Saint Francis*. A brief examination of his use of the earlier
hagiographical tradition will show how he locates the novelty of
Francis within the tradition of earlier saints. Finally, an examination of the vocabulary of "newness" in the *Life* will give the reader a
broad notion of the multiple uses of these terms to describe Francis.

A Newly Canonized Saint

The whole world positively beams with freshness and a feeling of
Spring in Thomas of Celano's description of the summer day when
Francis of Assisi was canonized as a saint in his hometown. Even the
natural world surrounding the crowd gathered at dawn reflects the
spiritual significance of the event, evoking a sense of a new beginning:

> The day is breaking, colored with radiant sunbeams.
> There are green *branches* of olive
> and fresh boughs *of other trees* (Mt 21:8).
> There all are dressed in festive clothing, shining brightly, while
> the blessing of peace gladdens the spirits of all.[1]

Evoking memories of Palm Sunday and Easter morning, Thomas
paints a charming scene of happiness in the Umbrian hills on July
16, 1228. Perhaps this brief description may serve as a fitting introduction to our theme, that of the "new" in *The Life of Saint Francis*,
the text composed in celebration of that canonization.

The theme echoes throughout the description of the 1228 canonization ceremonies in Assisi, as "the bright day grew brighter with
new lights."[2] The events surrounding the solemn declaration of
Francis as a saint repeat the theme of renewal:

---

1. 1C 126 (I, 296). All references are to section numbers in Thomas of Celano's *Life of
Saint Francis* (1C), and corresponding page numbers in *Franciscan of Assisi: Early
Documents* (FA:ED), vol. I, *The Saint* (Hyde Park, NY: New City Press, 1999).
2. 1C 123 (I, 293). Forms of the word "new" (including "renew") will be highlighted
in the text to facilitate identification.

> *All the people* (1 Sm 12:19) are waiting for *the cry of joy,*
> *the song of gladness* (Jer 25:10),
> a **new** song,
> a song full of sweetness. . . .[3]

The throng at the solemn ceremony join in the spirit of renewal, as they "*sing **new** songs* and the servants *of God* rejoice in the melody of the Spirit."[4] A few pages earlier, as he concludes the description of Francis's burial in the church of San Giorgio in Assisi, Thomas has already been setting the scene, as he shows that the saint continues his action on behalf of the people after his death: "At his tomb **new** miracles occur constantly"[5] as "he now *enlightens the world* (Jn 1:9) with a multitude of **new** miracles"[6] and "gladdens the whole world with the gift of **new** joy."[7] The change from sorrow at the passing of the saint to joy in his intercession has an enlivening effect on his surroundings: "With **new** light rising, the world is growing bright in these shining rays and feels all the darkness leave."[8]

These examples, from the Third Book of the *Life of Saint Francis* conclude a kind of litany of renewal chanted throughout the text. We can better appreciate the artistry of Thomas of Celano in sustaining this theme of "newness" if we take a moment to consider the framework he needed to use in telling the story of the Poverello, including both the demands of the canonization procedures themselves and the demands of a tradition of hagiographical literature.

Method: Virtue over Miracle

In Thomas's *Life* of Francis, the "new" includes method as well as content. He emphasizes the exercise of virtue during the saint's life as well as the evidence of miracles after his death, following the guidelines for papal canonizations promoted by Popes Alexander III, Innocent III, and by Thomas's patron, Gregory IX. This means that miracles after death are not the only, nor the most important

---

3. 1C 125 (I, 294–95).
4. 1C 126 (I, 296).
5. 1C 121 (I, 290).
6. 1C 118 (I, 286).
7. 1C 119 (I, 288).
8. 1C 119 (I, 289).

evidence of sainthood, but rather are complementary to the evidence provided by a way of Christian living, something of an innovation in the theology of sanctity in the twelfth and early thirteenth centuries. Under Gregory's watchful gaze, Thomas carefully points out the importance of this evidence.

In the *Prologue* Thomas explains that the First Book of the *Life* is "devoted principally to the purity of his blessed way of life, to his virtuous conduct and his wholesome teaching"; while, in something resembling a minor key, he notes that he "introduced a few of the many miracles which our Lord God deemed worthy to perform through him while he was *living in the flesh*" (Phil 1:22).[9] Note that even here the emphasis is on events, miraculous though they be, that occurred during the saint's lifetime. Thomas will return to the same point even more explicitly later in the text, as he explains: "we have not chosen to describe miracles—they do not make holiness but show it—but rather to describe the excellence of his life and the honest form of his manner of living."[10]

In an Epilogue following his account of the miracles of Francis, while continuing to insist on his theme of renewal, Thomas sounds a similar note, putting the miracles into their proper perspective:

> We have said a little about the miracles of our blessed father Francis, and have left out much, to inspire in those who wish *to follow his footsteps* (1 Pt 2:21) an eagerness to seek the grace of **new** blessings. Thus he, who so magnificently re**new**ed the whole world by word and example, life and teaching, might always graciously water the souls of those *who love the name of the Lord* (Ps 119:132) with **new** showers of heavenly gifts.[11]

The consistent emphasis on this "word and example" "life and teaching" and the restrained use of miraculous elements characterize Thomas's fidelity to what were, for his audience, relatively recent adjustments to the method of hagiographical writing. This means that in demonstrating Francis's holiness Thomas would have to focus on what was new in the saint's way of living, his words and

---

9. 1C Prol. 2 (I, 180).
10. 1C 70 (I, 243).
11. 1C 151 (I, 307–08).

example, without neglecting what was new in the miracles worked "in him" (during his life) and "through him" after his death.

Novelty and Tradition in Hagiography

For a religious and social culture in which novelty was not prized, but rather suspect, the "novelty" of the saint, Francis, was a problem that Thomas of Celano had to address. His task was made more difficult because he also needed to demonstrate Francis's similarity to earlier, well-established models of holiness. He found the way through this tension by considering Francis as a saint whose holiness includes and transcends earlier types of sanctity.

In introducing the reader to the Second Book, Thomas acknowledges the importance of the tradition of holiness, while insisting on a unique holiness for Francis (namely, the stigmata): "Yes, his glorious life reveals in even brighter light the perfection of earlier saints; the passion of Jesus Christ proves this, and His cross shows it clearly."[12] As Francis opens the gospel book to seek God's will, Thomas remarks, "In this he was led by the spirit of the saints and holy ones, as we read they did something similar with sincere devotion in their desire for holiness."[13]

Like Saint Antony of Egypt, Francis gives away all his possessions on hearing the gospel command.[14] Saint Martin of Tours, the soldier turned monk, later bishop, served as a measure of sanctity. Francis the soldier, called to conversion by divine grace, gives up dreams of military glory to become the *miles Christi*, the "soldier" or the "knight" of Christ. He echoes the opening of the *Life* of Martin by Sulpicius Severus in the opening of his own *Life* of Francis;[15] and notes that Francis (like Martin) was no "deaf hearer of the Gospel."[16] The lament of Martin's brothers at his passing echoes in Thomas's description of the death of Francis.[17] A careful early thirteenth century reader, or listener, would have been able to appreciate these evocations of classic hagiographical texts.

---

12. 1C 90 (I, 260).
13. 1C 92 (I, 262).
14. 1C 22 (I, 202).
15. 1C Prol. 1 (I, 180); see footnote a.
16. 1C 22 (I, 202).
17. 1C 109, 116–117 (I, 277; 285–86).

Augustine, the sinner turned saint, provides another point of reference: allusions to *The Confessions* can be found in the *Life* of the new saint. Like the young Augustine, Francis's neighbors fear being despised for their innocence;[18] and Francis, like the saint of Hippo, struts through "the streets of Babylon";[19] and learns God's will as he opens the Scriptures.[20]

The importance of the Cistercians in the early thirteenth century made it tempting for Thomas to gauge the sanctity of Francis against that of the pioneer Cistercian, Bernard of Clairvaux. Thomas uses allusions, and even direct citations from the writings of Bernard, for example, comments in "De consideratione" on the generally bad character of the Romans.[21] He describes events similar to those in Bernard's *Life of Malachy*;[22] and offers rather similar treatments of virtues (e.g., humility in the *Sermo I in Nativitate Domini*[23]); as well as similarities to the *legendae* of Bernard himself,[24] leading to the suspicion that the author had more than a passing acquaintance with Cistercian circles.

These examples, which could be multiplied to include Saints Benedict, Godric, Cuthbert and Anselm, serve to anchor the figure of Francis firmly in the hagiographical tradition, a necessary task for Thomas, who will play off against the traditional elements his insistence on the novelty inherent in the story of Francis as a saint.

"New": a Leitmotif in the Vita

As we have seen in the description of Francis's canonization, various forms of the word "new" serve as a leitmotif in the *Vita*. Francis is a "new" person; his words and example help to renew the life of the church; he founds a new Order; he renews devotion to the Incarnation and birth of Christ (Greccio); and he bears the new

---

18. 1C 1 (I, 183).
19. 1C 2 (I, 184).
20. 1C 92 (I, 262).
21. 1C 122 (I, 292).
22. 1C 9 (I, 190–91), 1C 18 (I, 197), 1C 23 (I, 203).
23. 1C 19 (I, 198).
24. 1C 23 (I, 203), 1C 27 (I, 206), 1C 40 (I, 219), 1C 42 (I, 221), 1C 83 (I, 253), 1C 85 (I, 256), 1C 97 (I, 266), 1C 115 (I, 284).

miracle of the stigmata on his body. A selection of phrases from the *Life* illustrate the frequency with which this vocabulary appears.

Francis is "the **new** *soldier of Christ*" (2 Tm 2:3),[25] and "the **new** athlete of Christ."[26] During his early experiences of solitude in caves near Assisi, "inspired by a **new** and extraordinary spirit he would pray to his *Father in secret*" (Mt 6:6).[27] As a result of God's action in him, "*renewed in spirit* (1 Sm 10:6), he now seemed to be *changed into another man*" (Ps 51:12).[28] So insistent is Thomas on this profound change visible in Francis that he will repeat it later: "He was so wholly taken up in joy, filled with pure delight, that he truly seemed a **new** person of another age."[29] The Saint of Assisi actually makes the "new" an element of sanctity itself: "*He did not consider that he had already attained* (Phil 3:13) his goal, but tireless in pursuit of holy **new**ness, he constantly hoped to begin again."[30]

Clearly, Thomas has shown respect for earlier models of holiness, but he does not allow these to overshadow what is clearly innovative in the holiness practiced and promoted by Francis. Novelty, far from being a vice, has been transformed into a virtue.

Francis and the Renewal of Life

The effect of Francis's word and example on others is a renewing action, producing in others what he has experienced in himself, "that through him the Lord might give sinners confidence in a **new** life of grace."[31] In a masterful summary of this renewing action of Francis in the church and the world, Thomas chooses a rich variety of scriptural images to depict the work of the saint:

In these *last times* (1 Pt 1:5)
a **new** Evangelist,
like *one of the rivers of Paradise* (Gn 2:10),
has poured out (Is 44:3)

---

25. 1C 9 (I, 189).
26. 1C 10 (I, 190).
27. 1C 6 (I, 187).
28. 1C 26 (I, 205).
29. 1C 81 (I, 251).
30. 1C 103 (I, 273).
31. 1C 2 (I, 184).

the streams of the gospel
in a holy flood *over the whole world* (Est 13:4).
He preached the way of the Son of God
and the teaching of truth in his deeds.
In him and through him
an unexpected joy and a holy **new**ness
came into the world.
A shoot of the ancient religion
suddenly re**new**ed the old and decrepit.
*A **new** spirit was placed in the hearts* (Ez 11:19) of the elect
and a holy anointing *has been poured out in* their *midst* (Ez 36:26).
This holy *servant of Christ* (Gal 1:10),
like one of the *lights of heaven* (Gn 1:14),
shone from above with a **new** rite and **new** signs.
The ancient miracles have been re**new**ed through him.
In the desert of this world
a fruitful vine has been planted
in a **new** Order but in an ancient way,
bearing *flowers, sweet*
with the *fragrance* of holy virtues (Sir 24:23; Ps 52:10)
and *stretching out* everywhere *branches* (Ez 17:6-7)
of holy religion.[32]

People of all social categories rush to be with Francis, because of "the wonders which the Lord worked a**new** in the world through his servant."[33] His appeal is to men and women, provoking a similar response, because "through his spreading message, the Church of Christ is being re**new**ed in both sexes."[34] The effect of the saint among the people was like that of the breaking of day after a long night, as "through the presence of Saint Francis and through his reputation, it surely seemed a **new** light had been sent from heaven to earth."[35]

In a rare description of papal mirth, Thomas pictures the former Cardinal Hugolino, now Pope Gregory IX, as he prepares to canonize Francis:

32. 1C 89 (I, 259–60).
33. 1C 36 (I, 215).
34. 1C 37 (I, 216).
35. 1C 36 (I, 215).

He rejoiced and exulted, dancing with joy,
for in his own day he was seeing
the Church of God being re**new**ed
with **new** mysteries that were ancient wonders.[36]

The New Order

As Francis attracted followers, an Order was born, and Francis is pictured as a parent, "the devoted father instructed his **new** sons *not so much in words* and *speech but in deed and truth*" (1 Jn 3:18),[37] "forming his **new** sons with **new** instruction."[38] These lesser brothers were "Christ's **new** students in the school of humility."[39] "What a great flame of charity burned in the **new** disciples of Christ!"[40]

As with other initiatives of the time, this family was opposed by unidentified enemies:

There were many who plotted to destroy
the **new** *planting* (Ps 144:12) of the Order at its beginning.
There were many trying to suffocate the *chosen vineyard* (Jer 2:21)
which the Lord's hand had so kindly planted a**new** in the world.[41]

The Order itself shares in the characteristic note of newness ascribed to the saint himself. It represents a force for renewal, particularly in the service of Gregory IX, and the enemies of that renewal were to be opposed to the Order he fostered.

Renewed Devotion to the Incarnation

Thomas of Celano presents Francis's vivid sense of the Incarnation and Passion of Christ as hallmarks of his spirituality. In different circumstances, during the short span of months from

---

36. 1C 121 (I, 291).
37. 1C 41 (I, 220).
38. 1C 26 (I, 205).
39. 1C 34 (I, 213).
40. 1C 38 (I, 217).
41. 1C 74 (I, 246).

December 1223 to September 1224, these two mysteries of the life
of Jesus are re-enacted in Francis's own experience and, through
him, become present to others in ways that were previously
unheard-of. As Francis sets out to recreate the circumstances of the
birth of Jesus in an Italian hilltown, at Christmas of 1223, his efforts
bring the reality of the gospel account of the birth of Christ to life:
"out of Greccio is made a **new** Bethlehem."[42] This innovative
approach to depicting a theological mystery becomes an occasion
for and outpouring of devotion. The reaction of the inhabitants of
the town betrays wonder ("The people arrive, ecstatic at this **new**
mystery of **new** joy"),[43] and the celebrant of the Mass joins in this
experience ("the priest enjoys a **new** consolation").[44]

The Stigmata

Because of his devotion to the Passion of Christ, Francis spends a
time in prayer and fasting on the mountain of La Verna in the Fall of
1224. There he sees, in a vision, a crucified man covered with wings
like a Seraph. Francis's reaction, in Thomas's text, is one of wonder,
provoked by the very novelty of the vision itself: "While he was
unable to perceive anything clearly understandable from the vision,
its **new**ness very much pressed upon his heart."[45] Marks on Francis's body (stigmata) appeared after this vision, and these he carefully concealed during the two remaining years of his life. But at his
death people were able to see them, and in the midst of their sorrow,
this "**new** miracle turned their minds to amazement."[46] Thomas
attributes these stigmata to the action of God, who "*gives **new** signs
and works **new** wonders*" (Sir 36:6)[47] while acknowledging that not all
accept the genuineness of the stigmata, precisely because they were
unprecedented (". . . to allay suspicion about the **new**ness of this
miracle").[48]

---

42. 1C 85 (I, 255).
43. 1C 85 (I, 255).
44. 1C 85 (I, 256).
45. 1C 94 (I, 264).
46. 1C 112 (I, 280).
47. 1C 114 (I, 282).
48. 1C 114 (I, 282).

With the declaration of this new miracle, Thomas has brought his theme to its highest point. The very body of Francis becomes the evidence that he is a new kind of saint, one conformed to Christ both in his inner self and externally, visibly, in his flesh.

Conclusion

Thomas of Celano faced a number of challenges when beginning the composition of his *Life* of Francis of Assisi: using a new hagiographical method; rooting his text firmly in earlier hagiographical tradition; and insisting that there is something fundamentally new about the Saint from Assisi.

Under the direction of his patron, Pope Gregory IX, he had the responsibility of presenting the saint according to new norms for canonization, emphasizing the virtues of the saint during his life, and not only the miracles worked at his tomb after death. That he was aware of this responsibility can be learned from his repeated affirmations about the greater importance to be ascribed to the saint's virtues.

Drawing on a rich hagiographical formation, Thomas does succeed in placing his narrative of the life of Francis in some continuity with the examples of earlier *Lives* of saints. But he also does something more, and dedicates a good deal of energy to the effort: he evokes the figure of a "new" saint, who brings a new kind of holiness into the tradition, even in his physical conformity to the body of Christ. Closely associated with the depiction of Francis himself as someone "new," Thomas describes the Order founded by Francis as a force of renewal, and the effect of Francis and his brothers as one promising renewed life in the church and the world.

On completing his commission in writing the earliest hagiographical text about Francis of Assisi, Thomas of Celano deserved to receive high praise from his papal patron, Gregory IX. With the skill of the very best authors in Christian hagiographical literature, this rather poorly known friar satisfied the requirements of a papal canonization procedure, placed Francis of Assisi within the great tradition of earlier Christian saints, and still managed to depict for us a saint who remains ever new.

Figure 1

Francis Naked and Clothed

A Theological Meditation

Lawrence S. Cunningham

> For Christ, desire to enter into complete nakedness,
> emptiness, and poverty in everything in the world.
>
> *Saint John of the Cross*

Introduction

It has been fashionable, from at least the time of Paul Sabatier, to condemn Brother Elias of Cortona for turning Saint Francis from a humble icon of the life of Christ into just another medieval saint whose tomb became a pilgrimage destination. The evidence for this charge comes, of course, from the basilica which began to be raised in Assisi almost immediately after the canonization of the saint in 1228. Within twenty-five years not only had the funds been raised to build the great romanesque church, which is the basilica of Saint Francis, but the church saw completion around 1253. The building itself is a somewhat forbidding fortress but, in fairness, it is not as crushingly ugly as the *settecento basilica of Santa Maria degli Angeli* in the valley below Assisi which truly is a monument to staggeringly bad taste. The only merit in that latter building is that it makes a stunning contrast to the humble little chapel of the Portiuncula which is housed inside it — a chapel so appealing that Simone Weil, in a penetrating passage in *Waiting on God*, says that when she entered it, she felt compelled "by something stronger than I was" to fall on her knees and pray for the first time in her life.[1]

Between 1253 and the early part of the next century a whole host of preeminent artists — one thinks of Giunta Pisano, Cimabue, Pietro Lorenzetti, Giotto, and Simone Martini came and added visually to the basilica of Saint Francis. If there is one thing to be said in favor of Brother Elias it is this: he built a monument that to this very day brings thousands of visitors to the city where they learn something, however fleetingly, of the life of Francis of Assisi.[2]

Among the many glories of the basilica of the saint is the series of frescoes in the upper church which depict scenes from the life of Saint Francis. Once thought to be the work of the great master, Giotto, they are now almost universally ascribed to an unknown artist (from the school of Giotto?) who is known simply as the "Master of the Saint Francis cycle."[3] It was part of that series of frescoes which suffered devastating damage during an earthquake in 1997. It has only been in recent times that the basilica has been reopened for visitors while work on the damaged frescoes goes on apace.[4]

There is one particular fresco in the cycle that will serve as the focus of our reflections in this essay (see Fig. 1). It is the scene where Francis, having been called before the bishop of Assisi, renounces his earthly goods, stripping himself naked while handing his clothes back to his father, Pietro Bernardone. The painter of this scene would have been inspired by the description of the incident in Saint Bonaventure's *Legenda Major* since when he painted (very early in the fourteenth century) that was the only extant source for the life of Francis.[5] We might recall here the salient points that

---

1. Simone Weil, *Waiting on God* (New York: Harper, 1952), 34.
2. It was not always so. When Goethe visited Assisi in the early nineteenth century he measured the Roman Temple in the main square and left in haste with no interest at all in either the architecture or the art of the city.
3. See the discussion by Alistair Smart in *The Assisi Problem and the Art of Giotto* (Oxford: Clarendon, 1971).
4. For a discussion of the damage, see George Bonsanti's *The Basilica of Saint Francis: Glory and Destruction* (New York: Harry Abrams, 1998).
5. Smart argues that tag lines from Bonaventure were inscribed under the scenes but were erased in the nineteenth century; it is not clear if the citations from Bonaventure were contemporary with the frescoes or not.

Bonaventure makes as he describes this particular scene in chapter two of his *Legenda Major*:[6]

(1) Bonaventure puts this scene in the context of a raging father who is irate over his son squandering money and of bringing dishonor to the family.

(2) Francis goes willingly to the bishop where he gives back everything including all of his clothes and renounces his earthly name by calling God his father.

(3) The bishop clothes the naked Francis with his own mantle. Bonaventure tells us that Francis had stripped off all of his clothes including his underwear (which gets translated modestly as "trousers").

(4) Francis re-clothed himself in a cheap cloak taken from a farmer who worked for the bishop. Francis then chalks a cross on the back of this cloak. Bonaventure then draws out the point of the narrative with a focus on the nakedness of Francis: "Thus the servant of the Most High King was left naked that he might follow his naked crucified Lord whom he loved."

The Master of the Saint Francis Cycle tells that story with vivid drama: to the left of the scene the grandees of Assisi frame the irate father Pietro Bernardone whose right hand is restrained from attacking his son by a figure behind him. There is a slight blank space in the fresco that separated the figure of the naked Francis, arms raised in prayer toward a heavenly hand which gestures down toward the saint. That gap vividly demarcates the separation of the world of Peter and the world of Francis, i.e., the world of the temporal and the world of the spiritual. Bishop Guido, complete with mitre, envelops Francis with the right side of his episcopal cope while two tonsured clerics stand just behind him.[7] Francis is bathed in a glow of light. In the background of the scene on the left and the right are highly stylized sets of architecture symbolizing again the mercantile world of Pietro and the church world of Guido — the temporality and the spirituality.

---

6. LMj 2.3–2.4 (II, 537–38). All abbreviations and citations are from *Francis of Assisi: Early Documents*, edited by Regis J. Armstrong, J. A. Wayne Hellmann and William J. Short, vol. 2 (Hyde Park, NY: New City Press, 2000).

7. Arnaldo Fortini has attempted to identify the retinues who would have attended this confrontation in his *Francis of Assisi*, translated by Helen Moak (New York: Crossroad, 1981), 227–29.

It takes little sophistication in religious iconography to grasp the main theme of the scene itself. Francis leaves the world represented by his father and his father's world. This scene, in short, represents the old ascetic topos of *fuga mundi* — flight from the world and the radical demands that such a flight entails. Behind that ascetic theme stands some of the sternest demands of Jesus recorded in the synoptic gospels: "No one can serve two masters . . . You cannot serve God and wealth" (Mt 6:24), and "I have not come to bring peace but the sword. For I have come to set a man against his father . . . whoever loves father or mother more than me is not worthy of me" (Mt 10:34–37).

However, there are some deeper themes that derive from this scene that are alluded to in the fresco[8] but that are fleshed out more fully in the corpus of the early writings about Francis. Those themes are (1) the symbolic value of exchanging one kind of clothes for another; and (2) the theme of nudity in the story of Francis. We will take up each of those themes in turn.

Clothing and Unclothing

The act of changing clothes, their wearing, and the kind of clothing one wears can be interpreted as a kind of code — this is obvious and a commonplace in the field of anthropology and social theory. The putting on of new clothes has a definite symbolic value in Christianity as everything from donning a baptismal robe at the beginning of the initiation rites to assuming a religious habit or vesting for the liturgy makes clear.

One cannot view the scene of Francis giving back to his father his clothes without thinking of the highly charged symbolism such an act entails. Exchanging clothes is a favorite metaphor in Saint Paul for the renunciation of sin and taking on Christ: "Do not lie to one another, seeing that you have stripped off the old self and have clothed yourself with the new self" (Col 3:9–10) or, more pertinently, "You were taught to put away your former way of life, your

---

8. The same scene appears in the life of Francis cycle in the Bardi chapel of the church of Santa Croce in Florence which is from the hand of Giotto. The scenes differ in composition but the radical distance between father and saint are both highlighted.

old self, corrupt and debased by lusts and to be renewed in the spirit of your minds and to clothe yourselves with the new self created according to the likeness of God" (Eph 4:22–24).

Since Francis had earlier in his life decided to seek his fortune as a soldier even after his first ignominious experiences of warring against Perugia, his stripping off of his old clothes and assuming the rags of a peasant might well have an implicit military metaphor from Paul in mind who sees the Christian as "putting on the whole armor of God so that you may stand against the wiles of the devil" (Eph 6:11ff). After all, as Bonaventure notes, when Francis takes the peasant's cloak he chalks a cross on its back, thus making Francis a cross bearer — which is to say — a crusader, but surely a crusader against the standard type familiar in the world of Francis. That Francis's whole body is bathed in light echoes Paul's urgent demand to "cast off the works of darkness and put on the armor of light" (Rom 13:12).[9]

The symbolism of putting off the old and putting on the new, taken from the New Testament, as we have noted, stands behind the monastic custom of leaving aside secular clothes and adopting the monastic habit. It is worth noting that the early Franciscan sources were quite aware of that custom and its symbolic significance. Many of the early *legenda* distinguish Francis in terms of his apparel. Bonaventure opens his first chapter by a description of Francis's manner of life "in the attire of the world." Bonaventure borrows this theme from earlier writings. Thomas of Celano entitles chapter one of the first part of *The Life of Saint Francis* "How He Lived in the Clothing and Spirit of the World." Further on in his text, Thomas relates how after his conversion Francis wore the traditional habit of the hermit (gown, belt, shoes, staff), and then changed to a single tunic and a cord.[10] Indeed, one could kind of mark the conversion(s) of Francis by paying attention to the different ways he changed his dress in his early years.

The exchange of clothes before Bishop Guido had a profound social significance. Excess of dress was so conspicuous in the Middle

---

9. It would be otiose to cite all the times when Thomas of Celano and others explicitly depict Francis as a "soldier" or a "knight" of Christ; see the Index to FA:ED (IV, 73, 122).

10. 1C 21 (I, 201).

Ages that many places issued sumptuary laws detailing just what was and what was not permissible for people to wear. That civil finery was a sign of decadence and self-indulgence is a commonplace complaint of the period.[11] One must think of that complaint by recalling the long chapter in the Rule of 1221 about the kind of clothing the friars are to have which ends with the exhortation "not to seek expensive clothing in this world so that they have a garment in the Kingdom of Heaven."[12] It would be difficult to read this move from secular finery to the rough clothing Francis adapts without thinking of the words of Jesus when speaking of Saint John the Baptist: "What did you go out to see? Someone dressed in soft robes? Look, those who are dressed in soft robes are in royal palaces" (Mt 11:8). Nor is it without significance to recall that Pietro made the money which Francis shunned from the selling of cloth.

Nudity

The sources that describe Francis and his father before Bishop Guido all note that as he stripped off his secular clothing he ended up standing naked in the public square before all those who were in attendance. Francis's nakedness is alluded to in the frescoes but his body is covered by the cope of the bishop. There is a spiritual dictum that went back many centuries before the time of Francis that, in its classic formulation, spoke of "nakedly following the naked Christ" (*nudus nudum Christum sequi*) — a formula that goes back at least to the time of Saint Jerome who uses it, in almost those exact words, in one of his letters.[13] The patristic tradition loved to play with the theme of the Christ child born naked and later stripped naked by the Roman soldiers before his crucifixion. The

---

11. One thinks, for example, of the warnings to the women of Florence that Dante puts into the mouth of Forese Donati in *Purgatorio* xxiii.
12. 1C 13 (I, 65).
13. The background of this theme is fully explored in the entry "Nudité dans la littérature mystique," in the *Dictionnaire de spiritualité*, fasc. lxxii–lxxiii (Paris. Beaucschene, 1981), 513–17. Michael Robson [*St. Francis of Assisi* (London: Chapman, 1997), 36] reads this allusion as a naked follower of Christ wrestling naked with the adversary that I do not think is correct. That theme does appear later in the death scene in the life of Francis.

latter stripping was an attempt, of course, to bring shame upon the malefactor during the process of execution.

The Christian spiritual tradition saw in the nakedness of Jesus as an infant an indication of his true humanity as well as a recapitulation of the nakedness of the first Adam who, in edenic innocence, was naked and without shame. The soon to be crucified Christ was left naked as a sign of shame. The traditional reading of that act of the Romans was almost always done in the light of the famous kenosis passage of Christ's self-emptying: "though he was in the form of God, did not regard equality with God as something to be exploited but emptied himself, taking the form of a slave, being born into human likeness, And being found in human form, he humbled himself and became obedient to the point of death — and even death on a cross" (Phil 2:6–8). It might be worthwhile, in passing, to note that this famous passage may be indirectly comparing Christ to Adam — the latter who did try to become an equal to God by not humbling himself.[14]

It is a reiterated theme in the Franciscan tradition that Francis linked the life of poverty under the rubric of self-emptying. The cross is the shorthand paradigm example of dying in poverty and humility. Those who studied the life of Francis linked his poverty with the passion of Christ. Dante seems to have understood this perfectly well. In the eleventh canto of the *Paradiso* where Saint Dominic praises Francis, he says that at Calvary Mary stood at the foot of the cross but Lady Poverty climbed up the cross to embrace Jesus in his death. Simone Weil said that those words were among the most beautiful ever written by a poet: "*Dove Maria rimase giuso/ ella* [i.e. Lady Poverty] *con Cristo salse in su la croce.*"

Dante may or may not have known the allegorical text called the *Sacrum Commercium* written more than a decade after the death of Francis. That allegorical work makes the strongest case possible for the Franciscan understanding of poverty and does so under the rubric of nakedness. Francis, searching for Lady Poverty, queries two ancients (representing the Old and New Testaments?) about her location only to be told that she lives on top of a high mountain and "if you wish to reach her, brother, take off your clothes of

---

14. On the Adam/Christ parallel see Frank Matera, *New Testament Christology* (Louisville, KY: Westminster/John Knox, 1999), 129ff.

rejoicing and put aside every burden and sin clinging to you for, unless you are naked, you will not be able to climb to her in so high a place."[15] When Francis does find Lady Poverty she is seated naked upon a throne.[16] In conversation with Francis she tells him that she once walked nakedly with Adam in the garden of paradise before the Fall.[17] Towards the end of their long conversation and a simple meal of bread and water, Lady Poverty lies down to rest "naked upon the naked earth."[18]

Lady Poverty's rest upon the naked earth is an anticipation of the manner of the saint's own death. In the fourteenth chapter of the *Legenda Major* Bonaventure says that before his death Francis threw himself "naked on the naked ground" so that he might "wrestle naked with the naked."[19] Bonaventure is not slow to draw the moral from this incident (which, incidentally, is not reported by Thomas of Celano in the *The Life of Saint Francis* but is recounted in his second life of the saint):[20]

> In all things
> He wished without hesitation
> to be conformed to Christ crucified,
> who hung on the cross poor, suffering and naked.
> Naked he lingered before the bishop
> At the beginning of his conversion;
> and, for this reason,
> at the end of his life
> he wanted to leave this world naked.[21]

What Bonaventure notes, in the above passage, is a kind of recapitulation of the converted life of Francis. He considers the encounter of Francis and his father before Bishop Guido as the beginning of his new way of life even though Francis, in the *Testament*, marks his

---

15. ScEx 11 (I, 532).
16. ScEx 15 (I, 534).
17. ScEx 25ff (I, 537ff).
18. ScEx 63 (I, 552).
19. LMj 14.3 (II, 642). It is here that the other topos of nakedly fighting the demonic one nakedly is heard. There are two themes to disentangle: nakedly following the naked Christ and nakedly wrestling the naked adversary. The image comes from Gregory the Great.
20. 2C 216 (II, 388).
21. LMj 14.4 (II, 642–43).

conversion to the time when he was able to look on lepers without loathing. Furthermore, after the episcopal encounter there were further stages that followed Francis as we have seen: the exchange of the traditional garb of the hermit for the patched tunic and cord characteristic of his new way of living. It might be better, in fact, to think of Francis's life as a series of conversions after the manner of a pilgrimage.[22]

Be that as it may, Bonaventure does make the serious point that Francis's change of clothing/stripping naked before the bishop does mark an easily recognizable moment in the life of Francis. It was the kind of gesture that anyone familiar with entrance into the religious life would have recognized immediately. That he then repeated that stripping to nakedness at the very end of his life carried with it a gesture, not of eccentricity, but of finality: "In one silent gesture he portrayed the lesser brother's attitude to life: to be a disciple of the new Adam, 'man of earth' inspired by God's Spirit . . . He wished to show this in a final dramatic gesture. Even Christ's stigmata, which until now he had managed to keep hidden from virtually everyone became visible, exposed, without covering."[23]

A final note on nudity: some early writers contrast Francis and Adam in terms of their respective nakedness. Thus Henri d'Avranches: "Exposed was the shamefulness of Adam, while no shame / is discovered in him. Where is the shame in a naked body / when the vesture of its soul is honor?"[24] The observation that Francis did not experience shame in his nakedness because of the purity of his soul alludes to an old theme in Christian spirituality that crops up as early as the Cappodocians and is frequent in Dionysian literature. Those who have undertaken the spiritual ascent recover, in the final stages of their contemplative life, the unsullied and naked state of Adam before the Fall. The movement of this ascent is twofold: the stripping away of the impulses towards sin and the recovery of the innocence of Adam in his nakedness that he enjoyed before the Fall.[25]

---

22. This is the argument of Pierre Brunette's *Francis of Assisi and His Conversions* (Quincy, IL: Franciscan Press, 1997).
23. Edith van den Goorbergh and Theodore Zweerman, *Respectfully Yours: Signed and Sealed, Francis of Assisi* (St. Bonaventure, NY: Franciscan Institute, 2001), 361.
24. VL 150 (I, 449).
25. This theme is adumbrated in the entry "Nudité dans la litterature mystique" in *Dictionnaire de Spiritualité*, 513–17.

Exegesis as Performance

Ewert Cousins has argued that Francis of Assisi inaugurated what he describes as the "mysticism of the historical event" by which he means the experience of someone who "recalls a significant event in the past, enters into its drama and draws from it spiritual energy eventually moving beyond the event toward union with God."[26] Cousins argues that this new form of mysticism, initiated by Francis, would lead in a straight line to the shape of Ignatian mysticism found in the *Spiritual Exercises*. It would not be possible to detail in any fashion the argument Cousins puts forward; but it is possible — without getting into the thorny issue of mysticism in general or the mysticism of Francis in particular[27] — to indicate something a bit more modest, namely, that Francis does exemplify to a high degree a kind of scriptural exegesis that can be called "performative." Following on this, Francis is, *sui generis*, a theologian.

What is performative theology? Frances Young gives a useful analogy to understand the concept.[28] She asks us to think of the music of someone like Mozart. We possess autograph musical scores of his work. Scholars establish the reliability of the texts but their true meaning only happens when those texts are performed. Some perform at a perfunctory or beginning level but others perform at a skilled level with the best who play at the level of the virtuoso. So with the scriptures: we need scholars to give us the correct text and the best of translations and interpretations but it is only in the performance of the texts in various settings (by ritual acts in liturgy; by acting on ethical demands in the text; by preaching/teaching the meaning of the texts to others; etc.) that the true meaning becomes transparent. Some do this at a mediocre level while others bring the performance to a high level of meaning. The latter group are the virtuosi whom we call in the tradition, saints.

---

26. Ewert Cousins, "Francis of Assisi: Christian Mysticism at the Crossroads," in *Mysticism and Religious Traditions*, edited by Steven Katz (New York: Oxford University Press, 1983), 166.
27. See the careful remarks of Bernard McGinn in *The Flowering of Mysticism: Men and Women in the New Mysticism* (New York: Crossroad, 1998), 41–69, especially 58ff for a discussion of Cousins.
28. Frances Young, *Virtuoso Theology: The Bible and Its Interpretation* (Cleveland: Pilgrim, 1993).

What is important to remember (as in the musical example) is that the performance is tied to the same text; it is the depth of the acting out of the text that marks the distinction between those who act at a superficial level and those who understand the text profoundly.

It is not difficult to see how Young's paradigm fits Francis. In a series of conversions he attempted to live out the themes of the gospel in a quite literal fashion: if the gospel said to eschew money, he would disdain it; if the gospel said to preach to all persons he would attempt to do that. His program was part of that great reform movement, initiated by Pope Gregory VII, which attempted to answer this simple question: What is the *vita evangelica*? How does one live according to the form of the gospel? Many different persons and groups attempted to answer that question in the twelfth century.[29] Indeed, some moments from Francis's life attempt to model some of those experiments: as a servant to the lepers; as a mendicant in Rome; as a "man of penance" in Assisi; as a hermit, etc.

When Francis settles on his life as a lesser brother he embarked on a process of discovering a way of life which would interest him centrally until the day he died. One can see his life as an ongoing experiment in scriptural exegesis, not at a scholar's bench, but in his gestures, activities, reflections, prayers, acts of charity and preaching, and so on. Francis's relation to the word of God was, in fact, complex: he was a hearer of the Word (hearing the gospel was a trigger point for his conversion); he was a preacher of the Word; he profoundly reverenced the Word and its expositors as his *Testament* makes clear; and most of all, he was a "Doer" or "Performer" of the Word. Both in the way he fashioned prayer from the Word but, most of all, by the way he lived. Thomas of Celano made the point succinctly: "For he was no deaf hearer of the gospel; rather he committed everything he heard to his excellent memory and was careful to carry it out to the letter."[30]

---

29. The range of attempts has been summed up by Duane Lapsanski's *Evangelical Perfection*, Theology Series 7 (Saint Bonaventure, NY: Franciscan Institute, 1977) which draws extensively on Herbert Grundmann's classic *Religiose Bewegungen im Mittelalter* (Berlin, 1935; reprinted Darmstadt, 1964); *Religious Movements in the Middle Ages* (Notre Dame: University of Notre Dame Press, 1995).

30. 1C 22 (I, 202).

Apart from the specific aims of the early writers on Francis — to remember his deeds, to celebrate them in the liturgy, to inspire his *religio* — we can also say that those writers and other artists also attempted to understand his charisms in the light of the Word of God. In other words, we have a process by which Francis attempts to be a living exegete of the Word of God and his commentators, in turn, try to understand his life in the light of the gospel.[31] That "reading" of Francis provides a trajectory for interpretations that will culminate in the approach of those who more directly interpret the life of Francis as "conformed" to the life of Christ. That trajectory will end up with some rather tendentious attempts to draw strict parallels between the life of Christ and the life of Francis which one detects in later elaborations of the saint's life as is clear from the opening lines of the *Little Flowers* which draws its inspiration from an earlier Latin text of the *Actus Beati Sancti Francesci* . The opening lines of the *Little Flowers* is typical, "We must first consider how the glorious Sir Saint Francis of Assisi was conformed to the blessed Christ in all the acts of his life . . ."[32] There is not much distance between the parallels found there (twelve apostles/twelve early companions; Judas/John of Cappella, etc.) and the excesses of Bartholomew of Pisa's *De conformitate vitae beati Francisci ad vitam domini Jesu*.

It is inevitable that there be a serious attempt to find the authentic Francis behind the various texts which have risen in response to his extraordinary life. It could not be otherwise since, as David Tracy argued, in a now classical work,[33] the "classic" (person, text, artifact) always possesses an excess of meaning — an excess that spills over into the reflections of those who look back and think about the meaning of the classic. What one can do, as a simple approach to reach up to the full meaning of Francis and his charism, is to look, first, at his words or gestures, and, then, look a second time, at how those words and gestures and events, were understood.

---

31. The editors of FA:ED I, 176–78 "read" the first life of Thomas of Celano as a depiction of Francis as a "mirror" of the Incarnation, Passion, and Resurrection.
32. LFl 1 (III, 566).
33. David Tracy, *The Analogical Imagination* (New York: Crossroad, 1978).

Conclusion

In this brief meditation on two incidents of unclothing and clothing in the life of Francis I see two stages that may invite a third.

First, Francis did certain things at crucial points in his life. He stripped himself naked before his father and Bishop Guido. He did that in a complex gesture that surely involved rejection of his father's way of life and his adoption of the *vita evangelica*. At the time of his death he took off his clothes and laid himself on the naked earth as, almost, an argument for the poverty he valued so supremely. Bonaventure tells us that on other occasions he would act in nakedness: in the snow to overcome lust; with a halter around his neck when he preached to the people of Assisi as penance for his own (perceived) gluttony.

Second, those who knew him or knew about him remembered and described those events both as historical moments and as highly emblematic gestures which could be understood against the background of an ancient spiritual tradition which linked Adam, Christ, and those who wished to lead the life of Christian perfection. In other words, they sought understanding from the reality of exigent facts. If Francis performed at the first level of gesture they wanted to deepen their understanding by the second level of reflection.

But what does that mean for those who live centuries after the time Francis lived and Bonaventure wrote? Already we see in the various legends an understanding that simply copying what Francis did was no guarantee that to be the best way of following the example of the saint. Those who witnessed Francis having himself dragged through Assisi naked with a halter about his neck "professed that his humility was easier to admire than to imitate." Bonaventure went on to observe, writing about this scene, that it was more like a portent or prophetic utterance than an example.[34] Likewise, Francis forbade Brother John the Simple from imitating

---

34. LMj 6.2 (II, 570).

his every movement. Francis admired his "simplicity, but gently told him not to do this anymore."[35]

How then do we recapture the particular insights that Francis can teach us about living out the gospel life? The short answer is that we not focus exclusively on Francis but on the kind of life he wanted to incarnate. To paraphrase an old Zen aphorism: when a Boddhisattva points to the moon, look, not at the finger, but in the direction that the finger points. Karl Rahner got it exactly right when he wrote that from the life of Christ and the lives of the saints one does not deduce a general theory of holiness; what the saints show us is that "a certain form of life and activity is a really genuine possibility; they show us experimentally that one can be a Christian even in 'this' way; they make this type of Christian believable as a Christian type."[36] So, then, the question becomes this: who shows us today, as Francis did in his time, what it means to wrestle nakedly with the naked Christ? It is a daunting and fearsome question.

35. In Thomas of Celano's awkwardly titled "The Remembrance of the Desire of a Soul," 2C 190 (II, 368–69). Other examples are cited and discussed by Hester Gelber in "A Theater of Virtue: The Exemplary World of Saint Francis," in *Saints and Virtues*, edited by John Stratton Hawley (Berkeley, CA: University of California Press, 1987), 15–35, especially 30–32.

36. Karl Rahner, *The Practice of Faith: A Handbook of Christian Spirituality* (New York: Crossroad, 1983), 157. The original essay on the saints may be found in *Theological Investigations III* (Baltimore: Helicon, 1967), 158–70.

Commercium

From the Profane to the Sacred

Michael Cusato

To translate or not to translate: this was one of the questions facing the American editors of the *Sacrum commercium beati Francisci cum Domina Paupertate* — and its problematic term *commercium* — in the recently edited corpus of sources, *Francis of Assisi: Early Documents*. It is a problem familiar to editors and translators the world over of the *fonti francescane*.[1] In the end, the Americans decided to translate the telltale phrase *"sacrum commercium"* by the somewhat inelegant phrase *"sacred exchange,"* attempting to retain an emphasis on the economic imagery connoted by the Latin term. More recently, Campion Murray, an Australian friar who published a private translation and commentary on the work in 1995, has recently issued an updated version of his translation. However, whereas in the first edition he had left the phrase in the title in its original Latin (as had been done, incidentally, in the earlier *Omnibus*

---

1. For example, the Italian *Fonti francescane,* 3rd ed. (Padua: Edizioni Messaggero, 1983) uses *"questa alleanza di salvezza"* (1636); the French *Saint François d'Assise. Documents* (Paris: Éditions franciscaines, 1968) uses *"cette alliance qui nous sauve"* (1403); the Spanish *San Francisco de Asís. Escritos, Biografías, Documentos de la época* (Madrid: Editorial Catolica, 1998) uses *"esta alianza de salvación"* (938); and in the German translation of the *Sacrum commercium* printed in his *Der Bund des heiligen Franzikus mit der herrin Armut* (Werl/Westfalen: Dietrich-Coelde-Verlag, 1966), Kajetan Esser uses *"dieses heilbringender Bund"* (101). All thus opt for the overtly religious meaning of covenant/alliance.

179

of Sources), his revised version now renders *sacrum commercium* by the more ambiguous phrase "holy agreement."[2] The effort to get this problematic phrase right thus continues unabated — mainly because most editors seem to believe that an accurate translation of the term is the key to unlocking the meaning of the wider document.

But is this really the case? Although the rendering of the Latin term into English (or any other language) still remains problematic, the real issue is not first and foremost one of correct translation but of correct comprehension: how is one to understand both the meaning and particular use that medieval authors made of this enigmatic phrase? For if it is axiomatic to assert that translations are really reflections of a translator's understanding (or lack of understanding) of a given text, then it is essential that we understand the meaning of the term *commercium* in this critical document of early Franciscan history.

The question is an important one for two reasons. First, the term itself as it enters into the High Middle Ages was polymorphous: therefore, when a given author uses the term, it is helpful to know whether the usage of the term was economic, relational or theological — or perhaps some combination of all three.[3] And second: prior to 1239 there were no fewer than three different documents in the Franciscan corpus that used the term *commercium*: Thomas of Celano's *Vita prima* of 1229, the *First Letter of Clare to Agnes of Prague* written in 1234 and the *Sacrum commercium* itself, which, by my reckoning, was drafted sometime between 1235–1238 by Caesar of Speyer. One can even add a fourth usage found in the so-called *Vita*

---

2. C. Murray, *The Holy Agreement between Saint Francis and Lady Poverty. Translation and Reflections on the* Sacrum Commercium, 2nd ed. (Orewa, New Zealand: Catholic Publications Centre, 2001). The change, however, is only reflected in the title of the work. In the body of the text, he retains, for the critical passage in c. 13, the same phrase he had used in his earlier translation: "this saving contract" (6); see *Reflections on the* Sacrum Commercium *with a New English Translation* (Orewa: Franciscan Institute of Oceania, 1995), 10. Thus, both recent English translations attempt to hold on to the economic import of the term.

3. See *Glossarium mediae et infimae latinitatis*, vol. II, edited by C. D. Du Cange (Paris: Niort, L. Favre, 1842), 477; *Lexikon totius latinitatis*, vol. I, edited by A. Forcellini (Padua: Typis Seminarii, 1940), 709; *Lexicon latinitatis nederlandicae medii aevi*, vol. II, edited by J. W. Fuchs, O. Weijers, and M. Gumbert (Leiden: Brill, 1981), cols. 614–15; *Mediae latinitatis lexicon minus*, edited by J. F. Niermeyer (Leiden: Brill, 1984), 217; and most especially *Mittellateinisches Wörterbuch*, vol. I/2 (Munich: Beck, 1959), cols. 956–59.

secunda of Celano in 1247. It will be my contention that the first three documents each use the term in a slightly different way and that the different manner in which the term is used is indicative of a different way of understanding the minorite charism. My purpose here is thus threefold: (1) to lay out how the term was used in the first three documents; (2) to shed light on the chronological dating of these documents and the evolutionary relationship between them; and (3) to highlight to what degree and in what manner the particular use of the term *commercium* illustrates the role played by economic concerns in the early Franciscan understanding of its charism.

However, before entering into an examination of the three documents in question, allow me to quickly review the varied nature of the term as it existed in the thirteenth century.[4] The term *"commercium"* is drawn from the commercial world of Antiquity. Originally, the word indicated the exchange of goods or merchandise (*merces* in the Latin) between two parties — a buyer and a seller — in an act that we would call "commerce." By extension, the term came to refer not just to the *act* of exchanging — the commerce conducted between two parties — but also to the *agreement* between commercial parties. And since the term focused on the mutuality required in such commercial exchanges (the agreed upon give and take of commerce), the word also came to take on the connotation of relationship. Again, by extension, the relational aspects of such exchanges began to encompass wider meanings such as "association," "personal relationship" or even "sexual intercourse." Finally, the term — that had begun in the economic realm and widened into the realm of social and sexual relationships — then entered into the theological realm as being descriptive of the Christian mystery itself. Here, the relationship between Christ and humanity is conceived as a kind of exchange where divinity and humanity become commingled in the mysteries of Incarnation, Redemption,

---

4. An excellent summary of the various levels of meanings that the word *commercium* could comprise is given by Edith A. Van den Goorbergh and Theodore Zweerman (see footnote 15). But see also the panoramic remarks of G. Todeschini, *"Quantum valet? Alle origini di un'economia della povertà,"* *Bullettino dell'Istituto storico italiano per il Medio Evo e Archivio Muratoriano* 98 (1992): 173-234, passim. For the liturgical associations, see in particular M. Herz, *Sacrum Commercium. Eine begriffgeschichtliche Studie zur Theologie der Römischen Liturgiesprache* (Munich: K. Zink, 1958).

and Eucharist; signaled most notably in the famous antiphon *"O admirabile commercium"* sung at Vespers on the feast of the Circumcision, where God takes on human nature and gives humanity, *in exchange*, his own divinity.

Now these levels of meanings are fairly well known to us — as they were, of course, to men and women of the thirteenth century. What is less well known or appreciated is the specific use that our Franciscan authors will make of the term.

The Vita prima *of Thomas of Celano (1229)*

The first document in the Franciscan corpus where the word *commercium* appears is the *Vita prima* of Thomas of Celano.[5] Begun in 1228 and officially accepted by Gregory IX in February 1229, this first life of Francis penned by the official hagiographer of the Order introduces us to the critical phrase in 1C 35. An understanding of the particular meaning given to the term *commercium*, however, is contingent on a clear understanding of the setting of 1C 34–35. The setting is the return of Francis and his early companions from Rome toward the Spoleto Valley, probably in the spring of 1209, after having received an oral approval for their *propositum*

---

5. The critical edition of the *Vita prima* of Celano can be found in *Analecta franciscana* 10 (Quaracchi: Collegio S. Bonaventurae, 1925–41). The secondary literature on this first work of the Celanese is surprisingly not very extensive. The classic study from the beginning of last century is N. Tamassia, *S. Francesco d'Assisi e la sua leggenda* (Padua: Fratelli, 1906), 31–81. English translations are: FA:ED I, 180–308, and *Saint Francis of Assisi and His Legend*, translated by L. Ragg (London: Fisher Unwin, 1910). More recently, the most significant studies are: S. Clasen, "Vom Franziskus der Legende zum Franzikus der Geschichte," *Wissenschaft und Weisheit* 29 (1966), 15–29; E. Grau, "Thomas von Celano. Leben und Werk," *Wissenschaft und Weisheit* 52 (1989): 97–140 [Engl. trans. of the first 2 of 4 parts (97–120 only) is available in *Greyfriars Review* 8 (1994): 177–200]; G. Pagani, *Fr. Tommaso da Celano (storico e poeta)* (Avezzano: Paolini Nobile, 1982), 79–105; E. Pásztòr, "Tommaso da Celano e la '*Vita Prima:*' problemi chiusi, problemi aperti," in *Tommaso da Celano e la sua opera di biografio di s. Francesco*. Atti del Convegno di studio (Celano, 29–30 novembre 1982) (Celano: Comitato del Centenario, 1985), 50–73; and F. Cardini, "Tommaso da Celano storico di Francesco," in *Frate Tommaso da Celano, storico et santo*. Atti del Convegno (Tagliacozzo, 6–7 agosto 1994), edited by N. Petrone (Tagliacozzo: Biblioteca Tommasiana, 1995), 51–71. An ambitious study on various aspects of the *Vita prima* has recently been published by R. Paciocco and F. Accrocca, *La leggenda di un santo di nome Francesco: Tommaso da Celano e la Vita beati Francisci*. Tau, 9 (Milan: Edizioni Biblioteca Francescana, 1999). Nonetheless, a definitive analysis of this seminal hagiographical text has yet to be written.

vitae from Innocent III. Having arrived at a deserted place, hungry and exhausted from the journey, they could find no food. Suddenly, a man appeared to provide them with the necessary nourishment, prompting the friars, we are told, to "a greater trust in divine mercy." From here, they moved on to a place near Orte at the mouth of the Spoleto Valley. Again in need of food, some of the friars went into the city to acquire what was necessary by begging door-to-door. Then Celano writes at the start of 1C 35:

> They had great joy, because they saw nothing and had nothing that could give them empty or carnal delight. As a result of this, in that place, they began to have commerce with holy poverty. Greatly consoled in their lack of all *things of the world*, they resolved to adhere to the way they were in that place always and everywhere. Only divine consolation delighted them, having put aside all *their cares* about earthly things. They decided and resolved that even if buffeted by tribulations and driven by temptations they would not withdraw *from* its *embraces*.[6]

The key Latin phrase here is *"coeperunt propterea cum sancta paupertate ibidem habere commercium* (as a result of this, in that place, they began to 'have commerce' with holy poverty").

Now the first thing to note is that the phrase *"habere commercium"* is somewhat unusual; its usage was not very common. Given that, one must ask why Celano would have chosen to use the phrase in his account. The Quaracchi editors of the critical edition of the *Vita prima* were on the right track by noting that the phrase *"habere commercium"* (to have commerce with) has a certain resonance with the phrase *"habere contubernium"* (have companionship with) employed in the treatise *De paupertate* attributed to Pseudo-Seneca.[7] This treatise is, in fact, nothing more than a compilation of numerous sentences on the matter of poverty excerpted from the

---

6. 1C 35 (I, 214): *Erat eis exsultatio magna, cum nihil viderent vel haberent quod eos posset vane seu carnaliter delectare. Coeperunt propterea cum sancta paupertate ibidem habere commercium, et in defectu omnium* quae sunt mundi *nimium consolati, disponebant, sicut ibi errant, ei ubique perpetuo adhaerere. Et quia, deposita* omni sollicitudine *terrenorum, sola eos divina consolation delectabat, statuunt et confirmant, nullis tribulationibus agitate, nullis impulse tentationibus,* ab *eius* amplexibus *resilire (AF* 10, 28).
7. *AF* 10, 28, footnote 9.

writings of Seneca which by the Late Middle Ages apparently came to be erroneously attributed to Martin of Braga, a sixth century bishop in Spain.[8] If accurate, Celano would have been consciously changing the relational image of *contubernium* (at root, a military image of comrades-in-arms together under a tent) to an economic image of *commercium*. In fact, the truth is much simpler. Celano is not altering a phrase from Pseudo-Seneca; he is citing Seneca himself who, in his *Epistola XVIII* to his friend Lucilius, urges him:

> Incipe cum paupertate *habere commercium*
> (Begin to *have commerce* with poverty).[9]

Now the context and content of Seneca's *Epistola XVIII* is crucial to understanding why Celano would decide to use it to elucidate minorite life on the return trip from Rome.

Seneca is writing one of his numerous letters to his friend Lucilius about the vicissitudes of life caused by abrupt and brutal shifts in the whims of Fortune. He asks: how is one to be prepared in the event of such an occurrence that could strip a rich man of his wealth and plunge him into destitution? Would one still be able to find happiness without the trappings of such wealth? In response to his own question, he cites the example of Epicurus, the teacher of pleasure *par excellence*, who was known to have observed certain times during which he satisfied his hunger with only minimal amounts of food. The same Epicurus, moreover, found that at such moments

---

8. Pseudo-Seneca, *"De paupertate, excerpta a Senecae epistulis,"* in *L. Annaei Senecae opera quae supersunt. Supplementum*, edited by Fr. Haase (Leipzig: Teubner, 1902), 56–59. The attribution of the work to Martin of Braga goes back to Gilbertus Cognatus whose edition of the works of the Spanish bishop in 1545 ascribed the excerpts to him. This attribution then carried on into this century. See *Martini Episcopi Bracarensis opera omnia*, edited by C.W. Barlow (New Haven: Yale University Press, 1950), 286. Haase correctly identified the text as nothing more than a series of excerpts on the subject of poverty compiled at a later time from Seneca's own writings. A section of this work containing the relevant passage on *contubernium* vs. *commercium* can be found at the end of this article in Appendix I.

9. *L. Annaei Senecae ad Lucilium epistularum moralium quae supersunt*, edited by O. Hense, in *L. Annaei Senecae opera quae supersunt*, vol. III (Leipzig: Teubner, 1914), 55–57, here 57. An English translation can be found in Seneca, *Ad Lucilium epistulae morales*, edited and translated by R. M. Gummere, in *Loeb Classical Library*, vol. I (London: William Heinemann / Cambridge, MA: Harvard Unviersity Press, 1934), 116–24. Relevant excerpts from the Latin text of this letter with accompanying English translation can be found in Appendix II.

the pleasure he was able to derive from the minimal fare he allowed himself — a diet consisting of water, barley-meal and scraps of bread[10] — was not a pleasure that was fleeting and precarious as most pleasures experienced in the world, but one that was steadfast and sure. Thus, having answered his own question, it is at this point that Seneca adds the key observation:

> So begin, my dear Lucilius, to follow the custom of such men and set apart certain days on which you shall withdraw from your affairs and make yourself at home with the minimum amount of food. *Begin to have commerce with poverty.* [Then, quoting Virgil, he adds:] "Dare, O friend, to scorn wealth and mold yourself so as to be worthy of God."[11]

Seneca is doing two things. First, he is urging his friend to build into his life a kind of ascetical regime — based on a detachment from wealth and a reduced or even minimal consumption of food — that will prepare him for the chance and cruel twists of Fate. Second, he is asserting that, contrary to common expectation, one can still find abiding happiness, pleasure and consolation even while having so little of what the world normally values.

To convey these ideas to his friend (especially how one could arrive at happiness while enjoying so little), Seneca has employed the economic image of *"habere commercium."* Both words are crucial. On one level, Seneca is describing a *commercium*, a business deal, in which there is an exchange of merchandise: wealth and security in exchange for poverty and apparent insecurity. But the Roman is not just describing a business *deal* (*commercium*); rather, he is inviting his friend to enter into a business *relationship* (*habere commercium*). In the context of that relationship, not only is something being exchanged but something is also being experienced; and that experience changes one of the parties in the relationship. For what is experienced is not only privation (as one would expect) but also happiness and consolation.

---

10. The importance of the particular Latin words used by Seneca in this passage — *"aqua et polenta aut frustum hordeacei panis"* — will become evident later on in this article (see footnote 35) and in Appendix III.

11. *Epistola XVIII*, 57: *Incipe ergo, mi Lucili, sequi horum consuetudinem et aliquos dies destina, quibus secedas a tuis rebus minimoque te facias familiarem;* incipe cum paupertate habere commercium: *"Aude, hospes, contemnere opes et te quoque dignum finge Deo."*

Given the content of Seneca's *Epistola XVIII*, it should now be
fairly apparent why Celano would have been drawn to it and what
he intended by using the image of *commercium* to describe the choice
the friars had made in their *propositum vitae*. Recall that he structures
his narration around the hunger of the friars: their need for food and
their ability to find the minimum amount — enough to survive —
through divine intervention and by begging from door-to-door.
This privation is the direct result of the choice they have made in
their *propositum* to embrace a life of poverty. Similar to Seneca's
comments, Thomas understands Franciscan poverty primarily as a
kind of ascetical regime: that is, as the renunciation of goods and
the embracing of hunger and want. This is their *commercium*: their
exchange of wealth and security for a life of privation and insecurity. Yet, like Seneca, they too had entered not only into a business
deal (*commercium*) but into a business relationship (*habere
commercium*): a relationship with poverty that yielded not only privation but also "a greater trust in divine mercy" and a deeper sense of
"divine consolation." In short, Celano uses the phrase *habere
commercium cum sancta paupertate* to describe an experience of grace
given to the friars in exchange for their embrace of voluntary material poverty.

Now before we take our leave of Thomas of Celano, notice that
up until now we have only encountered the phrases *habere
commercium* and *sancta paupertas*. What we have not encountered as
of yet is the phrase *sacrum commercium* nor the term *Domina Paupertas*
(Lady Poverty). In other words, thus far we have not been introduced to any personification of poverty as an allegorical figure.[12]
We do come a little closer, however, in 1C 51. Here, in a series of
chapters explaining how Francis served as an example to the other

---

12. The question of the chronological relationship between the *Vita prima* and the
Sacrum commercium will be discussed further on. The issue is: who borrowed from
whom? If the *Sacrum commercium* was written in 1227 (as some aver), then Thomas
would have known and probably used this text in composing 1C 35 (I, 214). If, on
the other hand, the *Vita prima* pre-dates the *Sacrum commercium*, then the author of
this latter text would have known and quite possibly used Thomas. Suffice it to say
at this point that, if the first scenario is accurate (i.e., that the *Sacrum commercium*
pre-dates the *Vita prima*), then Celano would have been consciously *de-allegorizing*
for his own uses the *allegorical* figure of *Domina Paupertas* — a most unusual
practice. My position will be that the second scenario (i.e., that the *Sacrum
commercium* post-dates the *Vita prima*) is the more probable one.

friars in living out the minorite charism, Celano makes the following succinct assessment:

> *Omni studio, omni sollicitudine custodiebat* sanctam et dominam paupertatem (He zealously and carefully safeguarded *holy and noble poverty*.)

Here, I have left the words in their original Latin because the formulation is significant. For 1C 51 and 52 go on to describe a number of specific habits of Francis in his practice of poverty: for example, his use of broken plates, his avoidance of cooked foods, the putting of ashes or cold water on his foods, his refusal to eat meat or drink wine, the composition of his bedding and clothing, etc. However, even here, it is important to point out that Celano is not allegorizing poverty under the image of *Lady Poverty* but merely personifying poverty as a noble virtue (*dominam paupertatem*).[13] Indeed, what Thomas is actually doing is evoking the very same image already used by Francis himself in his *Salutation of the Virtues* where poverty — as well as the other virtues of simplicity, humility, charity and obedience — all come to be personified:

> ... Lady Holy Poverty, may the Lord protect you with your sister, Holy Humility. Lady Holy Charity, may the Lord protect you with your sister, Holy Obedience ... [14]

Thus, although the presentation of poverty as the allegorical figure of *Domina Paupertas* will not make its appearance until a little later, Thomas has certainly established the groundwork for such an allegorization to take place.

---

13. Hence, my insistence that a more correct translation of the above-quoted phrase is "holy and noble poverty" rather than "Holy Lady Poverty".

14. SalV, in *Die* Opuscula *des hl. Franzikus von Assisi*, edited by K. Esser, in *Spicilegium Bonaventurianum, 13* (Grottaferrata: Collegium S. Bonaventurae, 1989), 427: *Ave, regina sapientia, Dominus te salvet cum tua sorore sancta pura simplicitate. Domina sancta paupertas, Dominus te salvet cum tua sorore sancta humilitate. Domina sancta caritas, Dominus te salvet cum tua sorore sancta obedientia* ... I owe an awareness of this parallel to Jean-François Godet, co-editor of the CEDOC volumes on the Franciscan sources.

The So-Called First Letter of Clare
to Agnes of Prague (1234)

The second document to be examined is the so-called *First Letter of Clare to Agnes of Prague*, written in 1234.[15] I say "so-called" because there has recently been some scholarly discussion about whether or not Clare was the actual or sole author of this letter and her three other letters.[16] I am going to assume as I begin my comments that Clare may not have been the primary author of this first letter; indeed I will contend that it emerged out of what we might call today a "textual community" whereby Clare would have collaborated with another or others in the composition of her letters.[17] At the end of this section, I will propose the name of a possible collaborator with Clare in the drafting of this letter, particularly on the basis of the use of the term *commercium*.

Whoever might have been the author or the possible collaborators in the redaction process, the letter was written in response to news received in Italy that Agnes of Prague, daughter of Ottokar I king of Bohemia and Constance queen of Hungary, was either

---

15. The critical edition of the four letters of Clare to Agnes of Prague was established by J.K. Vyskočil, *Legenda blahoslavené Aneky a ctyui listy sv. Kliry* (Prague: Nakladatelství Universum, 1932) [private English translation: *The Legend of Blessed Agnes of Bohemia and the Four Letters of St. Clare,* translated by Vitus Buresh (1963)]. The two most important contemporary editions are both based, with some corrections, on this text: *Opuscula S. Francisci et scripta S. Clarae Assisiensium*, edited by G. Boccali (Assisi: Edizioni Porziuncola, 1978), 410–48 and *Claire d'Assise. Écrits*, edited by M.-F. Becker, J.-F. Godet and T. Matura. Sources chrétiennes, 325 (Paris: Éditions du Cerf, 1985), 82–119. Two works have recently offered a detailed analysis of the four letters: E.A. Van den Goorbergh and T.H. Zweerman, *Light Shining Through a Veil: On Saint Clare's Letters to Saint Agnes of Prague*, translated by A. Looman-Graaskamp and Frances Teresa (Louvain: Peeters, 2000), and J. Mueller, *Clare's Letters to Agnes: Texts and Sources* (St. Bonaventure, NY: Franciscan Institute Publications, 2001). Both works present the letters in their original Latin along with an English translation.
16. See, for example, the judicious remarks of A. Marini, "'*Ancilla Christi, plantula sancti Francisci.*' Gli scritti di Santa Chiara e la Regola," in *Chiara di Assisi*. Atti del XX Convegno internazionale (Assisi, 15–17 ottobre 1992). SISF/CISF, 3 (Spoleto: Centro Italiano di Studi sull'Alto Medioevo, 1993), 127–33.
17. The allusion is to the famous thesis of Brian Stock, *The Implications of Literacy* (Princeton: Princeton University Press, 1983): 88–92. Although Stock's concern is primarily with the connections between orality, literacy, reform and heresy, the dynamics inherent to the creation of textual communities where texts emerge as the result of interaction (on the level of life) and collaboration (on the level of literary redaction) seem germane to the community of the companions of Francis that clustered around Clare and her sisters at San Damiano.

about to enter or had already entered the monastery of Poor Ladies, which she herself had built and endowed in 1232.[18] The content of the letter is an extended meditation on what it means to give oneself wholly to Christ through a form of life identified under one rubric: the way of highest poverty. Thus, whereas Celano used the term *commercium* in a rather narrow context to describe the privations embraced by the friars and the rewards of divine consolation received as a result, the author of the *First Letter to Agnes* frames the very notion of the religious vocation as a *commercium* — an exchange — between God and the aspirant.

What is the content of this exchange? The content is explicated in three different ways in different parts of the letter: at the beginning, near the end and most dramatically in the very heart of the letter.[19]

Just after the opening of the letter, in verses 5–7, the *commercium* into which Agnes has entered is presented in two sets of renunciations and rewards. First, Agnes is praised for having surrendered "the pomp and honors and grandeur of the world" *in exchange for*

---

18. In the critical edition of the writings of Clare (*Claire d'Assise. Écrits*, 18), Jean-François Godet, following the opinion of Englebert Grau [see "Die Schriften der heiligen Klara und die Werke ihrer Biographen," in *Movimento religioso femminile e francescanesimo nel secolo XIII*. Atti del Convegno internazionale (Assisi, 11–13 ottobre 1979). SISF, 7 (Assisi: Edizioni Porziuncola, 1980), 201–202], asserts that this first letter was written to Agnes before her entrance into the monastery on Pentecost (11 June) 1234. However, as he himself states, not all scholars share this position. Van den Goorbergh-Zweerman and Mueller assume the letter was written after news of her entrance had been received in Italy.

19. An excellent discussion of the contents of this *First Letter* and the spiritual focus of this *commercium* is given in Van den Goorbergh-Zweerman, *Light Shining through a Veil*, 43–74. Joan Mueller (*Clare's Letters*, 107–48, passim) has made a compelling case that the four letters of Clare to Agnes have all been influenced by the twelve lessons of the Office for the Feast of Saint Agnes of Rome — celebrated on 21 January and its octave — found in the Regula Breviary of the Friars Minor (and most probably used at San Damiano) after 1230 [see S.J.P. Van Dijk, *The Origins of the Modern Roman Liturgy. The Liturgy of the Papal Court and the Franciscan Order in the Thirteenth Century* (Westminster, MD: The Newman Press / London: Darton, Longman & Todd, 1960), 213–53]. However, two comments are in order. First, the linguistic resonances between the *First Letter* and this Office of St. Agnes occur only in verses 7–10. Hence, it must be said that the greater portion of the letter does not bear the imprint of the Agnes legend. Second, the primary structural motif used by the author(s) of the *First Letter* — the image of a *commercium* entered into between Agnes of Prague and God — does not come from the Office of Saint Agnes. Its origin, in other words, must be sought elsewhere. My contention is that the origin is to be found in the textual community at San Damiano: either Clare herself or — in my view, more likely — someone who had a rich scriptural and theological reservoir of images at his/her command.

"most holy poverty and physical deprivations."[20] Second, she is lauded for having refused marriage to Frederick II *in exchange for* a Bridegroom of a far more noble kind who will keep her virginity "inviolate." Hence this first statement fleshes out what Agnes has given up and what she is being given in return.

This exchange is again praised near the end of the letter in verse 30. Here the praise is once more presented in terms of what is given and what is received. This time, however, the exchange is explicitly framed as a *commercium*: *"Magnum quippe ac laudabile commercium!"*

Indeed, what a great and praiseworthy *commercium*!
to leave the temporal for the eternal,
to be promised the heavenly in exchange for the earthly,
to receive a hundredfold for one
and to possess blessed eternal life.[21]

But it is the central panel that actually names, in a triple hymn of praise, the specific means of that *commercium* as the embrace of poverty:

O beata paupertas!
Who guarantees eternal riches to those who love
and embrace her (v. 15);

O sancta paupertas!
To those who have her and long for her,
the Kingdom of Heaven is promised (v. 16);

---

20. 1LAg 5–7: *Hinc est quod, cum perfrui potuissetis prae ceteris pompis et honoribus et saeculi dignitate, cum gloria excellenti valentes inclito Caesari legitime desponsari, sicut vestrae ac eius excellentiae decuisset, quae omnia respuentes, toto animo et cordis affectu magis sanctissimam paupertatem et corporis penuriam elegistis, sponsum nobilioris generis accipientes, Dominum Jesum Christum, qui vestram virginitatem semper immaculatam custodiet et illaesam.*

21. 1LAg 30: *Magnum quippe ac laudabile commercium! Relinquere temporalia pro aeternis,promereri caelestia pro terrenis,centuplum pro uno recipereac beatam vitam perpetuam possidere.*

O pia paupertas!
Whom the Lord — who ruled and still rules both
heaven and earth —
. . . deemed worthy to be embraced before all others (v. 17).[22]

Whereas for Celano poverty is an important ascetical dimension to
the minorite vocation that inevitably draws one closer to God, for
the author of the *First Letter to Agnes* poverty *is* the minorite vocation
itself! It is the lens through which the whole religious journey is to
be seen. Hence, here we are witnessing a broadening and a deepening of the very concept of *commercium* — indeed, a fuller integration of the notion into Franciscan and Clarian life.

This is seen most strikingly in the two fairly dense verses (vv.
19–21) that follow the triple paean of praise to poverty:

If then such and so great a Lord, coming to the virginal
womb, wanted to be seen in the world as a scorned, needy
and poor man, so that those who were most poor and needy
(*pauperrimi et egeni*), suffering greatly from the lack of heavenly food, might, in him, be made rich by possessing the
Kingdom of heaven: exult then all the more and rejoice,
filled with great joy and spiritual happiness.[23]

This is a highly interesting passage. To grasp its significance, it is
important to point out the two key scriptural images that lie behind
this astonishing assertion. First, these verses are actually a restate-
ment of the mysterious *commercium* that Saint Paul had spoken
about in Second Corinthians 8:9 when he asserts:

---

22. 1LAg 15–17: *O beata paupertas, quae diligentibus et amplexantibus eam divitias praestat aeternas! O sancta paupertas, quam habentibus et desiderantibus a Deo caelorum regnum* (Mt. 5.3) *promittitur et aeterna gloria vitaque beata procul dubio exhibetur! O pia paupertas, quam Dominus Jesus Christus, qui caelum terramque regebat et regit, qui dixit etiam et sunt facta,* (Ps. 33.9; 148.5) *dignatus est prae ceteris amplexari!* See most recently C. Markert, "O Beata Paupertas. Zur Auslegung der Armut in den Briefen der hl. Klara an Agnes von Prag," in In proposito paupertatis. *Studien zum Armutsverständnis bei den mittelalterlichen Bettelorden,* edited by G. Melville and A. Kehnel. *Vita regularis 13* (Münster: LIT, 2001), 51–68.
23. 1LAg 19–21: *Si ergo tantus et talis Dominus in uterum veniens virginalem, despectus, egenus et pauper in mundo voluit apparere, ut homines, qui erant pauperrimi et egeni, caelestis pabuli sufferentes nimiam egestatem, efficerentur in illo divites regna caelestia possidendo* (2 Cor 8:9), *exsultate plurimum et gaudete, repletae ingenti gaudio et laetitia spirituali.*

> For you know the grace of our Lord Jesus Christ, that being rich (*dives*) he was made poor (*egenus*) for your sakes so that through his poverty (*inopia*) you might become rich (*divites*).[24]

The use of this text from Second Corinthians is not unheard of in the Franciscan sources. Indeed, Francis himself — in another instance of a textual community producing an important document for a larger audience — had already used the passage in the long version of the *Epistula ad fideles*.[25] The import of the image is that Christ, forsaking his rich estate and entering into the human condition, made himself poor so that human beings might in turn be drawn up into the riches of God. One becomes rich, so to speak, because Christ's descent into the human condition even to the extent of becoming poor and needy himself, has henceforth enabled all human creatures, their flesh ennobled, to be able to share in the richness of God. Such a broadening of the notion of *commercium* is due, at least in part, to a meditation on the significance of that *admirabile commercium* already celebrated in the liturgy of the church on the feast of the Circumcision. But there was much more impelling it forward: an awareness of the centrality of poverty as the way *par excellence* into God.

But how can one who is, in fact, poor become indeed rich? An answer to this crucial question is found in the second scriptural resonance. For verses nineteen through twenty-one are an evocation of the fruit of the first beatitude (already alluded to in verse sixteen) that is promised to those who embrace *sancta paupertas:* namely, the possession of the kingdom of heaven. This is an allusion, of course, to the text of Matthew 5:3: "Blessed are the poor in

---

24. 2 Cor 8:9: *Scitis enim gratiam Domini nostri Jesu Christi, quoniam propter vos egenus factus est, cum esset dives, ut illius inopia vos divites essetis.*
25. 2LtF 5 (I, 46); Esser, *Opuscula*, 208: *Qui,* cum dives esset (2 Cor 8:9) *super omnia, voluit ipse in mundo cum beatissima Virgine, matre sua, eligere paupertatem.* The precise dating of this famous letter — Esser calls it the *"Recensio posterior"* — and its relationship to the shorter version of the letter remains one of the great vexed questions of the early Franciscan sources. I hope to return in a later article to examine my contention that this longer version — at least in its present form — was written no earlier than 1220 and that Caesar of Speyer likewise had a hand in its redaction. If accurate, it could help to explain the use of 2 Cor 8:9 here as well as in the *First Letter to Agnes*. The text also comes to be used in the Rule of 1223 of the Friars Minor [LR 6, 4 (I, 103)].

spirit for theirs is *the kingdom of heaven*." However, we must not assume that this is some tepid allusion to the "spiritually poor" (as opposed to the materially poor). Rather, the allusion is specifically to those poor whose poverty comprises very real material poverty — those who, like Agnes and Clare, have voluntarily chosen to be *pauperrimi et egeni* — and who make this choice because they know and joyfully accept the spiritual ground of their being before God as inherently poor and needy creatures. In short: to know and to live in the knowledge of this primordial relationship with God, defined under the rubric of poverty, *is* to possess the kingdom of heaven.

Here, we are not too distant from the notion of *commercium* first advocated by Celano whereby hunger and privation drive one to cling more closely to God. But now the framework has almost entirely changed: for poverty has become not merely an ascetical means to a deeper experience of God but the very structure of creation's relationship to its Creator. *Commercium*, in other words, describes the very mystery of the Incarnation — that exchange where humanity and divinity commingle — which touches all human creatures, raises all human creatures into God and reveals to all human creatures their truest relationship to God. And in this, it is the voluntary poor — like Clare and her sisters as well as Francis and his companions — who serve as the vanguard and signpost of the wider universal Christian journey into God.

One final comment before I move on to the third document. It is significant, I think, that in verse seventeen, Christ is said to embrace *pia paupertas*. In other words, in the *First Letter of Clare to Agnes*, poverty is depicted as a separate figure: separate from Christ and not merely as a kind of extension of Christ whom one embraces *as if it were* Christ. The author, while probably dependent both on 1C 51 as well as the *Salutation of the Virtues*, has thus taken another step forward: toward creating Poverty as a self-standing figure. The next step — the full allegorization of *paupertas* as *Domina Paupertas* with her own speaking and acting parts in a large-scale drama — will only be taken in the next document written, I believe, by the same person who was the primary collaborator with Clare in her *First Letter to Agnes*.[26] That

---

26. This is not the place for a full-scale study of the connections between the *First Letter of Clare to Agnes* and the *Sacrum commercium*. However, a few preliminary remarks can be made. First, there is a striking similarity in the understanding of *commercium*

person was Caesar of Speyer — one of the central figures during the 1230s in the group known as the companions of Francis.[27]

Sacrum commercium beati Francisci cum Domina Paupertate (1235–38)

The *Sacrum commercium beati Francisci cum Domina Paupertate* is a polemical work written, in my estimation, by Caesar of Speyer sometime between 1235 and 1238.[28] It represents a stinging

in both documents (contrasted with the way that Celano understands and uses the term) as expressing the meaning of the minorite vocation as well as the creature-Creator relationship of all human beings — and that meaning is summed up in one word: poverty. If there are differences between the specifics of that expression in the two documents, they are attributable to the fact that the *First Letter of Clare to Agnes* was addressed to a woman beginning a vocation in a cloistered environment of contemplative prayer whereas the primary audience of the *Sacrum commercium* were First Order friars living and working in the world. Second, there is also a striking similarity between the reflections on poverty in the *First Letter* (vv. 15–22) and part of Francis's praise of poverty after he and his companions had ascended the mountain ScEx 19 (I, 535). Beyond the centrality of the terms *virgo/virginalis* and *pauperima/pauperrimi* in these verses, both documents also use the texts from Matthew 5:3 (on inheriting the kingdom of heaven) and Matthew 8:20 (where "foxes have holes and the birds of the air have nests, but the Son of Man has nowhere to lay his head") as the key scriptural images in their respective sections. Moreover, it is not without interest that the critical scriptural allusion providing the key to the polemical thrust of the ScEx — Matthew 5:14 as used in ScEx 39 (I, 543) — comes from the same section of the Sermon on the Mount. The question can rightly be posed: who then was borrowing from whom? Although an argument could be made that the author(s) of the *First Letter to Agnes* might have had the ScEx at her/their disposal in the composition of the letter (whereby the ScEx would be said to predate the *First Letter*), given the greater sophistication and complexity of the content of the ScEx and the evolution of the figure of *paupertas* into the allegorical person of *Domina Paupertas*, it would seem that the stronger argument is that the author of the ScEx was extending, broadening and deepening perspectives already advanced in the earlier *Letter to Agnes*.

27. For an overview of the life of Caesar (but without the associations made here), see A. Gattucci, "Cesario da Spira," in *I compagni di Francesco e la prima generazione minoritica*. Atti del XIX Convegno internazionale (Assisi, 17–19 ottobre, 1991). SISF/CISF, ns. 2 (Spoleto: Centro Italiano di Studi sull'Alto Medioevo, 1992), 119–65.

28. Several critical editions of the *Sacrum commercium* exist, each successive publication drawing on a wider network of manuscripts: "*Sacrum commercium beati Francisci cum domina Paupertate,*" *Analecta Ordinis minorum capuccinorum* 15 (1899): 276–87, 309–17; 16 (1900): 18–30, 50–57, 90–93, 109–17, edited by Edouard D'Alençon; *Sacrum Commercium Sancti Francisci cum domina Paupertate* (Ad Claras Aquas: Collegio S. Bonaventurae, 1929); and most recently, *Sacrum commercium sancti Francisci cum domina Paupertate*, edited by S. Brufani (Assisi: Edizioni Porziuncola, 1990). When referring to passages from the Latin text, I will cite the text from the

polemic from the camp of the companions of Saint Francis who were attempting to raise their voices against the new directions taken by the Franciscan Order with accelerating speed after the death of the founder in 1226 and particularly after the publication of the bull *Quo elongati* in 1230.[29] This opposition is expressed as a bitter critique of the leadership of the Order for having betrayed the very foundations of Franciscan life, encapsulated, once again, under a single rubric: poverty. In this work, the widespread betrayal of poverty will be symbolized most flagrantly by one particularly egregious action: the building of the massive complex on the *collis paradisi* consisting of the basilica of San Francesco, a papal residence and a new convent for the friars themselves, the ensemble being called by Gregory IX — much to the chagrin of these companions of Francis — the *caput et mater Ordinis* (the head and mother of the order).[30] Given the highly sensitive nature of his remarks, the

Brufani edition while following the traditional paragraph divisions proposed by the Quaracchi editors (since maintained in most translations). It is to be noted, however, that the different translations of the *Sacrum commercium* quite naturally reflect the translator's level of understanding (or lack of understanding) of the original intention of the text.

29. I have advanced my arguments on the polemical nature, structure and authorship of the *Sacrum commercium* in M. Cusato, "Talking about Ourselves: The Shift in Franciscan Writing from Hagiography to History (1235–1247)," *Franciscan Studies* 58 (2000): 37–75, especially 38–53. A more extensive treatment of the question of authorship can be found in the final section of chapter 2 of my dissertation, *La renonciation au pouvoir chez les Frères Mineurs au 13e siècle* (Ph.D. Diss., Université de Paris IV-Sorbonne, 1991), to be published in English translation in 2003. For the purposes of this article, when referencing this latter work, I will cite the page numbers from the French dissertation. Since the reading of the *Sacrum commercium* that I have proposed in the above works is fairly singular in its interpretation, I will refrain from citing most of the standard books and articles on the text in the secondary literature, with the exception of S. Brufani, "Il *Sacrum comemercium*: l'identità minoritica nel mito delle origini," in *Dalla "sequela Christi" di Francesco d'Assisi all'apologia della povertà*. Atti del XVIII Convegno internazionale (Assisi, 18–20 ottobre 1990). SISF/CISF, ns. 1 (Spoleto: Centro Italiano di Studi sull'Alto Medioevo, 1992), 203–22, and "Introduzione," in *Fontes Franciscani*, edited by E. Menestò and S. Brufani (Assisi: Edizioni Porziuncola, 1995), 1693–1703. However, two articles that each approach the text from very different perspectives echo several important aspects of my own reading of the *Sacrum commercium*: G. Ruggieri, "Dalla povertà all'uso e alla proprietà dei beni," *Cristianesimo nella storia* 5 (1984): 131–50 and D. Flood, "The Sacrum commercium and Early Franciscan History," *Haversack*, 1.1 (1977): 13–16; 1.2 (1977): 18–21; 1.3 (1978): 17–20; 1.5 (1978): 15–25; 1.6 (1978): 19–23.

30. The designation of the church of San Francesco (and by implication the whole complex on the *collis paradisi*) as the *caput et mater Ordinis* was made on 22 April 1230 by Gregory IX in his bull, *Is qui ecclesiam* (*Bullarium Franciscanum* I, 30). As I

author — a cleric trained at the University of Paris with a vast knowledge of the Scriptures — chose to craft his polemic as an allegory in order, I think, to be able to say obliquely what he could not say outright for fear of reprisal. Indeed, it is my contention that the drafting of the *Sacrum commercium* is precisely what caused its author, Caesar of Speyer, to be placed under house arrest by the Minister General and chief architect of the new basilica complex: Elias of Cortona.[31] Caesar was aware of the *Vita prima* of Celano — he had been Thomas's provincial during the first mission to Germany — and he was also quite possibly the primary collaborator in the *First Letter of Clare to Agnes*. He will now use both of them as the springboard for a new work representing the full allegorization of the poverty that lies at the heart of the minorite vocation, cast now under the figure of Lady Poverty (*Domina Paupertas*).

This magnificent work is constructed on the basis of two great pillars represented by the two old men in chapter eight whom Francis meets out on the plain, after he had left Assisi.[32] Each old man has a scriptural text to share with him and both texts serve as the two main themes of the entire work. The first cites Isaiah 66:2: a

---

have noted in my article ("Talking about Ourselves," 72–74), Thomas of Celano (2C 18) will subtlely yet decisively reject this identification of the basilica complex as the visible centerpoint of the Order to the world. Such a rejection, however, had already been made overtly by the companions of Francis — Leo, Rufino and Masseo — in what will eventually be called the *Compilatio Assisiensis*: their contribution to the call of Crescentius of Iesi in 1244 for more materials on the *fama et miracula* of Francis. Celano will undoubtedly draw on their polemical presentation of the Portiuncula (AC 56) in crafting his own more diplomatic statement on the matter.

31. M. Cusato, *Renonciation au pouvoir*, 323–326. This correlation of events in my reconstruction depends on the account of Caesar's imprisonment in the winter of 1238–1239 alleged by Angelo Clareno in his *Liber chronicarum sive tribulationum ordinis minorum*, edited by G. Boccali (Assisi: Edizioni Porziuncola, 1999), 290–316, especially 304–06. Such a reliance on Angelo in matters of fact and dating would be perilous if it were not for the slim evidence of two papal bulls, both under the standard formula *Cum secundum consilium*, issued on 16 January and 24 March 1238 (*Bullarium Franciscanum* I, 231, 235), requested specifically by Elias, which granted him authority to bring certain unruly and disobedient friars to heel. I associate the actions taken against Caesar by Elias — house arrest in a hermitage — as well as against other members of this group of companions (Bernard of Quintavalle, Angelo, Masseo, Rizzerio da Muccia, Simon of Collazzone, perhaps Andrew of Spello and *"alii non pauci,"* according to Angelo Clareno, 290) with this repression. See also the account reconstructed in L. Wadding, *Annales minorum*, 3rd ed. (Ad Claras Aquas: n.p., 1931) and the contemporary account offered in E. Lempp, *Frère Élie de Cortone. Étude biographique* (Paris: Fischbacher, 1901), 110–14.

32. M. Cusato, "Talking about Ourselves," 51–52.

text that praises the one who is poor; but it also contains a veiled critique of the basilica of San Francesco. The second old man quotes First Timothy 6:8 on being content with having a sufficient amount of food and clothing for the day. Once Francis and his faithful companions *ascend* the mountain, the content of these two texts will be expanded, broadened and deepened by Lady Poverty in her Grand Discourse *on the mountain*. Finally, after the friars *descend* the mountain — this time in the company of Lady Poverty — the same two themes will then be dramatized: the second, in their famous meal on the plain and, the first, in their bold rejection of the basilica complex on "a certain hill" as the place of their cloister, the place they would be proud to call their home.[33]

For our purposes, we need to go back to these two old men and, in particular, to the scriptural text quoted by the second. The text of First Timothy 6:8 reads as follows:

> We have brought nothing into this world and without a doubt we can take nothing out of it; but having food and whatever covers us, with these we are content.[34]

Now the first thing to note is that the passage from First Timothy is a text found in the earliest layers of the First Rule, in chapter nine of the *Regula non bullata*, going back to the very first years of the elaboration and development of the minorite charism. Hence, it is an absolutely foundational text for learning about early Franciscan identity. In fact, it is, I believe, the single most eloquent description of what will come to be called "Franciscan poverty" and the very bedrock of all discussion of Franciscan economics.

For the original minorite notion of poverty is not a matter of being poorer than the poor; nor does it have anything to do with a masochistic cult of destitution and indigence — as if these were values in themselves! Rather, the Franciscan poverty exemplified in the *Sacrum commercium* is first and foremost not a negative concept but a positive one that proposes living according to a particular ethic that has as its foundational principle the use of creation on the basis of honest human need. Such an ethic is grounded in the belief

---

33. M. Cusato, "Talking about Ourselves," 44–45, 52.
34. 1 Tm 6:8: *Nihil intulimus in hunc mundum, haud dubium quia nec auferre quid possumnus; habentes autem alimenta et quibus tegamur, iis contenti sumus.*

that creation is God's gracious gift to all his creatures; that God has
created and continues to sustain his creation through a fruitful and
abundant earth intended for all. As such, every creature — human
or otherwise — has a God-given right to be sustained at the table of
creation. However, human beings, accustomed to enjoying the
abundance of the earth, all too often twist the munificence of God
into an illusion of self-sufficiency. Forgetful of God and of the fact
that the earth is ultimately *God's* possession, they begin thinking of
themselves as possessors, acting as if creation were their own private
possession intended for their use alone. Assuming that others think
and act as they do, out of fear and insecurity they develop a spirit of
acquisitiveness, hoarding for themselves what might be desperately
needed by others. Such attitudes and actions, our Franciscan
asserts, are violations of the intent of creation. Indeed, any political
or economic system that impedes, prevents or deliberately denies
creatures the necessities of life is an unjust system and its perpetra-
tors living, as Francis says in his Testament, *in peccatis.*[35]

However, just as in the *First Letter to Agnes*, the Friars and Sisters
Minor — those who choose to be content to have sufficient food
and clothing for the day — stand as the vanguard and the signpost
to all Christians of the proper use of creation, using only what they
truly need, living simply — as we would say today — so that others
may simply live.

Now this cardinal thematic of Franciscan economics will move
from discourse to drama, after the descent from the mountain, in
the famous meal of the friars with Lady Poverty, depicted in chapters 59–62. This scenario is, in fact, built largely from materials
already mentioned in 1C 51 where, you may recall, the hagiographer had laid out a number of practices regarding poverty suppos-
edly espoused by Francis. To these elements Caesar has also,
however, very cleverly added several other elements found only in
Epistola XVIII of Seneca![36] Yet this meal with Lady Poverty is no

---

35. Test 1 (I, 124.) A wonderful contemporary reflection along the same lines,
    grounded in a biblical view of the purposes of creation, is offered in W.
    Brueggemann, "Options for Creatureliness: Consumer or Citizen," *Horizons in
    Biblical Theology* 23 (2001): 25-50.
36. The genius of what the author of the ScEx has wrought here is apparent when one
    compares the content of the meal drama in chapters 60–63 (I, 551–52) with the
    elements mentioned in 1C 51 (I, 227) and combined with those already noted in
    Seneca's *Epistula XVIII ad Lucilium* (i.e., the use of the terms *aqua, polenta* and

mere compilation; nor is it a romanticized and idyllic picture of Franciscan life, removed from the cares and concerns of real human life. The meal is a powerful, dramatized version of the second pillar, showing what it means to live according to the minorite ethic of creation, "having food and sufficient clothing, with these let us be content."[37]

What does this have to do with the notion of *commercium*? Just like in the *Letter of Clare to Agnes*, the minorite vocation of poverty — now understood as a positive ethic of the use of creation — *is* the *commercium* that the friars have made with God, now through the allegorical figure of Lady Poverty. Not merely the ascetical embrace of privations and hunger as in Celano, their *commercium* is quite simply the *forma vitae fratrum et sororum minorum*: the pledge to live as creation was intended to be lived by God in conformity with the poor Christ of history. *This* is the Kingdom of heaven, come down from on high, now made visible as a lived reality on earth.

Indeed so critical was this *forma vitae* of the friars for the very life of humanity, that Caesar will call it in chapter thirteen a *salutare commercium* — a *salvific* exchange: a form of life essential to transform the world into a reflection of God's original intentions for creation. And indeed: so critical was the fidelity of the friars to this life, that nothing must be allowed to impede them from living out what was, for them, not only a profound vision of Christian life but also, at

---

frustum hordeacei panis). I hope to return in a subsequent article to examine the content of these latter two documents as they relate to the composition of the meal narrative. In the meantime, one can consult a chart that I have prepared showing the parallels and resonances between the three documents in Appendix III.

37. The basilica complex being built under the auspices of the Friars Minor and carrying the appellation *caput et mater Ordinis* represents, for the author of the ScEx and many of his companions, the most flagrant example of how the friars have resumed the roles of power and importance in church and society they had previously forsaken and how they have once again bought into the way "the world" conceives of and uses the precious resources of the earth: as commodities to be used for personal advancement and self-aggrandizement (under the guise of accomplishing some noteworthy purpose) rather than as gifts of the Creator to be used for the benefit of all creatures, especially those men and women in need of the basic necessities of food and clothing. The basilica, in other words, represented for these friars the most vivid betrayal of the alternative economics grounded in the Scriptures and proposed by the early minorite community in their *Regula non bullata*. The famous story of Leo, on the instruction of Giles, smashing the urn placed in front of the basilica consruction site for contributions to the project is illustrative of their objections to this new and misguided orientation adopted by the leadership of the Order (see *AF* 3, 72).

root, a matter of conscience. For as Francis says to his brothers as they are about to ascend the mountain to meet Poverty:

> Wonderful, brothers, is the espousal of Poverty (*desponsatio Paupertatis*), yet we will be able to enjoy her embraces easily because the lady of the nations has been made as it were a widow, the queen of virtues made vile and contemptible to all. There is no one of our region who would dare cry out, no one who would oppose us, no one who would have the power to prohibit by juridical means (*jure*) this salvific exchange (*salutare commercium*).[38]

---

38. ScEx 13 (I, 533): *Mirabilis est, fratres, desponsatio Paupertatis, sed facile poterimus ipsius frui amplexibus, quia facta est quasi vidua domina gentium, vilis et contemptibilis omnibus regina virtutum. Nullus est qui e regione clamare audeat, nullus qui se nobis opponat, nullus qui iure hoc salutare commercium prohibere valeat.* This is a crucial passage not only because it is the only one in the entire ScEx where the word *commercium* actually appears but also because of the use of the critical — and controversial — phrase *"mirabilis est desponsatio Paupertatis."* According to the Quaracchi editors as well as Stefano Brufani in his more recent critical edition, the family of manuscripts that is considered to be more primitive and reliable (using the Assisi MS of the Biblioteca storico-francescana della Chiesa Nuova as its archetype) has the reading of *desponsatio* (espousal or betrothal) in this chapter. However, another family of manuscripts uses the word *dispensatio* (economy) in place of *desponsatio*. Editors are faced with a difficult choice and most have come down on the *desponsatio* reading. David Flood, following scholars no less formidable than Kajetan Esser and Englebert Grau, prefers the *dispensatio* reading as being the more accurate (see D. Flood, *"Sacrum commercium,"* *Haversack* 1.2 (1977) 18–21; K. Esser, "Untersuchungen zum *Sacrum Commercium beati Francisci cum domina Paupertate*," in *Miscellanea Melchior de Pobladura*, vol. I (Rome: Institutum Historicum O.F.M. Cap., 1964), 10–11 and footnote 34; K. Esser and E. Grau, *Der Bund des heiligen Franziskus mit Herrin Armut*, in *Franziskanische Quellenschriften 9* (Werl/Westfalen: Dietrich-Coelde-Verlag, 1966), 33–41. However, it is indeed curious — if not singularly significant — that the manuscripts that have the *dispensatio* reading also contain the date of 1227 at the end of the work! Now the use of the date 1227 to render a work more authoritative (since closer to the time of Francis) is not unheard of in the history of Franciscan sources. Paul Sabatier's discovery of what he claimed to be the so-called suppressed section of the *Legenda trium sociorum* (but which turned out to actually be a section of the much later *Speculum perfectionis* of 1318) also carried the 1227 dating. In other words, the 1227 date must be regarded with a certain amount of suspicion, especially if one accepts that the ScEx 31 (I, 539) represents a veiled diatribe against the issuance of the bull *Quo elongati* of 1230! David Flood, nevertheless, prefers the *dispensatio* reading for two other reasons: (1) he believes this explicitly economic term is more in keeping with the early Franciscan concern for creating a new economic vision of the world; and (2) he also believes that the presence of the term *desponsatio* in the family of manuscripts dependant on the Assisi codex shows that the later copyists had been unduly influenced by the espousal imagery used in 2C 55 (II, 284) where, in a pericope titled *De laude paupertate*, one reads: . . . *pater iste beatus communes filiorum hominum opes inopes dedignatur . . . inhiat paupertati. Hanc Filio Dei familiarem attendens . . . studet caritate perpetua* desponsare. However, as we have already seen,

I hear in these last words echoes of the attempt by the leaders of the Order to undercut the minorite vision of poverty through the legal mechanism of *Quo elongati* and the fierce intensity of the companions to try to remain faithful to their calling.[39]

To conclude: *commercium* — which began as an economic term in classical Antiquity — was one of the primary terms used in the first decades of Franciscan history to describe the heart of the *novitas franciscana*. Celano himself will use the term again in 1247 but, perhaps due to its association now with a work highly critical of the new directions taken by the Order, he will change — and ultimately weaken — its meaning.[40] Moreover, the earlier appropriation of the

---

this marital imagery was already present both in 1C 35 (I, 214) as well as in the *First Letter to Agnes* (v. 17) with the use of the terminology of "embraces" (*amplexio/amplexor*). Indeed, the latter document uses the image of *desponsare* (v. 5), albeit in referring to Agnes's refusal to betroth Frederick II. In short, one can make a strong case that the author of the ScEx uses and builds on the marital imagery already present in the two previous documents and that it is Celano — known for using terms and images from previous documents in his own unique way — who borrows the espousal imagery from the 1230s, most particularly ScEx 13 (I, 533), in formulating his account in 2C 55 (II, 284).

39. See M. Cusato, "Talking about Ourselves," 46–48 where I present my argument that c. 31 of the *Sacrum commercium*, seemingly a pericope about the testament of Jesus to his disciples before leaving the earth, is actually a cleverly worked out denunciation of *Quo elongati* and its annulation of the juridical force of the *Testament* of Francis which he left his disciples before leaving the earth.

40. In 2C 70 (II, 294), Thomas states the following: "The holy man would often repeat this: 'As far as the brothers will withdraw from poverty, that far the world will withdraw from them; they will seek,' he said, 'but will not find . . . but if they would only embrace my Lady Poverty, the world would nourish them, for they are given to the world for its salvation.' He would also say: 'There is an exchange *(commercium)* between the brothers and the world: they owe the world good example, and the world owes them the supply of necessities of life. When they break faith and withdraw their good example, the world withdraws its helping hand, a just judgment.'" In other words, whereas in 1229 the *commercium* was made between the friars and poverty [1C 35 (I, 214)] and in 1234 the *commercium* was made between the aspirant and God by means of highest poverty (*First Letter to Agnes*) as it will be in the *Sacrum commercium*, for Thomas in 1247 the *commercium* is now said to be between the friars and the world. This new shift in the use of the image of *commercium* by Celano is due not only to the fact of the ongoing repression of the Caesarini (and their association with the polemical work of their hero, Caesar of Speyer) by the leadership of the Order during the mid–1240s but due also to one of Thomas's primary aims in writing his 1247 *memoriale*. For the hagiographer was deeply concerned about the negative effect that the bull *Ordinem vestrum* was having on the life of the friars, allowing them the freedom, if they so chose, to provide not only for their necessities but also their conveniences through the instrumentality of *nuntii* (see M. Cusato, "Talking about Ourselves," 66–72). By contrast, Thomas is telling the friars that God will assure that the world will provide for their subsistence if they remain faithful to what they have promised both God and the world: poverty.

term by Caesar from Thomas (1C 35) and his stress on the absolute
necessity of living this positive ethic of creation as a concrete realization of the kingdom of heaven here on earth will, by the end of
the thirteenth century, only be weakly reflected in the designation
of this magnificent work under a title that it never had at its incep-
tion and with words that were never found in the text itself: namely,
the *sacrum commercium*. *Sacrum* derives from the realm of Christian
religiosity and theology; *salutare* derives from the realm of Christian
truth and obligation. It is perhaps indicative that, with the
juridicization of the vocation of poverty over the next decades of
the thirteenth century by means of the legal categories of use and
lack of ownership,[41] this bold and original vision of the early Franciscan fraternity explicated so magisterially by Caesar would
become dimmed, blurred and ultimately misunderstood by the very
men and women who were the bearers of the minorite tradition: a
fate already feared and warned against by the ill-fated friar from
Speyer.

---

41. Signaled most notably in the bulls *Quo elongati* (1230) and *Ordinem vestrum* (1245)
    but also in the so-called *Exposition of the Four Masters* (1242).

APPENDIX I: PSEUDO-SENECA & SENECA COMPARED

"De paupertate, excerpta e Senecae epistulis," in *L. Annaei Senecae opera quae supersunt. Supplementum,* ed. Fr. Haase (Leipzig: Teubner, 1902): 56–59 (here: 57–58).	Parallels, with minor alterations to select passages from the letters of Seneca:
[17,11] Multis divitias parasse non finis miseriarum fuit, sed mutation. Nec hoc mirror: non in rebus vitium, sed in animo ipso est. Illud quod paupertatem gravem nobis fecerat, et divitias graves faciet. Quemadmodum nihil refert, utrum aegrum in lecto ligneo an in aureo colloces: quocumque illum transtuleris, morbum suum secum transferet: sic nihil refert, utrul aeger animus in divitiis an in paupertate sit: malum suum illum sequitur.	*Epistola XVII,* 11–12
[18,7] Ad securitatem non est opus fortuna. Quod enim necessitati sat est, dabit, licet irata.	*Epistola XVII,* 7b
[18,8] Ne imparatos nos fortuna deprehendat, fiat nobis paupertas familiaris. Securius divites erimus, si sciemus, quam non sit grave pauperes esse.	*Epistola XVIII,* 8b
[18,12] **Incipe cum paupertate habere** *contubernium.* "Aude, hospes, contemnere opes, et te quoque dignum finge deo." Nemo alius dignus deo est, nisi qui opes contempsit. Quare possessions tibi non interdico, sed efficere volo, ut illas intrepide possideas. Quod uno consequeris modo, si te etiam sine illis bene victurum speraveris, et si illas tamquam exituras adspexeris.	*Epistola XVIII,* 12b–13

APPENDIX II: SENECA, *EPISTOLA XVIII*

"Epistola VI (=18)," in *L. Annaei Senecae ad Lucilium epistularum moralium quae supersunt*, ed. Otto Hense. L. Annaei Senecae opera quae supersunt (Leipzig: Teubner, 1914) III: 54–58 (here: 55–57).	*"Epistle XVIII,"* in Seneca, *Ad Lucilium epistulae morales*, trans. Richard M. Gummere (London: William Heinemann / Cambridge, MA: Harvard University Press) I: 117–125 (here: 119–123).
[5] Ceterum adeo mihi placet temptare animi tui firmitatem, ut ex praecepto magnorum virorum tibi quoque praecipiam: interponas aliquot dies, quibus contentus minimo ac vilissimo cibo, dura atque horrida veste dicas tibi: "hoc est quod timebatur?" [6] In ipsa securitate animus ad difficilia se praeparet et contra iniurias fortunae inter beneficia firmetur. Miles in media pace decurrit, sine ullo hoste vallum iacit et supervacuo labore lassatur, ut sufficere necessario posit. Quem in ipsa re trepidare nolueris, ante rem exerceas. Hoc secuti sunt, qui omnibus mensibus paupertatem imitati prope ad inopiam accesserunt, ne umquam expavescerent quod saepe didicissent. [7] Non est nunc quod existimes me dicere Timoneas cenas et pauperum cellas, et quicquid aliud est, per quod luxuria divitiarum taedio ludit: grabatus ille verus sit et sagum et panis durus ac sordidus. Hoc triduo et quatriduo fer, interdum pluribus diebus, ut non lusus sit, sed experimentum: tunc, mihi crede, Lucili, exultabis dipondio satur et intelleges ad securitatem non opus esse fortuna: hoc enim, quod necessitati sat est, dat et irata.	[5] I am so firmly determined, however, to test the constancy of your mind that, drawing from the teachings of great men, I shall give you also a lesson: Set aside a certain number of days, during which you shall be content with the scantiest and cheapest fare, with course and rough dress, saying to yourself the while: "Is this the condition that I feared?" [6] It is precisely in times of immunity from care that the soul should toughen itself beforehand for occasions of greater stress, and it is while Fortune is kind that it should fortify itself against her violence. In days of peace the soldier performs manoeuvres, throws up earthworks with no enemy in sight, and wearies himself by gratuitous toil, in order that he may be equal to unavoidable toil. If you would not have a man flinch when the crisis comes, train him before it comes. Such is the course what those men have followed who, in their imitation of poverty, have every month come almost to want, that they might never recoil from what they had so often rehearsed. [7] You need not suppose that I mean meals like Timon's or "paupers' huts," or any other device which luxurious millionaires use to beguile the tedium of their lives. Let the pallet be a real one, and the course cloak; let the bread be hard and grimy.

[8] Non est tamen quare tu multum tibi facere videaris. Facies enim, quod multa milia servorum, multa milia pauperum faciunt: illo nomine te suspice, quod facies non coactus, quod tam facile erit tibi illud pati semper quam aliquando experiri. Exerceamur ad palum. Et ne inparatos fortuna deprehendat, fiat nobis paupertas familiaris. Securius divites erimus, si scierimus, quam non sit grave pauperes esse.

[9] Certos habebat dies ille magister voluptatis Epicurus, quibus maligne famem extingueret, visurus, an aliquid deesset ex plena et consummata voluptate, vel quantum deesset et an dignum quod quis magno labore pensaret. Hoc certe in his epistulis ait, quas scripsit Charino magistratu ad Polyaenum. Et quidem gloriatur non toto asse *se* pasci, Metrodorum, qui nondum tantum profecerit, toto.

Endure all this for three or four days at a time, sometimes for more, so that it may be a test of yourself instead of a mere hobby. Then, I assure you, my dear Lucilius, you will leap for joy when filled with a pennyworth of food, and you will understand that a man's peace of mind does not depend upon Fortune; for, even when angry she grants enough for our needs. [8] There is no reason, however, why you should think that you are doing anything great; for you will merely be doing what many thousands of slaves and many thousands of poor men are doing every day. But you may credit yourself with this item, — that you will not be doing it under compulsion, and that it will be as easy for you to endure it permanently as to make the experiment from time to time. Let us practice our strokes on the "dummy"; let us become intimate with poverty, so that Fortune may not catch us off our guard. We shall be rich with all the more comfort, if we once learn how far poverty is from being a burden. [9] Even Epicurus, the teacher of pleasure, used to observe stated intervals, during which he satisfied his hunger in niggardly fashion; he wished to see whether he thereby fell short of full and complete happiness, and, if so, by what amount he fell short, and whether this amount was worth purchasing at the price of great effort. At any rate, he makes such a statement in the well-known letter written to Polyaenus in the archonship of Charinus. Indeed, he boasts that he himself lived on less than a penny, but that Metrodorus, whose progress was not yet so great, needed a whole penny.

[10] In hoc tu victu saturitatem putas esse? Et voluptas est. Voluptas autem non illa levis et fugax et subinde reficienda, sed stabilis et certa. Non enim iucunda res est aqua et polenta aut frustum hordeacei panis, sed summa voluptas est posse capere etiam ex his voluptatem et ad id se deduxisse, quod eripere nulla fortunae iniquitas possit.

[10] Do you think that there can be fullness on such fare? Yes, and there is pleasure also, — not that shifty and fleeting pleasure which needs a fillip now and then, but a pleasure that is steadfast and sure. For though water, barely-meal, and crusts of barley-bread, are not a cheery diet, yet it is the highest kind of pleasure to be able to derive pleasure from this sort of food, and to have reduced one's needs to that modicum which no unfairness of Fortune can snatch away.

[11] Liberaliora alimenta sunt carceris, sepositos ad capitale supplicium non tam anguste, qui occisurus est, pascit: quanta est animi magnitudo ad id sua sponte descendere, quod ne ad extrema quidem decretis timendum sit. Hoc est praeoccupare tela fortunae.

[11] Even prison fare is more generous; and those who have been set apart for capital punishment are not so meanly fed by the man who is to execute them. Therefore, what a noble soul one must have, to descend of one's one free will to a diet which even those who have been sentenced to death have not to fear! This is indeed forestalling the spear-thrusts of Fortune.

[12] Incipe ergo, mi Lucili, sequi horum consuetudinem et aliquos dies destina, quibus secedas a tuis rebus minimoque te facias familiarem; **incipe cum paupertate habere commercium:** 'Aude, hospes, contemnere opes et te quoque dignum finge deo'.

[12] So begin, my dear Lucilius, to follow the custom of these men, and set apart certain days on which you shall withdraw from your business and make yourself at home with the scantiest fare. Establish business relations with poverty. "Dare, O my friend, to scorn the sight of wealth, and mold thyself to kinship with thy God." [13] For he alone is in kinship with God who has scorned wealth. Of course I do not forbid you to possess it, but I would have you reach the point at which you possess it dauntlessly; this can be accomplished only by persuading yourself that you can live happily without it as well as with it, and by regarding riches always as likely to elude you.

[13] Nemo alius est deo dignus quam qui opes contempsit. Quarum possessionem tibi non interdico, sed efficere volo, ut illas intrepide possideas: quod uno consequeris modo, si te etiam sine illis beate victurum persuaseris tibi, si illas tamquam exituras semper aspexeris.

APPENDIX III: THE MEAL WITH LADY POVERTY
PARALLELS AND RESONANCES

1C 51–52	Seneca, *Epistola XVIII*	*Sacrum Commercium* 60–63
[51] . . . Omni studio, omni sollicitudine custodiebat sanctam et dominam paupertatem, non patiens, ne quando ad superflua perveniret, nec **vasculum** in domo aliquod residere, cum sine ipso utcumque posset extremae necessitates evadere servitutem. Impossibile namque fore aiebat satisfacere necessitate et voluptati non obedire . . .	[5] Ceterum adeo mihi placet temptare animi tui firmitatem, ut ex praecepto magnorum virorum tibi quoque praecipiam: interponas aliquot dies, quibus contentus minimo ac vilissimo cibo, dura atque horrida veste dicas tibi: "hoc est quod timebatur?" . . . [7] Non est nunc quod existimes me dicere Timoneas *cenas et pauperum cellas*, et quicquid aliud est, per quod luxuria divitiarum taedio ludit: *grabatus ille verus sit et sagum et panis durus ac sordidus*. Hoc *triduo et quatriduo* fer, interdum pluribus diebus, ut non lusus sit, sed experimentum. [10] Non enim iucunda res est *aqua et polenta aut frustum hordeacei panis*, sed summa voluptas est posse capere etiam ex his voluptatem et ad id se deduxisse, quod eripere nulla fortunae iniquitas possit.	[60] "Placet quod dicitis", ait; "sed iam afferte aquam, ut manus nostras lavemus, et sindones, quibus tergamus eas". Illi vero citissime obtulerunt medium quoddam terreum **vasculum**, quia perfectum non erat ibi, **plenum aqua**. Et vergentes in manibus eius respiciebant huc atque illuc pro sindone. Cumque non invenissent eam, unus obtulit ei tunicam qua indutus erat ut cum ea tergeret manus. Ipsa vero, cum gratiarum actione illam suscipiens, magnificabat Deum in corde suo, qui talibus eam associavit hominibus. [61] Deinde duxerunt eam ad locum in quo mensa parata erat. Que, cum fuisset perducta, respexit et nil aliud videns quam *tria vel quatuor frusta panis hordeacei aut suricei* posita super gramina, vehementer admirata est dicens intra se: "Quis umquam vidit talia in generationibus seculorum? Benedictus tu, Domine Deus, cui cura

est de omnibus; subest enim tibi posse, cum volueris; docuisti populum tuum per talia opera placere tibi". Sicque consederunt pariter gratias agentes Deo super omnia dona sua.

[62] Iussit domina Paupertas apportari **cocta cibaria** in scutellis. Et ecce allata est scutella una **plena aqua frigida**, ut intingerent omnes in ea **panem: non erat ibi copia scutellarum nec coquorum pluralitas.** Petiit aliquas saltem herbas odoriferas crudas sibi preberi. Sed hortulanum non habentes et hortum nescientes, collegerunt in silva herbas agrestes et posuerunt coram ea. Que ait: "Parum salis afferte ut saliam herbas, quoniam amare sunt". "Exspecta — inquiunt — domina, quousque civitatem intremus et afferamus tibi, si fuerit qui prebeat nobis". "Prebete — inquit — mihi cultellum ut emundem superflua et incidam panem, quia valde durus et siccus est". Dicunt ei: "Domina, non habemus fabrum ferrarium qui nobis faciat gladios; nunc autem dentibus cultelli vice utere et postea providebimus."

[51] **Cocta cibaria vix aut rarissime admittebat**, admissa vero saepe aut conficiebat cinere, aut condimenti saporem **aqua frigida** exstinguebat. O quoties per mundum ambulans ad praedicandum Evangelium Dei, vocatus ad prandium a magnis principibus, qui cum miro venerabantur affectu, gustatis parumper carnibus propter observantium sancti Evangelii, reliquum, quod comedere videbatur, deponebat in sinu, manu ori adducta, ne quis posset perpendere quod agebat. De potu **vini** quid dicam, cum nec ipsam aquam, desiderio sitis aestuans, ad sufficientiam bibere pateretur?

[52] Accubitum vero suum, ubique receptus hospitio, nullis sinebat stramentis seu vestibus operiri, sed **nuda humus**, tunicula interposita, **nuda** suscipiebat membra. Cum quandoque corpusculum suum somni beneficio recrearet, saepius sedens, nec aliter se deponens dormiebat, pro cervicali ligno vel **lapide** utens ...

"Et **vinum** apud vos est aliquantulum?" dixit. Responderunt illi dicentes: "Domina nostra, **vinum non habemus, quia initium vite hominis panis et aqua**, et tibi bibere vinum non est bonum, quoniam sponsa Christi vinum debet fugere pro veneno".

[63] Postquam autem exsaturati sunt magis ex tante inopie gloria quam essent rerum omnium a b u n d a n t i a, benedixerunt Domino, in cuius conspectu tantam invenerunt gratiam, et duxerunt illam ad locum in quo quiesceret, quia fatigata erat. Sicque supra **nudam humum nudam** se proiecit.
Petiit quoque pulvinar ad caput suum. At illi statim portaverunt **lapidem** et supposuerunt ei.
Illa vero, quietissimo somno ac sobria dormiens, surrexit festinanter, petens sibi claustrum ostendi. Adducentes eam in quodam colle ostenderunt ei totum orbem quem respicere poterant, dicentes: "Hoc est claustrum nostrum, domina."

Saint Francis as Struggling Hermeneut

Marilyn Hammond

Writing this paper is like looking at a new photo album with old pictures. The album is the new three-volume translations and commentaries about Francis. The pictures are the writings of Francis and the stories about him. Some of the pictures are clearer than others. Some have been copied repeatedly and Francis is harder to see. Some have likely been retouched. I intend to choose a few of the pictures and look at them in a certain light. The light in which I will view these writings and stories is medieval fourfold (allegorical) exegesis. This old hermeneutic is not used here for biblical exegesis, rather, it is used to explicate the hermeneutic habits of Francis, which may help us recognize our own hermeneutic habits.

The fourfold hermeneutic provides a spectrum of interpretive possibilities from reductive to exponential. Reductive interpretation only uses one of the four senses. Exponential interpretation uses all four senses. Mixes and gradations occur between these two extremes. The four senses, with bracketed words added for contemporary use, are: 1) literal, historical [physical]; 2) allegorical, hidden, figurative [psychological]; 3) tropological, moral [choices and consequences]; and 4) anagogical, spiritual, mystical [relationship with God].

We are forced to be hermeneuts. We must "read" our experiences and make choices about how to live. Francis and his brothers had to do the same. Hermeneutic predispositions influence how we see ourself, others, institutions, cultures, and God. Hermeneutic assumptions can be modified, refined and expanded, which is part of becoming a mature person. I suggest that a reductive hermeneutic complicates life whereas a more exponential hermeneutic simplifies everyday living. I further suggest that Western culture, though today dominated by a reductive empiric-rational hermeneutic, is slowly expanding its hermeneutic horizons. This gradual shift was referred to by Pope John Paul II, in his 1994 book *Crossing The Threshold of Hope*: "In gaining some distance from positivistic convictions, contemporary thought has made notable advances toward the ever more complete discovery of [the human person], recognizing among other things the value of metaphorical and symbolic language."[1] I contend that metaphor and symbol help form a complex hermeneutic urgently needed in contemporary Western culture to understand desires. Without metaphoric and symbolic discernment desires are often misinterpreted and mislived as addictions and compulsions. This is discussed at the end of the paper. Before some of the writings and stories of Francis are addressed, a brief historical sketch of the old fourfold hermeneutic, which was an active part of church life for nearly fifteen-hundred years, must be presented.

Allegorical Ways of Knowing

Allegory is not well-understood in our culture, but was a prominent way of understanding throughout Western Europe in Francis's day and continued until the sixteenth century.[2] Erich Auerbach writes: "In the course of the sixteenth century the Christian-figural schema lost its hold in almost all parts of Europe."[3] However, allegory had a long and rich history before its demise.

---

1. Pope John Paul continues, "Contemporary hermeneutics — examples of which are found in the work of Paul Ricoeur or, from a different perspective, in the work of Emmanuel Levinas — presents the truth about man and the world from new angles" [*Crossing the Threshold of Hope* (New York: Alfred A. Knopf, 1994), 35].
2. Three cultural shifts during the sixteenth century converged to undermine allegorical ways of knowing: 1) emergence of the scientific method, which demanded quantifiable evidence; 2) religious reform movements which stressed literal interpretation of the bible; and 3) Ramism, a widespread educational "method" of Peter Ramus, which promoted a "plain-style mentality" that was not compatible with figurative/symbolic ways of understanding.
3. Erich Auerbach, *Mimesis: The Representation of Reality in Western Literature* (Princeton: Princeton University Press, 1953), 318.

Allegory is "extended metaphor"[4] or "every metaphor is a little allegory."[5] There are two distinct forms of allegory: 1) as a hermeneutic, and 2) as a literary genre. They are two sides of the same coin. Allegory as a hermeneutic *discerns* or *interprets* while allegory as literary genre *describes* or *expresses*.

Hermeneutic allegory is older than literary allegory and is thought to have begun in the fifth century B.C.E. when the Pre-Socratics wanted to keep both Homer and the new philosophy-science. Later, Philo of Alexandria solidified Jewish allegorical biblical commentary which had been ongoing for nearly two centuries in Alexandria. Following Philo, the Christian exegetes Clement and Origen refined the process. When used in biblical exegesis, interpretive (hermeneutic) allegory is sometimes referred to as *allegoresis*.[6]

Though Origen favored a threefold method of interpretation, as many as seven classifications of interpretation can be seen in medieval Christian exegesis.[7] However, by the fifth century, largely because of the efforts of John Cassian and St. Gregory the Great, allegoresis evolved into a rather standard fourfold way of understanding scripture.[8]

In the Church during Francis's lifetime, allegoresis was not the only kind of exegesis but the fourfold sense of scripture was still prominent.[9] R. E. McNally writes: "Two conceptions of the multiple (threefold and fourfold) senses of Scripture dominate medieval exegesis. The fourfold sense was generally preferred to the threefold to which it was reducible, and the spiritual was invariably preferred to the literal sense."[10] Allegorical interpretation was also

---

4. Quintilian's definition is in *Institutio oratoria* 9.2.46 [*The* Institutio oratoria *of Quintilian*, translated by H.E. Butler (Cambridge: Harvard University Press, 1961–1966)].

5. C.S. Lewis, *The Discarded Image: An Introduction to Medieval and Renaissance Literature* (Cambridge: Cambridge University Press, 1964), 60.

6. *Allegoresis* is used in Ernst Curtius's *European Literature and the Latin Middle Ages* (Princeton: Princeton University Press, 1953) and later in Maureen Quilligan's *The Language of Allegory: Defining the Genre* (Ithaca: Cornell University Press, 1979).

7. R.M. Grant, *A Short History of the Interpretation of the Bible* (New York: MacMillan, 1966), 119.

8. R.E. McNally, *The New Catholic Encyclopedia*, vol. 5 (New York: McGraw Hill, 1967), 708.

9. Henri de Lubac, *Medieval Exegesis: The Four Senses of Scripture*, vol. I (Grand Rapids: Eerdmans Publishing, 1959, English translation 1998), 15–74.

10. McNally, *The New Catholic Encyclopedia*, vol. 5, 708.

the basis of all secular textual interpretation.[11] Basically, allegory as a hermeneutic was an active part of European culture while Francis was alive. Allegory as literature was also part of his culture. An example of this is *The Sacred Exchange between Saint Francis and Lady Poverty*[12] written after Francis's death. This kind of writing began in the fourth century C.E. when the Latin poet Prudentius wrote *Psychomachia*, a poem about vices which beset the soul.

Though Assisi was not a center of learning and Francis's own education was limited, he likely heard allegorical interpretations in sermons and encountered literary allegory in the ballads and poetry of his day. It is not surprising that even as a young man he was able to *express* himself metaphorically, to use riddles and figures of speech when he didn't want others to know exactly what was going on in the early days of his conversion.[13] However, his ability to *discern* metaphorically is not as clear.

Hermeneutic Examples

The four senses of medieval exegesis are present in Francis's vow of poverty.[14] In the Rule, the brothers are to live *material poverty*, having only the bare necessities of clothing,[15] eating whatever food was set before them,[16] accepting no money or coins but instead receiving sustenance for the body from their work,[17] having owner-ship of no thing.[18] They are to live *interior poverty*, which is humility. The root word of humility is *humus*, which is the soil, the earth. A humble person is "down to earth," real, genuine, honest, true, sincere about who and what one is. Opposites of humility are pride, vainglory, envy, greed, worldly distractions and complaining.[19] The brothers are to live *moral poverty*, which is *compassion*, and means to "suffer with." They are to be united in the solidarity and welfare of

---

11. Curtius, *European Literature*, 205.
12. ScEx (I, 529–54).
13. 1C 6 (I, 187–88).
14. See FA:ED I, 133, footnote a.
15. LR 2.9 (I, 101).
16. LR 3.14 (I, 102).
17. LR 5.3 (I, 102), LR 4.2 (I, 102).
18. LR 6.1 (I, 103).
19. LR 10.7 (I, 105).

all the brothers,[20] and to live peaceably and non-judgmentally with everyone else.[21] The brothers are to live *spiritual poverty*, totally serving God in poverty and humility, which brings the kingdom of heaven, the fullness of life.[22]

The kinship between Francis's vow of poverty and the fourfold hermeneutic gives the impression that Francis was an exponential hermeneut. This is not always the case. There are times when Francis seems to have understood very literally and reductively. One example is about shoes. The Rule states "those who are compelled by necessity may wear shoes."[23] This stipulation in the Rule may corroborate Thomas of Celano's story that Francis immediately took off his shoes when gospel passages which included shoes were explained to him.[24] It is, of course, possible that not wearing shoes was part of Francis's personal struggle against materialism and/or his compassionate alignment with those too poor to have shoes. This is certainly possible. However, if Francis did literally take off his shoes, as Thomas says, is this more profound than understanding shoes metaphorically and symbolically? Not really.

Deeper meanings are also possible. Shoes are human-made coverings to protect our feet. We stand on our feet. Allegorically/metaphorically, feet allude to our *under-standing*, which is what stands under (is the foundation) of what we know and believe. The exhortation not to wear shoes could mean we are not to cover our understanding with human contrivances (to protect our egoistic views and beliefs). Rather, our understanding is to rest on humility. As mentioned above, the word humility comes from humus, the soil, the earth. Metaphorically, shoes (human-made

---

20. LR 6.7 (I, 103).
21. LR 3.10 (I, 102), LR 2.17 (I, 101).
22. LR 5.4 and 6.1–6 (I, 103). The sometimes simplistic adage "Let go and let God" can embody Francis's vow of poverty: Let go of possessions, lest they possess you. Let go of ego-centeredness, lest you be devoured by your own fears. Let go of judging others, lest you forget to serve them. Let go of God, lest you trust in your own notions of God.
23. LR 2.15 (I, 101).
24. 1C 22 (I, 201–02). Thomas says Francis "was no deaf hearer of the gospel; rather he committed everything he heard to his excellent memory and was careful to carry it out to the letter." The "letter" in this case included: shoes, as well as gold, silver, money, a wallet, a sack, bread, a staff, and two tunics. My comments metaphorically explicate only the shoes, but the other items could also be interpreted metaphorically.

understanding) can separate us from being "down to earth" (from being real, genuine, honest and truthful) about who we are and what we do. Quite simply, human understanding can keep us from being "grounded" in God. Francis certainly did not live by human standards. Instead he lived all of these symbolic shoe implications. I have used shoes here as an example of metaphoric *discernment*.[25] In contrast, an example of shoes as metaphoric *expression* is in Ephesians when Paul says:

> Stand therefore, and fasten the belt of truth around your waist, and put on the breastplate of righteousness. As *shoes* for your feet put on whatever will make you ready to proclaim the gospel of peace. With all of these, take the shield of faith, with which you will be able to quench all the flaming arrows of the evil one. Take the helmet of salvation, and the sword of the Spirit, which is the word of God.[26]

Like Paul, Francis knew how to express himself metaphorically. This ability is also corroborated in his writings:

> We are spouses when the faithful soul is joined by the Holy Spirit to our Lord Jesus Christ. We are brothers to him when we do the will of the Father who is in heaven. We are mothers when we carry him in our heart and body through a divine love and a pure and sincere conscience and give birth to him through a holy activity which must shine as an example before others. [27]

Francis's struggle was not with expressive/descriptive metaphor but with interpretive metaphor, metaphoric *discernment*.

The literalism above with shoes is again present when he is said to have interpreted a dream he had. Thomas wrote that Francis had a dream in the early days of his conversion experiences. Of course, Francis not telling us about his own dream is problematic. However, it is all we have. This is Thomas's report of Francis's dream:

---

25. Just like the example of taking off his shoes, Francis's reaction to "rebuild My house" at San Damiano is literal [LMj 2.1 (II, 536); LMn 1.9 (II, 688)]. Later writers would comment that what Francis really helped rebuild was the Catholic church of his day.
26. Eph 6:14–17, *NRSV*.
27. 1LtF 8 (I, 42), 2LtF 52 (I, 49).

It seemed to him that his whole house was filled with soldiers' arms: saddles, shields, spears and other equipment. Though delighting for the most part, he silently wondered to himself about its meaning. For he was not accustomed to see such things in his house, but rather stacks of cloth to be sold. He was greatly bewildered at the sudden turn of events and the response that all these arms were to be for him and his soldiers. With a happy spirit he awoke the next morning.[28]

Thomas adds that in waking life Francis was so impressed with a nobleman from Assisi who was gathering military weaponry getting ready for a military campaign in Apulia, that Francis also started gathering military necessities and planned to go to Apulia. Then Francis had the dream, which he felt predicted military success for him in Apulia. Thomas comments that Francis "should have been able to see his interpretation of it [the dream] was mistaken."[29] Of course, Thomas wrote this three years after Francis died and had the benefit of hindsight. Thomas's slightly reproachful remark that Francis should have known his interpretation of the dream was mistaken lends a human and perhaps authenticating touch to the story of Francis's dream.

---

28. 1C 5 (I, 186). I use this version of the dream because it seems unembellished. When Thomas wrote about Francis's dream eighteen years later [2C 6 (II, 245)], the dream took place in a beautiful palace (it was his father's house in the first version) and in addition to suits of armor there was also a lovely bride (not mentioned earlier) and Francis was called by name (not in the first version). Thomas's second account of the dream appears to be a conflation or inflation of other events or aspects of Francis.

29. 1C 5 (I, 186).

Today it is generally believed that dreams are almost never literal statements about external events but rather are metaphoric comments on psycho-spiritual aspects of the dreamer.[30] Metaphorically musing about Francis's dream with a modern mindset, "his whole house" was his father's house. The house represented his father's "frame of reference" where Francis also lived, symbolizing an aspect of Francis's personality that was like his merchant father. Military arms instead of stacks of cloth (material–materialism) symbolized Francis's ability to combat and conquer materialistic tendencies in his own personality. If Francis had understood his dream in this way he might not have had a broken relationship with his father. Instead, he would have been able to subjectively overcome his own materialism without externalizing it and breaking with his father, if this episode happened as the stories report. Also, knowing how Francis's life turned out, we can wonder whether the dream was a statement about Francis's capacity for spiritual warfare in a broader sense. Dreams sometimes reveal potential that can take years to actualize. It must be admitted that using a dream said to have taken place eight hundred years ago, reported by someone other than the dreamer is suspect! However, as used here, it demonstrates metaphoric *discernment*, which is "reading" an event by metaphorically musing about it and spotting similitudes in seemingly disparate situations. This can bring new impressions, insights, understandings, discernments. Whereas, in metaphoric *description* or *expression* one uses metaphor to couch or voice an already held impression or discernment.

Did Francis ever display metaphoric discernment? Yes. At least there is a story that when he was staying at the Portinuncula he had been tormented by a temptation for more than two years. One day while praying in the church, he heard in spirit the words of scrip-

---

30. Jungian analyst Robert Bosnak writes, "Learning to see metaphorical forms in literal images is essential for dreamwork" [*A Little Course in Dreams: A Basic Handbook of Jungian Dreamwork* (Boston: Shambhala, 1989), 116]; psychoanalyst Bruno Bettelheim says: "The unconscious reveals itself in symbols or metaphors" [*Freud and Man's Soul* (New York: Vintage Books, 1982), 37–38]; Montague Ullman and Nan Zimmerman write: "You have to get closer to the dream by addressing the images and learning how to look at them metaphorically" [*Working With Dreams* (Los Angeles: Jeremy P. Tarcher, 1979), 101]; and, "Our dreams may be thought of as metaphors in motion" according to Montague Ullman, Stanley Krippner, and Alan Vaughan [*Dream Telepathy: Experiments in Nocturnal ESP*, 2nd edition (Jefferson NC: McFarland & Company, 1989), 220].

ture: "*If you have faith like a mustard seed, and you tell* that *mountain to move* from its place *and move* to another place, it will happen" (Mt 17:19). Francis replied: "What is that mountain?" He was told: "That mountain is your temptation." "In that case, Lord, be it done to me as you have said!" And he was set free.[31] If this story was written for instructional purposes and never really happened to Francis, it still demonstrates metaphoric *discernment,* for the story has Francis knowing the mountain is a symbolic mountain, which is why he asks "*What* is that mountain?" He does not ask *where* the mountain is so as to find it in the external world.

There is another story, where a Dominican, who was a doctor of sacred theology, asked Francis to explain the words of Ezekiel to him: *If you do not warn the wicked man about his wickedness, I will hold you responsible for his soul* (Ez 3:18–20; 33:7–9). The story goes on to say that the unlettered Francis was reluctant to reply, but did so. "If that passage is supposed to be understood in a universal sense, then I understand it to mean that a servant of God should be burning with life and holiness so brightly, that by the light of example and the tongue of his conduct, he will rebuke all the wicked. In that way, I say, the brightness of his life and the fragrance of his reputation will proclaim their wickedness to all of them."[32] Though we cannot be certain this encounter between Francis and a Dominican theologian took place, we can learn a hermeneutic lesson. The story has Francis prefacing his answer by identifying it as being "in a universal sense." Today we might say "in the broadest sense." Then Francis, in the story, extrapolates the word "warn" to penetrating dimensions and interprets the bible passage with doubled-edged subtlety, placing responsibility back on the one who is doing the warning. Today's aphorism "actions speak louder than words" is present in this story about Francis. The story demonstrates exponential understanding at the outset by stating this is going to be a broad-based answer. The story shows metaphoric *discernment,* when the word "warn" is taken outside its usual connotation of verbally admonishing, chastising, remonstrating, exhorting, or commanding. The story illustrates metaphoric *expression* in "the light of example" and "the tongue of his conduct."

---

31. AC 63 (II, 165), 2C 115 (II, 324), BPr 12 (III, 43).
32. AC 35 (II, 140), 2C 103 (II,103).

A look at one of Francis's writings, *The Admonitions*, shows that Francis was able to translate bible passages into ordinary experiences of daily life.[33] His twenty-eight teachings show a Francis with nuanced (exponential) understanding. An example is his teaching about Adam and the tree of knowledge:

> He [Adam] was able to eat of every tree of paradise, because he did not sin as long as he did not go against obedience. For that person eats of the tree of the knowledge of good who makes his will his own and, in this way, exalts himself over the good things the Lord says and does in him.[34]

When we look at this teaching in light of the fourfold hermeneutic, Francis is turning a spiritual story into a psychological lesson about the will. He does something similar in *A Salutation of the Virtues*,[35] when he takes the virtues Wisdom, Simplicity, Poverty, Humility, Charity, Obedience and tells what they confound. Among other things, the virtues confound the body and all that alludes to the body. The wisdom of the body is confounded, carnal temptation and every carnal fear, as well as every corporal and carnal wish. The mortified body obeys the Spirit, obeys one's brother, is subject and submissive to everyone including beasts and wild animals to do whatever they want with it insofar as it has been given to them from above by the Lord.[36]

In light of the fourfold hermeneutic, what does Francis mean by the "body"? Is Francis speaking of the literal, physical, body or as "flesh" meaning the ego? Is he talking about desires that appear to be rooted in bodily cravings, but are, more precisely, misinterpreted psycho-spiritual longings that are attributed to the body, mislived through the body, and are today called addictions and compulsions? Francis's comments about the body in *A Salutation of the Virtues*, and in other of his writings are confusing. What did Francis mean by the "body" and did receiving the stigmata change his view of the body? We now turn to discuss these questions.

---

33. See the introduction to the *Admonitions* (I, 128).
34. Adm 2.1 (I, 129).
35. SalV (I, 164–65).
36. SalV 10–14 (I, 165).

The Body and the Stigmata

A contemporary author has written that receiving the stigmata forced Francis "to consciously accept the indwelling of God in his own despised body"[37] If Francis "despised" his body it was in the context of medieval asceticism that has been explained in the following way: "Control, discipline, even torture of the flesh, in medieval devotion, was not so much the rejection of physicality as the elevation of it–a horrible yet delicious elevation–into a means of access to the divine."[38] Such asceticism accounts for Francis being "excessively austere"[39] with his body and for practices which seem bizarre to the modern mind:

> [Francis] rarely or hardly ever ate cooked foods, but if he did, he would sprinkle them with ashes or dampen the flavor of spices with cold water . . . he refused to use a straw mattress or blankets . . . he would often sleep sitting up, not lying down, using a stone or a piece of wood as a pillow.[40] Since he had over many years chastised his body and brought it into subjection, he suffered infirmities often . . . his flesh rarely or never had any rest, as he traveled through many distant regions.[41]

Alongside stories like this are Francis's own seemingly harsh words about the body. A few years before receiving the stigmata Francis admonished and exhorted "we must hate our bodies . . . we must place our bodies under the yoke of servitude and holy obedience . . . let us hold our bodies in scorn and contempt."[42] Though each of these phrases ends with the purpose being to serve and obey the Lord, it cannot be assumed that Francis is simply talking about

---

37. Susan McMichaels writes that Francis's psycho-spiritual journey "required that he move from the young Francis who valued his body for the pleasure it gave him to the mature Francis who experienced it as the way to participate in the Incarnation" [*Journey out of the Garden: Saint Francis of Assisi and the Process of Individuation* (Mahwah, NJ: Paulist Press, 1997), 92].
38. Caroline Walker Bynum, *Fragmentation and Redemption: Essays on Gender and the Human Body in Medieval Religion* (New York: Zone Books, 1991), 182.
39. L3C 14 (II, 76).
40. 1C 51 (I, 227).
41. 1C 97 (I, 266).
42. 2LtF 37, 40, 45 (I, 48).

overcoming self-centeredness (ego) in these exhortations. Because in the middle of the statements he says, "we must not be wise and prudent according to the *flesh*."[43] Recent Franciscan interpretations contend that Francis was speaking of the ego and self-centeredness in his harsh body-comments.[44] One author says we need to question "the popular suspicion that Francis carried asceticism to a morbid extreme and held the body in utter contempt."[45] My reading of Francis is that he had a hermeneutic dilemma with the material body and medieval asceticism on one side and the Incarnation on the other side and that translating his body-comments as teachings against self-centeredness is too simple. More likely, in line with the medieval asceticism mentioned above, the body to Francis included those desires of the personality that seem strongly tied to bodily functions such as eating, sleeping, and sex, and in his medieval mindset these needed to be severely controlled, disciplined and even tortured in order to reach the divine.[46] His hermeneutic dilemma is clear when in the same writing where Francis exhorted hating the body, he extolled the Incarnation "in the womb of the holy and glorious Virgin Mary, from whose womb he received the flesh of our humanity and frailty."[47] It has been said that prior to receiving the stigmata Francis seems to have accepted the reality of Incarnation for Christ but not for himself.[48] The question then is

---

43. 2LtF (I, 48).
44. See footnotes c and e, 2LtF (I, 48) where it is is said "body" statements refer to self-centeredness, the egotistical self. The word "flesh" in the midst of these statements suggests either Francis purposely distinguished the two words or used them as synonyms. The editors say Francis's concerns in this writing are with fasting and abstaining as penitent Catholics, not because the body and material things are evil; also see footnotes a (46) and c (47).
45. Thaddeé Matura says that when Francis speaks about the body, he is not referring to the physical body but to the whole personality insofar as it opposes good and embraces evil [*Francis of Assisi: The Message in His Writings* (St. Bonaventure: Franciscan Institute, 1997), 94 and 133].
46. I deal with psychosomatic desires later in this paper. Francis's effort to emphasize the detrimental results of mislived psychosomatic desires as well as extraneous, inordinate preoccupations is found in footnote a, 2LtF (I, 50): "The word *detenti* (detain) found in the 1LtF 2.6 has been changed to *decepti* (deceive). While *detenti* (detain) may be understood as a variation of the Italian *detenere* meaning to imprison or to hold prisoner, it follows the sense of the general concept of being possessed. However such a meaning might have seemed too severe in this context and was perhaps theologically unsatisfactory. Its force, then, was weakened to the more acceptable *decepti*."
47. 2LtF 4 (I, 46).
48. McMichaels, *Journey out of the Garden*, 92.

whether receiving the stigmata changed Francis's understanding of
the body. To help answer this, two stories about Francis are
presented. Both stories involve Francis and his body after receiving
the stigmata. In neither story is Francis depicted as heroic, but as a
rather ordinary human. In the first story, Francis's conflict about
the body is evident. In the second, Francis reconciles with his body.

First, near the end of his life Francis is reported to have "jokingly"
said to his body: "'Cheer up Brother Body, and forgive me; for I will
now gladly do as you please, and gladly hurry to relieve your
complaints!'"[49] This "joking" comment took place when medical
remedies were being smeared on his body and he sought a brother's
opinion about their use, because Francis's conscience was bothering
him on the matter. After the brother's advice to care for the body
which had served Francis so well, Francis jokingly asks the body's
forgiveness for his having been reluctant about using the medical
remedies. If Francis could "joke" about something related to the
body does this show a new attitude about the body, or was it merely
a way to relieve the tension of reluctantly acquiescing to the medical
remedies?[50] One thing is clear, Francis was conflicted, his
conscience was bothering him about how to treat his body.

Second, Francis is reported to have "confessed on his death bed
that he had greatly sinned against 'Brother Body.'"[51] If this
happened, was the death bed "confession" a mere apology? Was
Francis saying it was unfortunately necessary that his body had to
be harshly subdued for the sake of sanctity? If this was true, would
the phrase "he had greatly sinned" been used? If not an apology,
was it instead a poignant scene showing he had a change of heart
about the value or necessity of treating the body harshly? This
death bed scene, unless a fabrication, is an incongruity in the life of
Francis and his relationship with the body and should not be
ignored, as it is one of the final statements of his life. Both stories
show that Francis had a hermeneutic struggle about the body that
he was still dealing with at the end of his life.

49. 2C 210 (II, 383).
50. 2C 210 (II, 382).
51. L3C 14 (I, 76).

However, for these two stories to validate that Francis changed his view of the body by the end of his life, a wider net must be cast by looking at historical circumstances that would have had an impact on him. Certainly, the Fourth Lateran Council (1215) was such an event for Francis who was likely in Rome at the time of the Council.[52] This would have made him poignantly aware of what the church considered heretical[53] in the dualistic errors of Cathars.[54] However, it may be that not until years later, upon receiving the stigmata, that Francis would experientially understand *why* Cathar dualism was heretical in the eyes of the church.[55] Could it be that with the stigmata he realized what the church found heretical in the Cathars was not far from what he sometimes exhorted and practiced about the body?[56] In theory Francis rejected Cathar dualism, in practice his behavior is not so easily interpreted. For instance, his harsh statements about hating the body, mentioned earlier, are in a

---

52. Herbert Grundmann writes, "The first source to confirm Francis being present in Rome at the time of the Council is the *Chronicle of the 24 General Ministers*." Grundmann notes that 2C records that Francis and Dominic once met in Rome in the house of Cardinal Hugolino. And finally, Grundmann concludes, "the most certain clue shows, even without Francis being present in Rome, that *something* happened in the context of the Council which protected the order beyond the oral approval: as the tradition of the order shows with some certainty, Innocent publicly announced to the Council his recognition of the order or its rule. All of this indicates that in all likelihood, Francis was in Rome in 1215 negotiating with the curia over matters concerning his order, and that Innocent expressed a new recognition of the order in public which protected it from being affected by the decree of the Council or compelling it to accept one of the older approved orders" [*Religious Movements in the Middle Ages* (Notre Dame, IN: University of Notre Dame Press, 1995), 95]; see also Bernard McGinn, *The Flowering of Mysticism* (New York: Crossroad Herder, 1998), 48.

53. Grundmann writes: "Very little is actually known about the course of the Council. We know almost nothing about the negotiations which took place before and during the council, nothing at all about the preliminary discussions in committees, and we have no idea of the forces which influenced its outcome. Only the decrees themselves survive. Among these decrees, the treatment of heresy takes primary place" (*Religious Movements*, 59).

54. Grundmann, *Religious Movements*, 53.

55. "In contemporary educational jargon, we would call [Francis] a kinesthetic learner; that is, he had to experience something through his body before he could understand it with his conscious mind" (McMichaels, *Journey out of the Garden*, 99).

56. Bynum comments, "By the thirteenth century the prevalent concept of person was of a psychosomatic unity, the orthodox position in eschatology required resurrection of body as well as soul at the end of time, and the philosophical, medical and folk understandings of body saw men and women as variations on a single physiological structure . . . medieval theology and natural philosophy saw persons as, in some real sense, body as well as soul" (*Fragmentation and Redemption*, 183).

document in which it is thought Francis was upholding the practices of penitent Catholics in contrast to the heretical dualistic
notions of the Cathars,[57] yet his statements seem to condemn the
material body. Congruity between theory and practice, linked by
experiential understanding, is the ultimate goal of discernment ever
striving for a truer conversion. Did the stigmata seal Francis's
conversion?

Francis left nothing in writing about the stigmata. And so we are
left to wonder whether it moderated his medieval asceticism or rein-
forced it, believing that austerities invited the stigmata. We are also
left to wonder whether his painful and prolonged illnesses changed
his ideas about the body. And last, did the awareness that his own
body would be venerated after death impact his views of the body?[58]
We cannot be certain. He does not mention the body in *The Canticle
of Creatures* except for Sister Bodily Death. However, the stories
where he joked about his body at the end of his life and more particularly the death bed apology to his body may nonetheless be clues
that Francis had a hermeneutic-shift about the body.

Concluding Remarks

Now, living eight hundred years after Francis, we still must make
choices about *body/flesh* desires, needs, and wants. Addictions and
compulsions show our struggle. Alcoholics Anonymous (*AA*) is one
source of help in the struggle and when examined closely *AA* has a
fourfold hermeneutic mirroring fourfold exegesis. *AA* acknowledges
a physical propensity (likened to an allergy) in alcoholism. Its literature recognizes many psychological traits in alcoholism, and the
Twelve Steps identify moral issues and above all, the longing for
Spirit instead of "alcoholic spirits." A fourfold interpretation of
alcoholism as having physical, psychological, moral, and spiritual

---

57. 2LtF Intro. (I, 45); see also line 32 and footnote c (47).
58. Eamon Duffy writes, "Francis probably appreciated well enough the likely fate of
his own relics. He understood perfectly well why the citizens of Assisi had sent an
armed guard to escort him in his last illness back to his home town, lest another
community should seize the precious body along the way" [*Finding Saint Francis:
Early Images, Early Lives: Medieval Theology and the Natural Body*, edited by Peter
Biller and A. J. Minnis (Great Britain: York Medieval Press, 1997), 199].

exponents is the likely reason that the *AA* format is effective with other addictions and compulsions.[59]

Today we overfeed the body (obesity) and starve it (anorexia, bulimia). The current term "comfort foods" recognizes eating for reasons other than bodily nutrition. Using the fourfold hermeneutic and descriptive metaphor, we may "hunger" in ethical, psychological, or spiritual areas and overeat or be "starved" and stop eating. We diet for cosmetic reasons rather than fast for spiritual reasons as medieval people did. We manipulate body chemicals with psychoactive drugs like "ecstasy" while medieval people sought spiritual ecstasy through ascetical practices. They flagellated their bodies. We get body piercings, tattoos, cosmetic surgeries. We are sleep-deprived because we are too busy to sleep while they stayed awake to pray and to spiritually discipline their bodies. Though we strive to be healthy, we do not always live more comfortably and wisely with our bodies than Francis and his contemporaries did.

Pedophile scandals (actually *ephebophile* scandals, as most of those molested have been teenagers, young adolescent boys) in the Catholic church today show the carnage from misinterpreted and mislived impulses, cravings, longings and fantasies. In pedophilia or ephebophilia, sexual fantasies about children (thoughts, mental images, feelings, moods, urges) are interpreted incorrectly and literally (physically) acted-out on children or teenagers. Understood metaphorically, sexual fantasies about children or teenagers are symbols alluding to compelling psycho-spiritual concerns. There may be an urgent need to get in touch with, embrace, become intimate with and bring to a climax (consciousness), *childhood or teenage* issues that need healing. Or the fantasies may allude to lost *childlike or adolescent* capacities to experience the numinous,[60] or to *childish,*

---

59. Twelve-Step Programs patterned after Alcoholics Anonymous include: Overeaters Anonymous, Narcotics Anonymous, Emotions Anonymous, Al-Anon, Sexaholics Anonymous, Alateen, Cleptomaniacs and Shoplifters Anonymous, Adult Children of Alcoholics Anonymous.

60. See Edward Hoffman's book *Visions of Innocence: Spiritual and Inspirational Experiences of Childhood* (Boston: Shambhala, 1992). On the psychological assessment, MMPI, adult child molesters have been found to have strong religious interests. See F. A. Johnston and S. A. Johnston, "Differences Between Human Figure Drawings of Child Molesters and Control Groups," *Journal of Clinical Psychology* 42.4 (1986): 638–47.

adolescent (immature) aspects of the personality that need to be dealt with. Considering pedophilia or ephebophilia as mere moral lapse is too simple. Yet the moral aspect cannot be ignored. In the fourfold hermeneutic it is not ignored. The moral (tropological) is included in this hermeneutic of checks-and-balances, and should alert one to the wrongness of some interpretations. Using the four-fold hermeneutic, pedophilia/ephebophilia is "symbolic confusion" "allusion confusion" "interpretive error,"[61] where urgent psycho-spiritual dynamics are misinterpreted and mislived through the body to the detriment of everyone involved. The fourfold hermeneutic is the framework and metaphoric discernment is the process to unravel psycho-spiritual symbols. Otherwise, we are left with symptoms. The undiscerned symbolic can become diabolic, in the language of Francis's day.

The wisdom in symbol and metaphor must be rediscovered by each person in each generation. Though earlier it was suggested that Francis lived in an allegorical age, it may be that despite allegoresis in the church and allegorical secular literature, metaphoric discern-ment and exponential understanding were never integrated into or commonplace in everyday medieval life.[62] They are not prevalent in contemporary culture either. However, one need not wait for culture to rediscover metaphor, symbol, or the fourfold herme-neutic, to develop a habit of using them in interpreting personal experiences. To be human is to be a struggling hermeneut. Obvi-ously, the Franciscan controversy after Francis's death was largely a hermeneutic struggle. Present-day sex scandals in the church show the ongoing urgent need to be astute in interpreting deep, intimate desires and longings.

Bonaventure, one of the leading commentators on the Fran-ciscan spirit, says Francis taught his brothers "to follow discern-ment as the charioteer of the virtues."[63] The fourfold method helps develop the virtue of discernment since the *literal, historical, physical*

---

61. American philosopher Ken Wilber uses Bonaventure's "three eyes" (flesh, reason, and contemplation) to illustrate "category error" [*Eye to Eye: The Quest for the New Paradigm* (Boston: Shambhala, 1990), 2–7]. Wilber's "category error" is substantially the same as the terms used here, "symbolic confusion," "allusion confusion," "interpretive error."
62. "What modern readers find most disturbing about medieval discussions is their extreme literalism and materialism" (Bynum, *Fragmentation and Redemption*, 13).
63. LMj 5. 7 (II, 565).

grounds us in the five-sense, time-space world while not being constricted to it or solely defined by it. The *allegorical, hidden, figurative, psychological* recognizes the need for interior healing and harmony without becoming engulfed in the process. The *tropological, moral, consequences of our choices* highlights the impact of our choices on our self and others without a strident or simplistic moralism. The *anagogical, spiritual, mystical, relationship with God* acknowledges our longing for and contact with something beyond ourselves and the world that guides the choices we must make, without devolving into exaggerated spirituality.

Francis's reliance on personal discernment is seen in a brief letter handwritten by him to Brother Leo to resolve some of the scruples which Leo experienced interpreting Francis's vision of gospel life:[64]

> Brother Leo, health and peace from Brother Francis! I am speaking, my son, in this way–as a mother would–because I am putting everything we said on the road in this brief message and advice. If, afterwards, you need to come to me for counsel, I advise you thus: In whatever way it seems better to you to please the Lord God and to follow his footprint and poverty, do it with the blessing of the Lord God and my obedience. And if you need and want to come to me for the sake of your soul or for some consolation, Leo, come.[65]

Francis, Leo's friend and spiritual mentor, knew Leo was spiritually mature enough to use his own discretion, and so Francis encouraged him to do so. The fourfold hermeneutic, rooted in the rich tradition of the church, can today bear fruit as a personal spiritual guide to encourage the maturity needed in discernment and discretion. *Metaphoric discernment* opens doors of understanding: to ourselves as symbolic creatures, to the wonders of a symbolic universe, and to a transcendent God who is best glimpsed through and in the medium of symbol. To discern without metaphor is an *illusion*, to discern with metaphor is always an *allusion*.

Only in discerning metaphorically can we ever hope to *embody* what Francis himself continually struggled to understand and to

---

64. FA:ED I, 36.
65. LtL (I, 122).

love experientially: "Consider, O human being, in what great excellence the Lord God has placed you, for he created and formed you to the image of His beloved Son according to the body and to His likeness according to the Spirit . . . we can boast in our weakness and in carrying each day the holy cross of our Lord Jesus Christ."[66] The fact that Francis links the body and spirit with Christ's cross indicates *how* and *where* Francis chose to wrestle as a struggling hermeneut.

---

66. Adm 5.1, 5.8 (I, 131); also note the Trinitarian dimension of Francis's admonition.

Into the Light: Bonaventure's Minor Life of Saint Francis

. . . and the Franciscan Production of Space

Timothy J. Johnson

To underestimate, ignore and diminish space amounts to the overestimation of texts, written matter and writing systems along with the readable and the visible, to the point of assigning to these a monopoly on intelligibility.[1]

Henri Lefebvre's *The Production of Space* continues to impact postmodern critical theory in diverse disciplines from geography and sociology to architecture and religion.[2] His admonition regarding the

---

1. Henri Lefebvre, *The Production of Space*, translated by Donald Nicholson-Smith (Oxford: Blackwell Publishers, 1991), 62. An example of stressing text at the expense of space in the study of Bonaventure and Gothic art and architecture is found in: Remigius Boving, *Bonaventura und die französische Hochgotik* (Werl i. Westfalen: Franziskus-Druckerei, 1930).
2. Concerning Lefebvre, space, and postmodernism, see David Harvey, *The Condition of Postmodernity* (Oxford: Blackwell Publishing, 1989), 218–19. On Lefebvre's work and religious-architectural studies, see Fraser MacDonald, "Producing Space in Presbyterian Scotland: Highland Worship in Theory and Practice," in *Arkleton Research Papers No. 2* (Aberdeen: Arkleton Centre for Rural Development Research, 2000): 1–36, and Megan Cassidy-Welch, *Monastic Spaces and Their Meanings* (Turnhout: Brepols, 2001), 2–4. See also Philip Sheldrake, *Spaces for the Sacred: Place, Memory, and Identity* (Baltimore: Johns Hopkins University Press, 2001), 21. On the life and work of Henri Lefebvre, see Rob Shields, *Lefebvre, Love, and Struggle: Spatial Dialectics* (New York: Routledge, 1999) and Andy Merrifield, "Henri Lefebvre: A Socialist in Space" in *Thinking Space*, edited by Mike Crang and Nigel Thrift (New York: Routledge, 2000), 167–82.

hermeneutical priority given to written texts at the expense of considering space, offers a compelling point of departure for a study of the
relationship between Franciscan hagiographical-liturgical *legendae*[3]
and church architecture.[4] Utilizing Lefebvre's insights, this essay
demonstrates that a crucial element behind Bonaventure's *Minor Life
of Saint Francis*[5] was the Franciscan production of space evident in the
major building program undertaken by the Minorite community in
the middle of the thirteenth century.

The obviation of space as a hermeneutical category in the interpretation of the *Minor Life of Saint Francis*, together with other
hagiographical-liturgical *legendae*, results in the concomitant failure
to recognize the spatial experience proper to medieval churches.
Lefebvre's classical study of space, although driven by albeit a
heterodox Marxist philosophy,[6] devoted sustained attention to the
Romanesque and Gothic churches of his native France. His delinea-
tion of space in terms of three dimensions, representations of space,
spaces of representation, and spatial practice, suggests an avenue of
reappraisal for *The Minor Life of Saint Francis* encompassing the
praxis of prayer, the architecture of the Minorite churches and
Bonaventure's theology. To begin, this essay will examine
Lefebvre's threefold understanding of space in relationship to
churches, then consider the production of space in thirteenth-century Minorite churches, and conclude claiming *The
Minor Life of Saint Francis* is the result of, and certainly better suited
to, the spatial practice of choir prayer during Bonaventure's tenure

3. On early Franciscan hagiographical-liturgical *legenda*, see Francesco Dolciami,
"Francesco d'Assisi: tra devozione, culto, e liturgia," *Collectanea Francescana* 71
(2001): 5–45, and Timothy J. Johnson, "Lost in Sacred Space: Textual
Hermeneutics, Liturgical Worship, and Celano's *Legenda ad usum chori*," *Franciscan
Studies* 59 (2001): 109–31.
4. On Lefebvre and the question of intelligibility, texts, and space, see Lindsay Jones,
Monumental Occasions: Reflections on the Eventfulness of Religious Architecture, vol. 1 of
The Hermeneutics of Sacred Architecture: Experience, Interpretation, Comparison
(Cambridge: Harvard University Press, 2000), 121–33, especially 127–29.
5. The English translation of Bonaventure's *Minor Life of Saint Francis* is found in: *The
Founder*; vol. 2 of *Francis of Assisi: Early Documents*, edited by Regis J. Armstrong, J.
A. Wayne Hellmann, and William J. Short (New York: New City Press, 2000),
684–717. All abbreviations to texts from *Francis of Assisi: Early Documents* will
follow the system delineated in *The Founder*, 26.
6. On Lefebvre and Marxism, see Merrifield, "Henri Lefebvre," 178–80. Shields
claims Lefebvre's university studies of Catholic philosophy and theology were
integral in the development of his nascent Marxism; see *Lefebvre, Love, and Struggle*,
8–12, 186.

as minister general than other available Franciscan hagiographical-liturgical *legendae*.

Henri Lefebvre on Space and Churches

As Andy Merrefield notes, Lefebvre's spatial triad is not a precise methodology but a preliminary, dialectical stance toward space that is employed in various ways by scholars in their research.[7] Churches, as monuments, encompass all three aspects of spatiality. The first term, representations of space, refers to conceived or conceptualized space dominant in any society and marked by the ideological concerns of power and knowledge embedded in monuments such as, but not limited to, churches, temples, and palaces.[8] Representations of space are constructed by social engineers, planners, canonists, and architects whose projects are not reducible to simple structures; their efforts have an undeniable spatial context with consequences for the production of space. Distinguished by intellectual systems articulated in verbal codes, monuments like churches represent an objectified conception of reality equated, by the planners, with the actual perception and lived experience of those who enter. Lefebvre claims, in particular, an intrinsic bond between representations of space in churches and the ultimate vitality of the Christian worldview:

> What is an ideology without a space to which it refers, a space which it describes, whose vocabulary and links it makes use of, and whose code it embodies? What would remain of a religious ideology — the Judeo-Christian one, say — if it were not based on places and names: church, confessional, altar, sanctuary, tabernacle? What would remain of the Church if there were no churches? The Christian ideology, carrier of a recognizable if disregarded Judaism (God the Father, etc.), has created the spaces which guarantee that it endures.[9]

---

7. Merrifield, "Henri Lefebvre," 173.
8. Lefebvre, *The Production of Space*, 38–39, 42, and Merrifield, "Henri Lefebvre," 174.
9. Lefebvre, *The Production of Space*, 44.

The second term of Lefebvre's spatial triad, representational space, is the realm of the everyday experience of perceived, lived space. Such space is dynamic; alive with affective, passionate, non-verbal systems of signs and symbols, it sparks the imaginative creativity of artists, and at times writers and philosophers, who seek only to describe, and not to appropriate and control. Churches are the loci of representational space as evident in the perceptions of those drawn into the poetic world of monuments.[10] Gazing accompanies hearing, silence unites with gesture, touch is embraced by scent, and the possible, visible gives way to the impossible, invisible, as worshipers are engaged in an antiphonal dialogue of private and public experience that may, or may not, conform to the intended representation of space of the architects, patrons, and planners. The immediacy, fluidity, and even subversive nature of this representational space assures the continual attempt to intervene and dominate it.[11]

Spatial practice, the third term from Lefebvre's insight into spatiality, concerns the dialectical of production and reproduction of space assuring continuity and cohesion of social interaction within a community.[12] For example, Rob Shields points out specific, historical places dedicated to remembrance and the dead, such as churches, evoke a spatialization, a "human space" indicative of society's quality of life. Space, ideology, and social formation converge in churches, thereby ensuring spatial competence and performance of individuals within society.[13] Spatial practice, according to Lefebvre, produces, masters, and appropriates space and is ultimately discerned, analytically, by deciphering the very societal space it secretes, or creates.[14]

The spatial triad, delineated by Lefebvre in *The Production of Space*, converges dialectically in churches, and specifically in cathedrals, where the initial, intellectual conceptualization of space of the planners evokes a symbolic realm of perceived experience and, through the responses of those entering, a spatial performance indicative of the society. Within a simple practice of everyday life,

---

10. Lefebvre, *The Production of Space*, 223–26.
11. Merrifield, "Henri Lefebvre," 174.
12. Lefebvre, *The Production of Space*, 33, 38.
13. Shields, *Lefebvre, Love, and Struggle*, 162.
14. Lefebvre, *The Production of Space*, 38.

visitors are initiated into a Christian worldview that is eminently social, commonly accessible, and ultimately revelatory. The entire person, body and soul, regardless of social status or occupational competency is caught up, and integrated in the dynamic of spatialization proper to a cathedral, which, for this reason, becomes emblematic of the specific culture that produced it, and threatening to those who oppose it:

> The use of the cathedral's monumental space necessarily entails its supplying answers to all the questions that assail anyone who crosses the threshold. For visitors are bound to become aware of their footsteps, and listen to the noises, to the singing; they must breathe the incense-laden air, and plunge into a particular world, that of sin and redemption; they will partake of an ideology; they will contemplate and decipher the symbols around them; and they will thus, on the basis of their bodies, experience a total being in total space. Small wonder that from time immemorial conquerors and revolutionaries eager to destroy a society should so often have sought to do so by burning or razing that society's monuments. [15]

The Franciscan Production of Space

Henri Lefebvre's keen interest in spatiality and churches included a comparison between Romanesque churches and Gothic churches that bears directly on the question of Minorite architecture and Bonaventure's *Minor Life of Saint Francis.* The medieval period, initially, was the heir of the representational space of Roman antiquity equated commonly with the basilica; yet this space was soon transformed in a process of "co-option" to produce innovative expressions of space replete with symbolic meaning producing a new spatial practice of worship, often joined to monuments honoring the deceased.[16] The tombs, crypts, sanctuaries, churches, and concomitant artwork of the aptly named Romanesque period are examples of

---

15. Lefebvre, *The Production of Space*, 220-21.
16. Lefebvre, *The Production of Space*, 45-46, 231, 245, 254-55, 368-69.

this space, which was familiar to the Umbrian layman, Francis of
Assisi and his early followers. While the transformation or, to use
Lefebvre's term, "co-optation" of the antiquity's representational
space produced elaborate churches requiring theorists and engineers,
the intellectual, codified representation of space proper to architects,[17] engineers, and even philosophers and theologians[18] is more
perceptible in the conceived order of the emerging Gothic cathedrals,
which transparent and suffused with light, towered over the
surrounding opaque Romanesque structures.[19]

Lefebvre's spatial perspective situates Francis of Assisi firmly
within the representational space of thirteenth-century Umbria.[20]
The stark Romanesque façade of the Cathedral of San Rufino in
Assisi, dedicated to the martyr bishop, dominated the square where
Francis may have preached.[21] The small, and often neglected, local
churches where he encountered the divine such as San Damiano[22]
and Santa Maria degli Angeli[23] were permeated by the symbolic
language of Romanesque-Byzantine architecture and art, which
often included austere biblical narratives.[24] The Romanesque representation of space, proposed by Rome and emanating throughout
Italy, was rooted in the far-reaching, long-lasting efforts of the

17. On the worldview of medieval architects, see Günther Binding, *Der früh-und hochmittelalterliche Bauherr als sapiens architectus* (Darmstadt: Wissenschaftliche Buchgesellschaft, 1998).
18. The collaborative roles of medieval masters and builders is treated in Charles Radding and William Clark, *Medieval Architecture, Medieval Learning* (New Haven: Yale University Press, 1992).
19. Lefebvre, *The Production of Space*, 256–61.
20. On the lingering influence of Romanesque-Byzantine art in Italy, see Michael Camille, *Gothic Art* (London: Calmann and King, 1996), 105–06.
21. Francesco Santucci, "La Cattedrale e il Francescanesimo," in *La Cattedrale di San Rufino in Assisi*, edited by Francesco Santucci (Cinisello Balsamo: Arti Graphice Amilcare Pizzi, 1999), 88–91.
22. On the Romanesque origins of San Damiano, see Marino Bigaroni, "San Damiano-Assisi: The First Church of Saint Francis," *Franciscan Studies* 47 (1987): 45–97, especially 56, 63–64.
23. On Santa Maria degli Angeli and other churches of the early Franciscan community, see Marcello Salvatori, "Le prime sedi francescani" in *Lo spazio dell'umiltà: Atti del convegno di studi sull'edilizia dell'ordine dei minori* (Fara Sabina: Centro francescano Santa Maria in Castello, 1984), 77–106, especially Appendice 89–105.
24. Hans Belting, "The New Role of Narrative in Public Painting of the Trecento: Historia and Allegory," in *Pictorial Narrative in Antiquity and the Middle Ages*, edited by Herbert Kessler and Marianna Simpson, in *Studies in the History of Art*, vol. 16 (Washington D.C.: National Gallery of Art, 1985), 151.

preceding Gregorian reform; it fostered sacred images of martyrs and the communal life witnessed in the Acts of the Apostles.[25]

Romanesque crypts, crosses, and altars, in particular, mediated the presence of God. San Damiano, the earliest church and perhaps the only church rebuilt by Francis,[26] appears to have exhibited the common combination of a lower crypt and upper platform altar popular throughout thirteen-century Umbria.[27] According to Lefebvre, crypts speak the cryptic language of cross;[28] they linked the underworld of deadly darkness to the eschatological future as the entombed saints await divine justice like the martyrs buried under the altar of Revelation 6:9–11. The altar of the church arose upon the sacrifice of saints, whose crypt assured the sacredness of the church.[29] Francis's spatial practice, marked by prayer, witness, and resistance to persecution in San Damiano, suggests a faith challenged like that of the martyrs, yet sustained by the gratuitousness of God's mercy. In prayer before the painted, *Christus triumphans* image of the Crucified, Francis confessed his struggles and received confirmation of his calling.[30]

Francis's writings, in the reverential awe and praise ascribed to Christ present on the altar and on the cross, echo his experience of ecclesial, representational space.[31] *The Testament* displayed his

25. Hélène Toubert, *Un'arte orientate: riforma gregoriana e iconografia*, translated by Lucinia Speciale (Milano: Jaca Book, 2001), 11–18.
26. Johnson, "Lost in Sacred Space," 116–17.
27. Bigaroni, "San Damiano-Assisi," 63–64.
28. Lefebvre, *The Production of Space*, 369.
29. Arnold Angenendt, *Heilige und Reliquien: Die Geschichte ihres Kultes vom frühen Christentum bis zur Gegenwart* (Munich: C.H. Beck, 1997), 167–82, especially 172–73.
30. L3C 13–24 (II, 75–83). Some manuscripts of the L3C contain *The Prayer before the Crucifix* (I, 40) when they relate this story of the young Francis in San Damiano. This simple, yet elegant prayer speaks of Francis's yearning for God's assistance. This story has liturgical implications; see LMn 1 (II, 686, footnote a). The San Damiano Cross is an example of the painted, Byzantine-Romanesque art of the period. On the history of this cross, see Servus Gieben, "Die Tafelkreuz von S. Damiano in der Geschichte. Mit einem ikonographischen Anhang," *Collectanea Francescana*, 1–2 (2001): 47–63.
31. Francis refers on several occasions to the altar and the presence of Christ, see: 1 Adm 9 (I, 128), 1 Adm 18 (I, 18), 1LtCus 3 (I, 56), 1LtCus 7 (I, 57), 2LtF 11 (I, 46), 2LtF 33 (I, 47), LtOrd 26 (I, 118), LtOrd 37 (I, 119). In 2LtF 11, Francis brings together the image of the cross and the altar, "His Father's will was such that His blessed and glorious Son, Whom He gave to us and Who was born for us, should offer Himself through His own blood as a sacrifice and oblation on the altar of the cross." On the significance of the altar in medieval spirituality and church architecture, see Arnold Angenendt, *Geschichte der Religiosität im Mittelalter* (Darmstadt: Primus Verlag, 2000), 452–56.

exuberance regarding the ability of this representational space to
invoke a declaration of faith:

> And the Lord gave me such faith in churches that I would
> pray with simplicity in this way and say: 'We adore you
> Lord Jesus Christ, in all Your churches throughout the
> world and we bless You, because by your holy cross You
> have redeemed the world.'[32]

The Legend of the Three Companions, detailing Francis's admonitions
to the first brothers sent into the world to preach the gospel, notes
he taught this prayer of adoration and blessing to them, "For they
believed they would find a place of God wherever they found a cross
or church."[33]

Although Francis and his brothers found sanctuary in crypts and
churches,[34] the itinerant dynamic of evangelical preaching did not
require the acquisition or possession of churches. Edith Pásztor
evinces the pastoral care offered by Francis and the nascent fraternity consisted in urging men and women, with word and example,
to embrace the reign of God.[35] The initial relationship between the
brothers and churches is perhaps best illustrated by the account of
Brother Bernard, the first companion of the Poverello, in Florence.
The Legend of the Three Companions relates how Bernard and a
companion sought refugee from the bitter cold of the night, as was
their custom, in the porticoes of churches and homes. Despite the
rebukes of her husband, a local woman allowed them to sleep near
an oven in the family portico. On the following morn, the two
brothers prayed in a nearby church, in the company of the poor,

---

32. Test 4 (I, 124–25).
33. L3C 37 (II, 90). The Latin text reads, *"Credebant enim simper invenire locum Dei
ubicumque crucem vel ecclesiam invenissent." Legenda trium sociorum*, n. 37 in *Fontes
Franciscani*, ed. Enrico Menestò and Stefano Brufani (Santa Maria degli Angeli:
Edizioni Porziuncula, 1995), 1410. The usage of *"locum Dei"* underlines the
particular sacredness of the locale. Although God, like the universe, is everywhere
(*ubique*) just as the center of a circle is everywhere and the circumference is
nowhere (*nullibi*), a prominent medieval concept of place, according to Edward
Casey, envisions it as a "closely-confining circuit of place as perimeter" spoken of
as "lodging." See Edward Casey, *The Fate of Place: A Philosophical History* (Berkeley:
University of California Press, 1998), 114–16. Bonaventure uses a similar example
of the circle when speaking of God in *The Journey of the Soul into God*, 5.8 (V, 310a).
34. 1C 39 (I, 218), 1C 71 (I, 244).
35. Edith Pásztor, "La chiesa dei frati minori tra ideale di S. Francesco ed esigenze
della cura delle anime," in *Lo spazio dell'umiltà*, 63.

where their devotion confirmed the generosity of their hostess and appearance evoked the compassion of a wealthy man. He often came to the church to distribute alms and was so taken by Bernard's refusal to accept money from him that he invited the mendicants to stay with him.[36]

Bernard's unwillingness to receive money in the Florentine church and Francis's readiness to find sanctuary in churches belonging to others, underscore the poor, itinerant nature of the early brotherhood of beggars. Although Francis insisted upon poverty as integral to the evangelical life, the peripatetic presence of the brothers gave way, within a brief decade from 1210–1220, to a nascent conventual life organized around preaching and the Divine Office.[37] An expression of this fundamental shift was the gradual acceptance of churches and other dwellings; albeit poor and for the brothers' use alone.[38] *The Assisi Compilation* chronicles how, soon after his return from Rome in 1209, the increase in brothers induced Francis to seek out a poor church in the Assisi environs where they could pray and construct a simple dwelling. The Poverello was delighted when the Benedictine monastery on Mount Subasio offered reputedly the poorest church in the area, Santa Maria degli Angeli, to the fledgling fraternity.[39] The first admonition of Francis's *Testament*, dated between 1224 and his death in 1226, demonstrates he never abandoned his insistence on the need for the representational space proper to the poor churches that shaped his initial spatial practice in San Damiano and the ecclesial experience of his first companions:

> Let the brothers be careful not to receive in any way churches or poor dwellings or anything else built for them unless they are according to the holy poverty we promised in the Rule. As pilgrims and strangers, let them always be guests there.[40]

---

36. L3C 38–40 (II, 90–92).
37. On this organization dynamic among the early brothers, see Kajetan Esser, *Origins of the Franciscan Order*, translated by Aedan Daly and Irina Lynch (Chicago: Francisca Herald Press, 1970), 137–201.
38. Edith Pásztor, "La chiesa dei frati minori," 64–65.
39. AC 56 (II, 154–55).
40. Test 24 (I, 126). On Francis and the structures of the early community, see Jacques Dalarun, "Les maisons des frères matériaux et symbolique des premiers couvents

The *Testament*, together with *The Letter to the Entire Order* from 1225–1226, indicate the final years of Francis's life witnessed the widespread acceptance of existent and, perhaps, newly constructed churches, by Minorite communities in Italy and beyond.[41] Wolfgang Schenkluhn opines the church in Magdeburger Neustadt, built explicitly for the brothers, may date as early as 1225.[42] Papal directives, such as Honorius III's *Quia populares* in 1224,[43] fostered a separate, autonomous liturgical praxis in these Franciscan churches outside the parochial structures suggested by the earlier narrative of Brother Bernard in Florence. While the brothers shifted the locus of liturgical prayer away from local parishes, their pastoral ministry, supported by papal declarations as early as *Cum dilecti*[44] in 1219, remained firmly focused on these same parish churches administered by secular clergy.

Gregory IX's bull of February 1230, *Si Ordinis Fratrum Minorum*, marked a watershed in the Franciscan spatial practice of prayer and ministry; it granted the Minorites the opportunity to construct churches for the care of the faithful.[45] This initiative followed by the definitive papal interpretation of Francis's *Testament* in *Quo elongati* in September of the same year, together with the growing clericalization of the Lesser Brothers,[46] heralded a shift in ecclesial perception and spatial practice among many. Instead of gratuitous representational space pregnant with the promise of God's revelation in the spatial practices of fraternal life, churches became potentially contested arenas of pastoral care where clerical brothers competed with their secular counterparts in the administration of sacraments. Regardless of the eventual outcome of this struggle, the urban landscape of Europe would be forever altered, for the

franciscains," in *Le village medieval et son environnement: Etudes offertes à Jean-Marie Pesez*, edited by Laurent Feller, Perrine Mane, and Françoise Piponnier (Paris: Publications De La Sorbonne, 1998), 75–95.
41. Luigi Pellegrini, "La prima fraternità minoritica," and Marcello Salvatori, "Le prime sedi francescani," in *Lo spazio dell'umiltà*, 43–45 and 81–83 respectively.
42. Wolfgang Schenkluhn, *Architektur der Bettelorden: Baukunst der Dominikaner und Franziskaner in Europa* (Darmstadt: Primus Verlag, 2000), 31, 33.
43. *Quia populares* (I, 561–63).
44. *Cum dilectis* (I, 558).
45. Edith Pásztor, "La chiesa dei frati minori," 65.
46. Lawrence Landini, *The Causes of the Clericalization of the Order of Friars Minor* (Chicago: Franciscan Herald Press, 1968), 61.

Minorites were free to follow their mendicant brothers, the Friar Preachers, and produce their own representations of space, determined by a growing ideology of identity and mission.

Although the promulgation of *Si Ordinis Fratrum Minorum* fostered a Minorite construction program, the most notable church associated with the brothers preceded this papal bull. The origins of the Basilica of Saint Francis in Assisi lie in Gregory IX's desire, evident in his solicitation of funds through the generous offering of spiritual blessings,[47] to construct a sepulcher church dedicated to the Poor Man of Assisi. Gregory himself laid the first stone of the basilica on July 17, 1228, one day after Francis's canonization liturgy.[48] As plans for the Basilica of Saint Francis became evident, they offered a poignant reminder to brothers and laity alike of the past and future trajectory of Franciscan spatial practice. The lower church containing the entombed remains of the Poverello, evidenced the Romanesque crypt style familiar to Francis and the first companions, some of whom would eventually be buried in his shadows. The sweeping Lombard Gothic of the upper church, however, "decrypted," as Lefebvre might suggest,[49] the darkness

---

47. *Recolentes qualiter* (I, 564).
48. Elvio Lunghi, *The Basilica of Saint Francis*, translated by Christopher Evans (Florence: Arti Grafiche, 2000), 8. A possible chronology for the building of the Upper and Lower Basilica is offered in Antonio Cadei, "The Architecture of the Basilica," in *Patriarchal Basilica in Assisi Saint Francis: Artistic Testimony Evangelical Message*, edited by Paola Urbani and translated by Kate Singleton (Milan: Gruppo Editoriale Fabbri, 1991), 43–76, especially 54–55. Cadei maintains the initial plans for the basilica did not necessarily include a double church, as material evidence points to stages in the building process indicative of alterations in the architectural design. He theorizes there was an initial design that both immediately preceded and coincided with the canonization of the saint. The proclamation of the church as *caput et mater* of the Minorites by the papal bull *Is qui* of April 22, 1230 promoted design changes, including, perhaps, the addition of an upper church above the sepulcher church. While there may have been a temporary halt to construction due to the turmoil surrounding Brother Elias's dismissal in 1239, purchase of additional land for the church square indicates continued building, and perhaps, additional changes in design were under way in by 1246. The Upper Basilica was not completely finished when the altars were consecrated in 1253.
49. Lefebvre, *The Production of Space*, 256–57. Differences between Romanesque and Gothic manifest decidedly different understandings of architectural space and are not reducible to simple technical or stylistic features; see Radding and Clark, *Medieval Architecture, Medieval Learning*, 96. On the contrasting architecture and purposes of the Lower and Upper Basilica, see Schenkluhn, *Architektur der Bettelorden*, 37–43.

and death of the lower church is radically new, ordered representation of space, both luminous and alive with color. While the Upper Basilica of Saint Francis of Assisi is not the singular, definite model for other Franciscan churches, variegated expressions of its representative Gothic architecture mark much of the subsequent, significant Minorite ecclesial construction.[50]

The Gothic Ascent and the Urban Minorites

The Gothic "decrypting" of space, evident in the Basilica of Saint Francis and often emulated in other Minorite churches became a harbinger of the Franciscan urban trajectory. As Lefebvre notes, the rise of Gothic cathedrals in the thirteenth century inverts the space of earlier Romanesque religious structures resulting in the diffusion of meaningful space from the darkness of the hidden, underground cryptal sanctuaries onto medieval towns above ground.[51] Soon after *Si Ordinis Fratrum Minorum* and the construction of the Assisi basilica, towns and cities across Europe took on a decidedly mendicant appearance. Between 1240–1260 Franciscan communities embarked upon a widespread abandonment of small, poor churches outside the cities in exchange for churches, often built *ex novo*, in the burgeoning urban centers. There are, from 1244–1247 alone, more than a hundred extant papal documents regarding the transfer of Minorite residences and churches.[52] Numerous papal concessions concerning the ownership of churches, use of liturgical vessels and books, dispensation of the sacraments, the exercise of preaching, and acceptance of tithes culminated in *Cum tanquam veri* of Innocent IV in 1250, which established conventual churches, with all the accompanying ecclesial rights, dedicated to urban ministry.[53]

50. L. Barbaglia, "Mendicanti, Ordini (Architettura) in *Dizionario degli istituti di perfezione*, vol. 5 (Roma: Edizioni Paoline, 1978), 1189–1210, and Schenkluhn, *Architektur der Bettelorden*, 43, 56–63, 240. See also Antonio Cadei, "The Architecture of the Basilica," 70.
51. Lefebvre, *The Production of Space*, 256–57, 260.
52. John Moorman, *The History of the Franciscan Order* (Oxford: Oxford University Press, 1966), 118–19. See also Edith Pásztor, "La chiesa dei frati minori," 65, and Gabriella Villetti, "L'edilizia mendicante in Italia," in *Lo spazio dell'umiltà*, 227.
53. Salvatori, "Le prime sedi francescani," 82–84. See also Lorenzo Di Fonzo, Giovanni Odoardi, and Alfonso Pompei, *I Frati Minori Conventuali* (Roma: Curia Generalizia, O.F.M. Conv., 1978), 40–41.

The Minorite movement into urban churches fostered a division, both literal and symbolic, between the ever-increasing clerical communities clearly evident in the Gothic choirs where the brothers celebrated the Divine Office. Wolfgang Schenkluhn observes Franciscans opted in their town churches for enclosed choirs, separated from the rest of the church, and thus the laity, by a screen or wall.[54] While myriad architectural variations appear in these churches, the ubiquitous, systematic creation of two distinct areas is an evident Minorite attempt to produce space conforming to an emerging ecclesial hierarchy. This deliberate representational space, at the very center of the meaningful space Lefebvre attributes to medieval towns, is paralleled by an Order wide pictorial depiction of Francis as the exemplar of holiness. The separated choir area of these urban churches, dedicated to liturgical prayer and frescoed with scenes from the miraculous life of the Poverello, allowed the Minorite community to define the image of the saint for themselves first of all, and then for the laity.[55]

Since the canonization in 1228, the brothers celebrated the Octave of the Feast of Saint Francis, inscribed in the calendar of the Roman Curia, from October 4–11.[56] Architecture, liturgical performance, wall and panel paintings, together with the reading of a hagiographical-liturgical *legenda*, offered a compelling vision of the poor man from Assisi during prayer.[57] The Minorite Thomas of Celano authored a preliminary *legenda* shortly before the saint was

---

54. Schenkluhn, *Architektur der Bettelorden*, 81–83, 239–40. On various aspects of this question, including the pastoral activities of the mendicants in their churches, see Isnard Frank, "Bettelordenskirchen als multifunktionale Kulträume. Ein Beitrag zur Bettelordenskirchenforschung," *Wissenschaft und Weisheit* 59.1 (1996): 93–112. The separation of the church, and an accompanying emphasis on the choir, is also evident in the architectural and artistic regulations from the *The Constitutions of Narbonne*. Only the apse of the church is to be vaulted and no stained glass is to be installed except in the principal window of the choir; see Bonaventure, *Writings Concerning the Franciscan Order*, introduction and translation by Dominic Monti (St. Bonaventure: Franciscan Institute, 1994), 86, footnotes 17–18.
55. On the Franciscan interest in painted images and prayer within the Gothic environment of France, see George Duby, *Art and Society in the Middle Ages*, translated by Jean Birrell (Malden: Polity Press, 2000), 57–59.
56. Dolciami, "Francesco d'Assisi," 23.
57. Dieter Blume, *Wandmalerei als Ordenspropoganda: Bildprogramme im Chorbereich Franziskanischer Konvente Italiens bis zum Mitte des 14. Jahrhunderts* (Worms: Werner'sche, 1983), 100–01.

buried in the Lower Basilica in Assisi as early as the spring of 1230.[58] This *Legend for Use in the Choir*, compiled from Celano's earlier *Life of Saint Francis*, presented a truncated narrative permeated by the singular image of the saint as thaumaturgist.[59] The genesis of *The Legend for Use in the Choir* lies in the Romanesque sepulcher church of the Lower Basilica and the veneration of the saint's remains. The emphasis on cryptal tomb and miracles, indicative of Romanesque production of space, is presaged in an account of what took place at the Church of Saint George, where Francis was initially laid to rest in 1228:

> On the very day that he was buried, Francis scattered signs dazzling as lightning. He restored to her regular height a young girl whose body had been bent and twisted. Thereafter, he poured out everywhere the grace of health on those who were afflicted by grave illness, but especially on those who came to his memorial shrine.[60]

The miracle thematic of *The Legend for Use in the Choir* is mirrored in the first phase of the artistic representation of space promoted by the Minorite community. Early panel paintings of Francis from San Minato (1228), Pescia (1235), and Pisa (1240) illustrate the thaumaturgies consonant with the efficacious intercessory power of the newly proclaimed saint.[61] Undertaken immediately after the canonization in 1228 and intended for choir use during Octave of the Feast of Saint Francis, this liturgical medium appears to be unique to the Franciscans and limited to the thirteenth century.[62]

---

58. Johnson, "Lost in Space," 127.
59. Johnson, "Lost in Space," 125–31.
60. LCh 15 (I, 324). This miracle is represented already in the Pescia panel painting of Bonaventura Berlingheri from 1235; see Eamon Duffy, "Finding Saint Francis: Early Images, Early Lives," in *Medieval Theology and the Natural Body*, edited by Peter Biller and A. J. Minnis (Suffolk: York Medieval Press, 1997), 207. On this miracle in the latter Bardi dossal in the Minorite church of Santa Croce in Florence, see Chiara Frugoni, *Francescao un'altra storia* (Genova: Casa Editrice Marietti, 1988), 31–32.
61. Klaus Krüger, "Un santo da guardare: l'immagine di san Francesco nelle tavole del Duecento," in *Francesco d'Assisi el il primo secolo di storia francescana*, edited by Attilio Langeli and Emanuela Prinzivalli (Torino: Giulio Einaudi, 1997), 152–53. See also Blume, *Wandmalerei als Ordenspropoganda*, 107.
62. Krüger, "Un santo da guardare," 145 and 158.

The second phase of panel paintings in Florence and Pistoia (1250–1255) evidence a shift away from earlier, frequently posthumous miracle accounts toward a selected, biographical narrative. Two stories from these narratives, already present in panel depictions of the Poverello, emerge as well in frescoes of Franciscan choirs: the sermon to the birds and the stigmata.[63] Both images of Francis became emblematic of the Minorite ideals of preaching the gospel throughout creation and the compassionate union with Christ. An example, dating to around 1250, is found in the choir of San Fermo Maggiore in Verona.[64] The construction of large churches throughout the urban centers of Europe assured the propagation of these frescoed choir images and the eventual demise of the smaller, often antiquated panel paintings.[65]

As the visual images of Francis were transformed from canonized miracle worker to exemplar of religious holiness during the massive construction which Dieter Blume terms the "Bauboom" between 1240–1260,[66] the Minorite production of space, especially in the choir areas of urban churches, is marked, not by the Romanesque style of the Lower Basilica of Saint Francis, but by the Gothic architecture of the Upper Basilica. While the Order's architecture and art conformed to clearly articulated representation of space, *The Legend for Use in the Choir* remained the standard, if not universally utilized, hagiographical-liturgical *legenda* for the Feast of Saint Francis. The brothers chose, however, not to embrace Celano's *legenda* with the conviction evident in the architectural and artistic aspects proper to the emergent Franciscan production of space.[67] This is not surprising since *The Legend for Use in the Choir* presupposed and articulated a markedly dissimilar representation of space than the predominant Gothic choirs of the Franciscans. Another Minorite, Julian of Speyer, composed a popular rhythmic *Divine Office of Saint Francis* in the period of 1232–1235 apparently

63. Krüger, "Un santo da guardare," 152–57.
64. Blume, *Wandmalerei als Ordenspropoganda*, 10–13.
65. Blume, *Wandmalerei als Ordenspropoganda*, 20–21, 107, and Krüger, "Un santo da guardare," 157–61.
66. Blume, *Wandmalerei als Ordenspropoganda*, 9.
67. It should be noted that there was not universal acceptance of the burgeoning Franciscan production of space. Echoes of disapproval and resistance, perhaps from around 1240, are heard from a textual community linked to the earlier representational space of Francis; see AC 106 (II, 212).

without, however, a concomitant *legenda* for Matins.[68] *The Umbrian Choir Legend*, dated later between 1255–1259, focuses on the stigmata while retaining regional characteristics such as references to Brother Elias, and a list of miracles beginning with the healing of the crippled girl at the provisional burial site of Saint George.[69] Numerous other choir legends circulated, both inside and outside the Order, before the appearance of the definitive *legenda*, Bonaventure's *The Minor Life of Saint Francis*.[70]

The Spatial Theology of the Minor Life

The presumed presentation of Bonaventure's choir *legenda* at the General Chapter of Pisa in 1263, and subsequent universal diffusion within the Minorite community,[71] raises the complex issue of the motivation and intent behind this liturgical work. While the diversity of liturgical texts indicates there was no requisite choir *legenda* among the brothers there is, likewise, no convincing, textual evidence as to why they envisioned the composition of the *Minor Life of Saint Francis*.[72] Scholars, however, marginalize this unique

---

68. On the composition and dating of Julian's work, see Fernando Uribe, *Introducción a las hagiografías de San Francisco y Santa Clara de Asís* (Murcia: Editorial Espigas, 1999), 133–42. See also *Introduction*, FA:ED I, 312–15. For Julian's text, see FA:ED I, 327–45. Concerning the possibility that Julian also composed a *legenda ad usum chori* for Matins, see Théophile Debonnets, "La diffusion du culte de saint François en France d'apres les breviaries manuscripts étrangers à l"Orde," *Archivum Franciscanum Historicum* 75 (1982): 169–74. The *legenda* text Debonnets offers is intriguing from a number of perspectives, not the least being that it contains no reference to the canonization, the provisionary burial of Francis at Saint George, or the translation of his remains to the Lower Basilica in Assisi. The last lesson refers to the stigmata.

69. *Introduction*, FA:ED II, 471–72. For the anonymous text, see FA:ED II, 473–82.

70. Dolciami, "Francesco d'Assisi," 25–26, and Johnson, "Lost in Sacred Space," 121–23. Théophile Debonnets' study of the French breviary manuscript tradition demonstrates the diversity of *legenda* material used during the Feast of Saint Francis even after the introduction of *The Minor Life*; see Debonnets, "La diffusion du culte de saint François," 153–215.

71. On the question of Bonaventure's "mandate" to write a new hagiographical account of Francis and the various interpretation of the subsequent texts, see Jacques Dalarun, *La Malavventura di Francesco d'Assisi* (Milano: Edizioni Biblioteca Francescana; 1996), 160–75. English translation, *The Misadventure of Francis of Assisi: Towards a Historical Use of the Franciscan Legends*, translated by Edward Hagman (St. Bonaventure, NY: Franciscan Institute, 2002).

72. Dolciami, "Francesco d'Assisi," 25–29. The silence of sources referring to *The Minor Life of Saint Francis* leads Jacques Cambell to suggest that the liturgical *legenda*

hagiographical-liturgical *legenda* if they attempt to reduce it to an unimaginative, abbreviated version of the *Major Life of Saint Francis*.[73] Equating *The Minor Life of Saint Francis*, implicitly or explicitly, with the understanding of Bonaventure's hagiographical efforts as merely the means to diminish divisions and eliminate dissent, fosters a problematic metanarrative, which obscures the exceptional spatial theology of *The Minor Life of Saint Francis*.[74] A consideration of the Franciscan production of space, evident in the choir areas dedicated to fraternal prayer and illustrated with images of the Poverello, suggests Bonaventure composed his choral *legenda*, not to simply reduce tensions concerning issues like poverty and ministry, but to foster the liturgical remembrance of Francis in conformity with the prevailing Gothic architecture and spirituality of the urban churches.

Bonaventure entered the Minorites in Paris in 1242 or 1243 when, through the efforts of Haymo of Faversham and others, the clerical constitution of the Order was already firmly entrenched.[75] This thriving city on the Seine, where he had first come to study with the Faculty of Arts in 1235, remained his religious, academic, and legislative point of reference until his death in 1274. His Parisian liturgical life, like that of his confreres, centered on the choir of the Minorite church of Ste.-Madeleine. The Lesser Brothers arrived in Francis in 1217 and lived until 1230 near the city tower adjacent to Saint-Denis. As early as 1236 they began the construction of the church named after the Magdalene, and Alexander of Hales moved his chair of theology there in 1245. At the time of the blessing in 1262, Ste.-Madeleine measured over ninety meters long, with the

---

was written after the favorable reception of Bonaventure's *Major Life of Saint Francis*. This would put the composition of the *Minor Life* after the Paris Chapter of 1266 and before Bonaventure's departure from Paris before the winter of 1268; see Jacques Cambell, "Une tentative de résoudre la question franciscaine," *Miscellanea Francescana* 69 (1962): 203. Another hypothesis places *The Minor Life* before *The Major Life*. Bonaventure may have been requested to compose a liturgical *legenda* when elected Minister General in 1257. On this question, see Dolciami, "Francesco d'Assisi," 26–29, especially 28, footnote 88.

73. For an overview of *The Minor Life of Saint Francis* with reference to the wide diffusion of this text, see Uribe, *Introducción a las hagiografías*, 259-61.

74. For an initial attempt to develop the spatial theology of *The Minor Life of Saint Francis*, see Introduction, FA:ED II, 502-03.

75. Luigi Pellegrini, *Introduzione, Opusculi Francescani/1* in *Opere di San Bonaventure* (Roma: Città Nuova Editrice, 1993), 11.

majority of the space dedicated to the choir area. In appearance and
function, Bonaventure's church seemed like two different churches,
one for the laity and the other for the brothers. The variegated
Gothic influence, prevalent throughout the city, was evident in
certain aspects of Ste.-Madeleine.[76]

Bonaventure's celebration of Matins during the Octave of the
Feast of Saint Francis in Ste.-Madeleine, together with other liturgical experiences throughout the Paris environs and in numerous
Minorite churches during his travels as Minister General, may be
mirrored in the structure and content of *The Minor Life of Saint
Francis*. While it is impossible to delineate what Lefebvre might
refer to as Bonaventure's representational space, the theological
elements of Gothic architecture, such as light and order,[77] are
certainly concomitant aspects of the Franciscan representation of
space. They appear, in contradistinction to *The Major Life of Saint
Francis*, at the outset of *The Minor Life*:

> The grace of God, our Savior, has appeared in these last days
> in his servant Francis. The Father of mercy and light came to
> his assistance with such an abundance of blessings of sweet-
> ness that, as it clearly appears in the course of Francis's life,
> God not only led him out from the darkness of this world
> into the light, but also made him renowned for his merits
> and the excellence of his virtues. He also showed that he was
> notably illustrious for the remarkable mysteries of the cross
> displayed in him.[78]

---

76. Schenkluhn, *Architektur der Bettelorden*, 71–72, and Wolfgang Schenkluhn, *Ordines
studentes: Aspekte zur Kirchen architektur d. Dominnnikaner u. Franziskaner im 13. Jh.*
(Berlin: Gebr. Mann Verlag, 1985), 76–84, especially 83. Schenkluhn states
Ste-Madeleine shared few aspects common to High Gothic cathedral designs.
While the church was not constructed in High Gothic, Schenkluhn does leave
open the possibility that the choir area was of such design. Corrado Bozzoni
maintains that, in general, the mendicants in the area of Paris where more open to
the influence of High Gothic; see Corrado Bozzoni, "L'edilizia mendicante in
Europa" in *Lo spazio dell'umiltà*, 291. On the development of Gothic architecture in
Paris, see *L'abbé Suger, le manifeste gothique de Saint-Denis et la pensée victorine*, edited
by Dominique Poirel (Turnhout: Brepols, 2001), especially Patrice Sicard,
"L'urbanisme de la Cité de Dieu: constructions et architectures dans la pensée
théologique du XIIe siècled," 109–40.
77. Sheldrake, *Spaces for the Sacred*, 53.
78. LMn 1.1 (II, 684).

The pronounced emphasis on light, and the visual dynamic of perception, is notably absent from the prologue of *The Major Life*. These initial lines of *The Minor Life of Saint Francis* are already ample reason to view this finely crafted hagiographical-liturgical *legenda* as far more than an abbreviated version of *The Major Life*. Bonaventure's predilection for light as the preferred metaphor for grace, especially in the context of prayer, is evident throughout his writings.[79] The light of grace illuminates, reforms, refreshes, and enlivens as it descends from the Father of Lights and leads those who pray upward to the fontal source.[80] Light, understood as grace, conforms and orders those who pray to Christ through the virtues so prominent in *The Minor Life*.[81]

The thematic of light is particularly applicable to Matins for the Octave of Saint Francis since this ancient form of vigil begins in the darkness of night, yet awaits the promised light of dawn.[82] Bonaventure begins, therefore, *The Minor Life* with theological imagery corresponding to the highly suggestive, descending-ascending ordered lines of Gothic choir architecture, emphasizing and contrasting both the darkness and light of the choir and of the journey into God. The darkness and light appear most intensely, paradoxically together, in the fifth chapter within a travel narrative;[83] they provide a compelling theological link, not found in *The Major Life*, to the sixth chapter on the stigmata where Francis, the

---

79. Timothy J. Johnson, *The Soul in Ascent: Bonaventure on Poverty, Prayer, and Union with God* (Quincy, IL: Franciscan Press, 2000), 81–84.

80. The scriptural reference is to James 1:17, one of the most frequently quoted biblical texts in Bonaventure's works. For Bonaventure's theological use of the light theme with reference to the *reductio*, see *On the Reduction of the Arts to Theology*, edited by Zachary Hayes in *Works of Saint Bonaventure*, vol. 1 (St. Bonaventure: Franciscan Institute, 1996).

81. The virtues are emphasized in LMn 3.1–9, 6.9, 7.9 (II, 694–98, 712, 717 respectively). The Christological dimensions of the virtues appear as early as Bonaventure's Parisian *Commentary on the Sentences*; see *III Sent*, d. 34. p. 1. a. 1, q. 1, concl. (III, 737a). The numeric pattern of their appearance in the *Minor Life* underscores the *reductio* dynamic of the choir text and architecture.

82. The thematic of light and darkness in the monastic Divine Office is treated in Cassidy-Welch, *Monastic Spaces*, 96–100. On Matins in the medieval period, see John Harper, *The Forms and Orders of Western Liturgy from the Tenth to the Eighteenth Century: A Historical Introduction and Guide for Students and Musicians* (Oxford: Claredon Press, 1991), 86–97. In regard to the Octave of Saint Francis, see Dolciami, "Francesco d'Assisi," 39–44.

83. LMn 5.9 (II, 707–08). On the apparent paradox of light and darkness in Bonaventure's theology of prayer, see Johnson, *The Soul in Ascent*, 167–68.

apocalyptic angel of the sixth seal,[84] is lifted up into God and transformed by compassion into the image of the Crucified.[85]

The seventh chapter of *The Minor Life* continues the descending-
ascending theme with Francis's return down from Mount LaVerna
to evangelize anew with the greatest degree of charity.[86] This
descent from the mountain into ministry is simultaneously an
ascent, as divine and human loves are inextricably melded in the
stigmatized flesh of the Poor Man. Just as he is continually lifted up
by the fire of love, Francis longs to be brought down to his humble
origins. The themes of preaching and compassion, integral aspects
of the Minorite production of space through the medium of choir
frescoes, are proclaimed in the seventh chapter, on the seventh day
of the Octave of Saint Francis. This seventh day is not the final day
for the cycle of Matins includes the eighth day, when the *legenda*
readings from the first day are repeated. This day, according to
Bonaventure's *Collations on the Six Days*, brings body and soul back
to the beginning, transformed, however, by the passage.[87] As the
desired dawn draws nearer, *The Minor Life of Saint Francis* returns the
brothers on the last day of the Octave into darkness from which the
Poverello emerged, with the enduring promise of the divine light
that descends from above.

Conclusion

Although *The Minor Life of Saint Francis* became the canonical choir
legenda for the Minorites, it was marginalized due to the histori-
cal-critical significance accorded Bonaventure's *The Major Life of
Saint Francis* within the complex debate referred to simply as "The
Franciscan Question." Examination of *The Minor Life* against the
background Lefebvre's interpretative appreciation of space underlines the need for renewed research into this unique, albeit ignored
text. Admittedly heuristic, this hermeneutic suggests Bonaventure
composed his liturgical *legenda* because *The Legend for Use in the*

---

84. LMn 7.1 (II, 714, footnote b).
85. LMn 6.2 (II, 709–10).
86. LMn 7.1 (II, 714). On the relationship between the ascent-descent theme in
    Bonaventure's theology and contemplative love, see LMn 7.1 (II, 714, footnote a).
87. *Hex* 3.31 (V, 348b).

Choir, and other similar legends, were no longer considered appropriate for liturgical use of urban Minorites. *The Minor Life* emerges as a choir *legenda* better suited to the didactic-contemplative requirements of the Order, given the Franciscan production of space throughout Europe. If Lefebvre is correct in suggesting that spatial practice may precede texts, attempts to relegate *The Minor Life* to the margins as inconsequential, truncated version of *The Major Life of Saint Francis* suggest if not demonstrate, a hermeneutical preference linked to the prevailing metanarrative of ideology and control intimated by Lefebvre's critique of the inordinate emphasis given to texts over and against space.

Speculum: Form and Function in the *Mirror of Perfection*

Daniel T. Michaels

The *Mirror of Perfection* or *Speculum Perfectionis* (hereafter 2MP),[1] compiled in the early fourteenth century (1318), brings forward a number of the earlier thirteenth century sources that speak of Francis and the Lesser Brothers. The 2MP sorts these earlier texts into a compilation divided into twelve major divisions, comprised in total of 124 pericopes, including editorial glosses. Selections of the *Assisi Compilation* (1244–1260) and the *Remembrance of the Desire of a Soul* (1245–1247) are the principal texts from which the 2MP compilation draws. With the exception of the glosses, the unknown redactor of the 2MP took the early stories of Francis, told from the perspective of "those who where with him,"[2] and compiled them thematically under the title *"Speculum."*

This study evaluates the form and function of the 2MP as a text insofar as it was shaped by the medieval genre of mirror

---

1. This study is based on the critical edition originally prepared by Paul Sabatier: *Speculum (Le) Perfectionis ou Mémoires de frère Léon sur la seconde partue de la vie de Saint François d'Assise*, edited by Paul Sabatier and Andrew George Little (Mancester: British Society of Franciscan Studies 13, 1928), 1-350; and reprinted in *Fontes Franciscani*, edited by Enrico Menestò, et al. (S. Maria degli Angeli-Assisi: Edizioni Porziuncola, 1995), 1849-2053. In FA:ED III, 207-372, the Sabatier text is abbreviated 2MP, while the Lemmons edition, once thought to be earlier, is abbreviated 1MP.
2. *Nos qui cum eo fuimus* (we who were with him), repeated throughout the 2MP, captures the importance of eyewitness testimony claimed by the authors. See Raoul Manselli, *Nos qui cum eo fuimus* (Rome: Library of the Capuchin Historical Institute, 1980).

(speculum).[3] The word *"Speculum"* in the title places it within a monumental tradition of texts.[4] In fact, as described below, the title *"Speculum"* and its protocol fills a significant number of manuscripts collections within the Franciscan tradition alone. The symbolic continuity of the 2MP within the corpus of Franciscan texts is lost, or at least incomplete, without a proper understanding of the popular and influential medieval genre of the mirror. Ultimately, I argue that the significance of the form of the 2MP as a medieval *"Speculum"* has been overlooked. This has created some of the confusion among modern exegetes regarding its chronological and theological place among the early sources. Furthermore, this simple oversight has veiled the full function of this text.

While the volume of medieval mirror texts is too massive to summarize in detail here, it is nevertheless possible to quickly identify three dominant categories of mirror texts that significantly contribute to a more comprehensive interpretation of the 2MP: 1) mirror texts that are formed by selections from scripture, 2) mirror texts that focus on virtue, and 3) mirror texts that are primarily compilations or encyclopedic texts. These three groups of texts share a lineage of function, following a protocol of mirror conventions. Each mirror text, while distinct, develops and applies the metaphor of mirror in a consistent manner. The *Mirror of Perfection*

3. This study shifts attention from the more usual preoccupation of date and position within the corpus of sources for the life of Francis (source criticism) to the less explored literal and symbolic form of the text itself (form criticism). Since its discovery by Paul Sabatier in 1898 until recently, the 2MP fueled the debate over the primacy and authenticity of early Franciscan sources (hagiography, legends, compilations, etc.). Commonly referred to as the *"question franciscaine"* or "Franciscan question," the debate over chronology of texts has been for the most part solved. See Daniele Solvi, "Lo 'Speculum Perfectionis' et le sue Fonti," *Archivum Franciscanum Historicum* 88 (1995): 377–472.
4. Due to the abundance of mirror literature it is necessary to limit discussion to the form and function of texts entitled mirror (*speculum*). For more information on the function of texts entitled "mirror" see Rita Mary Bradley, "Background of the Title *Speculum* in Medieval Literature," *Speculum* 29 (1954):100–15. For the development of the mirror metaphor in spiritual literature see Margot Schmidt, "Miroir" in *Dictionnaire de Spiritualité Ascétique et Mystique: Doctrine et Histoire*, vol. 10 (Paris: Beauchesne, 1980), 1290–1303. For a partial index of medieval Latin mirror texts see the appendix of Herbert Grabes, *Speculum, Mirror and Looking Glass. Kontinuität und Originalität der Spiegelmetapher in den Buchtiteln des Mittelalters und der englischen Literatur des 13. bis 17. Jahrhunderts* (Tübingen: Grabes, 1973), 246–351.

is no exception and, as such, will be analyzed in light of the development of this tradition.

Mirrors of the Scriptures

The medieval mirror tradition, as received in the West, was initially formed upon Augustine's use of the term, particularly as it referred to the scriptures. First Corinthians 13:12 (*For now we see in a mirror dimly, but then we will see face to face*) captures Augustine's understanding of "mirror" as a statement concerning the nature of human understanding. According to Augustine, the experience of knowing God in part, or having "just a tantalizing reflection in a mirror" of God, inspires the "longing for a greater certainty"[5] toward complete knowledge of God. The full significance of the ascent is not realized until after death in an encounter with God *face to face*. Until then, however, God gave humanity the sacred Word to have some understanding of God's Truth through enigmas. Humanity thus gazes into the mirror of scripture to know of its state and aspire toward perfect knowledge in God.

Augustine's mirror imagery has a twofold function: "in its resplendence it shows you what you will be, that is, pure of heart; and it shows you what you are, that you may confess your deformity and begin to adorn yourself."[6] The form of the mirror, which for Augustine is to be found in scripture, reveals the course of salvation history, thereby showing who we are: past, present, and future.

The metaphor of mirror so aptly captured Augustine's attempt to unite the Word with the development of the soul, that, near the end of his life (ca. 427), he compiled a collection of Old and New Testament precepts in one work entitled *Speculum*.[7]

[The *Speculum* was] an aid to all, whether or not they were capable of reading many books, [Augustine] extracted the divine precepts and prohibitions from the two inspired Testaments, the Old and the New. He wrote a preface for

5. Augustine of Hippo, *Confessiones* 8.1, *Corpus Christianorium, series latina* 27, 113/10. English translation, *The Confessions*, translated by Maria Boulding (Hyde Park, NY: New City Press, 1997), 184.
6. Bradley, "Backgrounds of the Title *Speculum*," 103.
7. Augustine of Hippo, *Speculum Scriptorum, Patrologia Latina* 34, 887–1040.

the collection and made it into a single book so that those who wished might read it and see to what extent they were obedient or disobedient to God. This work he wished to be known as Mirror (*Vita* 28.3).[8]

In short, for Augustine the form of the mirror is the scriptures, and the function is a twofold recognition of who you are, and who you should be. That is, first scripture demonstrates the relationship between creation and revelation, showing "who you are" with respect to God. Secondly, as humanity discerns their state through such enigmas, they are inspired to move closer to a pure reflection of God, that is, to become "who you should be." This dialectic between revelation and moral ascent continues to influence the form of mirror texts and metaphors throughout medieval literature.

Mirrors for Formation (Exemplary Texts)

Margot Schmidt identifies two major categories of medieval mirror texts that emerge in the wake of Augustine's moral model in the form of the scriptures: 1) exemplary mirrors and, 2) instructive mirrors.[9] Like Augustine's *Speculum* these texts function to show "who you are" — instructive, and "who you should be" — exemplary, thus serving as two models of formation. These two models center on moral development so that the reader may discover in them the depth of their own personal weakness and find in them a measure of their progress. Moving beyond Augustine, however,

---

8. Possidius, *Vita Sancti Aurelii Augustini* 28.3, *Patrologia Latina* 32, 57, col. 788bc. See Allen D. Fitzgerald, "Speculum," in *Augustine Through the Ages: An Encyclopedia* (Grand Rapids: William B. Eerdmans Publishing Company, 1999), 812. Interestingly, as described by Fitzgerald, the passages that Augustine includes in his *Speculum,* some of which are not elsewhere, "are severe calls to order . . . identifying the deterioration of society in North Africa by the invasion of the Vandals." Thus, Augustine offers the first "mirror," or *speculum* text in the West to be used as the locus of moral reform.
9. Schmidt, "Miroir," 1292. Among the instructive spiritual literature there is, for example, the *Speculum Ecclesiae* (1160–70) of Hugh of St. Victor, and *Speculum Universale* (1200) of Raoul Ardent. Among the major works in the exemplary spiritual literature, leading to moral purification, there is, for example, the *Speculum Fidei* (1148) of William of St. Thierry, *Speculum Caritatis* (1166) of Aelred of Rievaulx (1143), and the *Speculum Virginum* (ca. 1140, author unknown).

these mirror texts reflect the scriptures through the intercession of saints, rules of life, and treatises on virtue. No longer did the medievals directly and solely access the moral lessons of scripture, but they engaged the scriptures in light of an influential person or way of life. The saint, rule, or virtuous program, functioning as either instructive or exemplary, thus became the way to realize the fullness of scripture. The exemplary form in particular came to dominate much of the medieval mirror genre.

Bernard of Clairvaux (1091–1153), for example, was one of the first to develop the idea of this formational mirror. According to Bernard, "The examples of holy men, and the testimony of the scriptures are also called mirrors, and men are enjoined to meditate on these writings, where all things shine forth as in a mirror."[10] The popularity of the mirror text as revealing the actual life of a saint(s) never enjoyed great popularity. In fact, even mirror texts with the name of a saint in the title seldom, if ever, presented the actual life of the saint. Instead, consistent with Bernard's idea of moral lessons from holy lives, these mirror texts focused on the virtuous acts exemplified in the saint identified in the title (e.g., *Speculum beatae Mariae Virginis,* 1279). These texts belong to a massive collection of mirror texts that promote examples taken from the lives of the saints.[11]

Hugh of St. Victor (1100–1041) in his *Commentary on the Rule of Augustine* made this exemplary connection between virtue and scripture more explicit by literally identifying "ethical writings," or "rules" of saints as mirrors:

> This little book may be called a mirror. In it we are able to examine our condition, whether it is beautiful or ugly, that is to say, whether it is just or unjust. . . . For scripture shows us a likeness of our interior, making known what is beautiful and what is deformed within the soul . . . [It indicates] how we may adorn ourselves with the glory of virtues, and how we may cleanse away every stain of sin.[12]

---

10. Bernard of Clairvaux, *Instructio Sacerdotis* 2.11, *Patrologia Latina* 184, 788bc as cited in Bradley, "Background," 111.
11. Schmidt, "Miroir," 1293–95.
12. Hugh of St. Victor, *Expositio in regulam beati Augustini, Patrologia Latina* 176: 924a.

Hugh's commentary on Augustine's Rule is particularly noteworthy because, not unlike 2MP, he uses the mirror to underscore a rule or way of life (*Expositio in regulam beati Augustini*), which, in turn, serves the function of purification through virtue. His intention was ultimately to lead his readers back to the purity of scripture. Hugh emphasizes the moral dimension of the mirror by appealing to James 1:25, in which the *perfect law of liberty* stands as the model for one who is not a *forgetful hearer,* but a *doer of the work.* Hugh's text reveals a dialectic between rule and virtue and the evangelical way which, as explained below, comes to dominate the 2MP.[13]

By the thirteenth century, and particularly by the fourteenth century, exemplary mirror texts were widely distributed, even among Franciscan collections. In fact, among thirteenth century Franciscan manuscripts, particularly those by or attributed to Bonaventure, there are more than twenty collections entitled "*Speculum.*"[14]

These mirror texts, all contemporaries of the 2MP, were almost exclusively devoted to the formation of virtue. They followed the Victorine mirror tradition of presenting a moral code to be followed (mirrored) by the reader, with the intention of again echoing, "who you are," and "who you should be." Among these, a classic example of the exemplary mirror is Bernard of Besse's *Speculum disciplinae* (1300–1304), which was intended as an instruction manual for novices and organized around the principal virtues of Francis (poverty, humility, obedience, charity, etc.) as expressed in various duties of a brother. This manual identifies the same virtues that dominate the collection of stories concerning the companions of Francis in the *Mirror of Perfection.*

Mirror Texts as Encyclopedic and Instructive Manuals

Medieval mirror texts since their beginnings in the early church always guide readers to scripture — even if, as described above, the

---

13. Hugh's *Rule Commentary* also eloquently incorporates mirror imagery from Augustine's Psalm commentaries and Augustine's *Speculum.*
14. For a partial listing of works, most of which are spuriously attributed to Bonaventure, see the Appendix at the end of this article. For a more detailed listing of these manuscripts see Balduinus Distelbrink, *Bonaventureae Scripta: Authentica Dubia Vel Spuria Critice Recensita* (Rome: Istituto Storico Cappuccini, 1975).

path is through a saint or virtuous way. This model is rooted in the medieval connection between the Word and Creation. The fullness of creation, or the Book of Creation, is revealed in the Book of Scripture. This is quintessentially Augustine's concept of the mirror of scripture as revealing who we are and who we should be. The end result of this is that humanity must utilize all of creation, not just saints, as a guide toward understanding personal deformity and subsequently making progress in salvation. Thus, not only do the saint and instructional rule texts serve as models toward understanding scripture, but every facet of creation, particularly the sciences of history and theology become important "instruction" on the road toward salvation. As a result, there was an increased popularity in encyclopedic texts entitled *Speculum* in the Middle Ages.

The *Speculum* of Vincent of Beuvais (four volumes compiled from 1244 to 1254) was perhaps one of the greatest encyclopedic instructive mirror texts. The *Speculum* was an encyclopedia of all the sciences — natural science, theology and history. The historical part of it, *Speculum Historiale,* is a history of the world told through extracts from a vast number of recognized authorities (similar to Lombard's *Sentences*), including brief commentary, inserted where necessary, to link the passages together. The work served as a database for later compilers, saving them the trouble of consulting the originals. What makes this and other encyclopedic/compilation mirror texts unique from other compilations are their sensitivity to progress. If understood properly the reader should find a development of perfection and harmony in the many different branches of history, art and science. In fact, the historical account of the world itself becomes the model for moral growth. History instructs the readers as to "who they are" (past and present) so that they might progress to the next level of salvation, "who they should be."

In total, mirror texts (exemplary and instructive) reflected all of the various levels of order: mirror of scripture (divine), mirror of saints (heavenly), and mirrors of saintly texts (human). Augustine first identified the model of mirror in scripture, and from this there was a prompting to explore the nature of creation to further unlock the mystery of scripture. It is no small wonder that in successive generations after Augustine the reflection of God became more clearly articulated, from scripture to creation and creation to scripture. In retrospect, it is evident that each of the forms of mirror texts supported the double function of revealing one's identity and leading one to purity of life: "who you are," and "who you should be."

The Mirror Genre and the Mirror of Perfection

The above overview of the protocol for the formation of medieval *speculum* texts makes it possible to make some very specific observations about the particular form of the 2MP. The most obvious is that the redactor of the 2MP chose the very popular organizational scheme of "*speculum.*" As Duncan Nimmo suggests, "the merit of the author of the *Speculum* was to take this material (*Assisi Compilation* and *Remembrance for the Desire of a Soul*) and completely re-organize it, according to a literary plan of his own. Moreover, the plan he chose was a familiar and popular one in medieval devotional literature, that precisely of the 'mirror' reflecting virtues to be followed by the reader."[15] As such, the compiler of the 2MP follows the exemplary program of forming a moral way of life. However, the 2MP is shaped by much more than a moral code.

Four dominant forms highlight the architecture of the *Mirror of Perfection*: 1) authority of testimony, 2) *Rule,* 3) virtue, and 4) compilation. In other words, the 2MP borrows from the vocabulary of the mirror tradition in four ways: 1) scripture and testimony of the companions, 2) exemplary *Rule,* 3) exemplary virtue, and 4) instructive compilation. Thus, 2MP weaves together these four major elements of mirror form.

Divine Revelation and Scripture

The *Mirror of Perfection* is guided by an overarching thematic of authority supported by the arrangement of very specific stories of Francis told from the perspective of "those who were with him."[16] These stories recount the testimony of the *rotuli,* or scrolls, now

---

15. See Duncan Nimmo, *Reform and Division in the Medieval Franciscan Order* (Rome: Capuchin Historical Institute, 1995), 323; also see Sophronius Clasen, *Legenda Antiqua S. Francisci* (Leiden: Brill, 1967), 324–29.
16. See Raoul Manselli, *Nos qui cum eo fuimus* (Rome: Library of the Capuchin Historical Institute, 1980).

believed to be partly collected in manuscript 1046 of Perugia (*Assisi Compilation*). Portions of these so-called *rotuli* provided substantial quotations for what Ubertino de Casale declared to be the written work of brother Leo.[17] The provocative possibility of Leo's first generation testimony led Ubertino in 1305 to search for the *rotuli,* declaring that, "these rolls have been dispersed, and perhaps lost." However, he believed that a copy of them was kept "in the cupboard of the brothers at Assisi."[18] Shortly after this discovery in 1311, the *Mirror of Perfection* (1318) was orchestrated as a compilation of texts — based on the *Assisi Compilation* — that is now known to contain the same such *rotuli.*

Turning to these early sources takes the reader not only to the first generation followers of Francis but points to Francis and finally to Christ and scripture through revelation. Only scripture and divine revelation can provide the perfect model for purification. In fact, the 2MP invokes the name of the Lord (God, Christ, etc.) more than five hundred times throughout the text. Sixty percent of these references are used to verify the primary virtues of Francis (chapters 1–3). Many of these sources are direct revelations from God: "God has placed in my mouth" (no. 3), "The Lord has called us . . . " (no. 10), "The Lord revealed to him" (no. 19), "the Holy Spirit will inspire them . . . " (no. 22), "Therefore, the Lord willed and revealed to him" (no. 26), etc.

Virtue

"Pure observance of the Gospel,"[19] becomes the battle cry for Francis and his brothers as they progress in the perfection of virtue. The compiler of the 2MP clearly organized the text to exemplify virtue. Unlike its parent texts (*Assisi Compilation* and *Remembrance for the Desire of a Soul*), the 2MP is completely and solely a thematic

17. Leo's testimony as recorded by Ubertino in the *Arbor Vitae Crucifixae* (1305) comes from what is known as the *Intentio Regulae* (intention of the Rule) and forms the first numbers of the first chapter of the 2MP (2, 3, 4, 11, also 72–73). Both Ubertino and the 2MP quote the *Intentio* as fundamental for understanding poverty.
18. Ubertino reported the *rotuli* lost in 1305, but by 1311 (roughly 7 years before the 2MP) he had some of them in his possession. Heinrich Denifle and Franz Ehrle, *Archiv für Literatur und Kirchengeschichte des Mittelalters,* III (Berlin/Freiburg, 1885–1900), 168.
19. See for example, 2MP 70 (III, 315): *in pura observantia evangelii*

compilation, divided according to the central virtues of Francis. The largest portion of the *Speculum Perfectionis* (numbers 2–75, chapters 1–3) addresses the virtues of charity, poverty, humility and obedience as they are contained in and expressed in the *Rule* of Saint Francis (76–84, chapter 4). At the heart of the text is a reflection on the suffering of Christ and Francis (91–93, chapter 6), surrounded by stories demonstrating specific virtues that characterize the Lesser Brothers (prayer, joy, virtuous deeds, etc., 85–91, chapter 5, and 94–97, chapter 7). Finally, the divine nature of Francis as perfect exemplar of virtue and holiness, even to lordship over all creation, is expressed by his continual prophesies, even unto his death (98–124, chapters 8–12).

The virtues are arranged to help the reader progress from the purifying virtues of Francis, namely, poverty, humility, obedience, and charity, through a reflection on the suffering of Christ, and then subsequently upon the death and glorification of Francis. In other words, a process of conversion is built into the text. Each pericope exemplifies and challenges the Lesser Brothers to embrace the perfect observance of virtue. Ultimately, from this observance the brothers will embrace a way of life that emerges from the text. That way is the evangelical way of Christ as manifest in Francis. Thus, 2MP forms the brothers through virtue that is based on scripture while exemplifying Francis as the virtuous one. As Francis achieves perfection, so too should the brothers imitate his conversion: "the closer he [Francis] approached death, the more careful he became in considering how he might live and die in complete humility and poverty **and in the perfection of every virtue.**"[20]

Rule

The *Rule* of Francis occupies a central theme in the 2MP. In the introduction, discussion about the creation and observance of the *Rule* initiates a sequence of commentary that carries through to the end of the text. Even the division of the 2MP into twelve units mimics the divisions of the *Rule*. It appears that the compiler

---

20. 2MP 46 (III, 292): *quanto magis appropinquabat morti, tanto magis erat sollicitus considerare quomodo in omni humilitate et paupertate et omnium virtutum perfectione posset vivere atque mori.* Bold text indicates new material inserted by 2MP author/editor.

intends to present a corrective to the many papal declarations that in his view have damaged the true calling of the Lesser Brothers. Appealing to a higher authority, it is Christ who says: "Francis, nothing of yours is in the *Rule*: whatever is there is mine. And I want the *Rule* observed in this way: to the letter, to the letter, to the letter, and without a gloss, without a gloss, without a gloss."[21]

The 2MP denounces abuses of clothing, money, the office of prelacy, etc., through multiple references to the *Rule*. In fact, the *Rule* directly and/or indirectly occupies more than half the work. The *Rule* is explicitly discussed in the first major section of the work, which covers twenty-five numbers (2–26). As presented by the compiler, the *Rule* is equivalent to the perfect evangelical life. The *Rule* becomes *the* perfect model of salvation and, as such, no other rule is to be observed.[22]

The significance of the *Rule* is further emphasized through a symbolic application of the church of the Portiuncula. The compiler of 2MP identifies and applies Saint Bonaventure's representation of the Portiuncula as symbolically concluding Francis's conversion and initiating the formation of the Lesser Brothers. The Portiuncula, or "Our Lady of the Angels" symbolizes the Blessed Mother and her conception of Jesus through the Holy Spirit. Like Mary, Francis gives birth to the friars minor. In 2MP there is a stylistic division at the end of chapter 4 (Zeal For Profession of the *Rule* and the Entire Religion) leading into chapter 5 (Zeal for the Perfection of the Brothers). This division is in the form of a long prayer (numbers 83–84) known as the "Portiuncula Prayer," at the end of the four chapters (1–4) laying out the virtues of Francis. Like Bonaventure's *Life of Saint Francis*, the official life of Francis, the church of the Portiuncula in this prayer symbolizes the final stage in the conversion of Francis and, also like Bonaventure's text, initiates the remaining chapters that deal with the "perfection" of the brothers and the formation of their Religion. Furthermore, the completion of Francis's conversion and subsequent "birth" of the order hinges on the relationship between conversion (evangelical perfection) and adherence to the *Rule*. In fact, the *Rule* —

---

21. 2MP 1 (III, 254): *Francisce, nihil est in regula de tuo sed totum est meum quidquid est ibi; et volo quod regula sic servetur ad litteram, ad litteram, ad litteram, sine glosa, sine glosa, sine glosa.*
22. 2MP 68 (III, 314).

inspired by the Spirit and instituted by Christ (2MP, prologue) — provides the framework through which the Religion can be born. And, therefore, the Portiuncula and Mary also come to be associated with the *Rule*.

Compilation

Like other influential compilation mirror texts, the 2MP warrants its authority by gathering writings from primary witnesses — in this case the companions of Francis. This tactic not only imparts a sense of authority as suggested above but it gives the compiler of the 2MP the freedom to re-present the early sources, demonstrating not only what they said but what they would say if they were still present. As a compilation the mirror can literally reflect the broad scope of the tradition ("who you are") while shaping and correcting the spiritual direction of the community ("who you should be").

Conclusion

In light of the mirror tradition, and the inclusion of its various forms, the 2MP shapes a vision of the Lesser Brothers that goes far beyond a mere thematic re-organization of the *Assisi Compilation* and *Remembrance for the Desire of a Soul*. From the perspective of the form and function of the "mirror," the 2MP is a hagiographical master-piece. The 2MP eloquently develops three primary themes (Virtues of Francis, *Rule*, and authority) and in so doing the 2MP calls the Lesser Brothers to re-form with respect to their roots in Francis ("who they are") and their final rest in God ("who they should be"). Thus, the genre of "mirror" provided the perfect vehicle for transmitting the varied collection of sources from which it is composed.

The *Mirror of Perfection*, as it conforms to the context within which every mirror text was formed, eloquently inculturated itself within three types of mirror texts. It should likewise be noted that no mirror text in the history of Christianity initiates a tradition. In other words, a mirror is always a reflection of an already established norm, often arising many years after the formation of a tradition. Augustine's *Speculum* was written during a time of reform and it utilized a body of writing (scripture) that was written centuries prior. Mirrors of saints and mirrors of virtues always follow an earlier established tradition. Encyclopedic or compilation mirrors of the world simply cannot exist without previous history. In short, the *Mirror of Perfection*, like *every* other mirror text, is a calculated reflection upon an established tradition. Had Paul Sabatier understood the mirror genre he would not have drastically misplaced the date of the text, even though he encountered an error in the dating of a manuscript and did not have the benefit of modern research on the *Assisi Compilation*.

Similarly, the moral consistency of all mirror texts as revealing identity and leading to purity (exemplary or instructive) implies that the primary function of the *Mirror of Perfection* is formation, not the establishment of a tradition. Like its textual mirror peers, 2MP is driven by moral development. Therefore, this text, like other mirror texts, is not a life or biography. The function of the text is not to impart the story of the saint, but to nurture the story of the reader. The text itself forms a subjectivity, mirroring the life and development of the reader in dialogue with the life of Francis and the life of the Lesser Brothers. The mirror assumes the facts, theology and authority of the previously written *Life of Saint Francis* by St. Bonaventure. Thus, while the 2MP has an agenda for reform, or formation, it was never intended to supplant Bonaventure's official *Life of Saint Francis*.[23]

Finally, the identification of form in this application of the mirror genre within 2MP lifts the text above and beyond the century old question of textual sources (Franciscan Question). While the taxonomy of Franciscan sources is critical for an understanding of the tradition in general and the 2MP specifically, it is essential to also view this text within the broader Christian tradition. The genre of mirror, as only one of many images, connects the *Mirror of Perfection* to the broad scope of interpreting the scriptures as they continue to reveal, "who we are" and "who we should be."

---

23. Duncan Nimmo suggests in *Reform and Division*, 335–44, that the genre of compilations, aside from any consideration of mirror form, was a tradition that developed as a way to further an understanding of Francis as brothers continued to honor Bonaventure's one official *Life of Saint Francis*. The protocol of mirror texts explains and substantiates this suggestion.

Appendix:
Bonaventure and spurious Bonaventure texts entitled "Speculum"

Speculum amoris (Bonaventure) Mirror of Love (a.k.a. *De triplici via*)

Speculum animae (Bonaventure) Mirror of the Soul (a.k.a. *De triplici via*)

Speculum mentis in Deum (Bonaventure), Mirror of the Mind toward God
(a.k.a. *De triplici via*)

Speculum conscientiae (spuria) Mirror of Conscience

Speculum animae (spuria) Mirror of the Soul (a.k.a. *Speculum conscientiae*)

Speculum disciplinae ad novitios (Bernard of Besse) Mirror of Instruction
for Novices

Speculum disciplinae religiosorum (Bernard of Besse) Mirror of Religious
Instruction (a.k.a. *Speculum disciplinae*)

Speculum sancti Bonaventurae (Bernard of Besse) Mirror of St. Bonaventure
(a.k.a. *Speculum disciplinae*)

Speculum beatae Mariae Virginis (spuria) Mirror of the Blessed Virgin Mary

Speculum concionatorum de doctrina cordis (spuria) Mirror of a Speech
Concerning the Doctrine of the Heart (a.k.a. *De doctrina cordis*)

Speculum munditiae cordis (spuria) Mirror of a Pure Heart
(a.k.a. *De modo confitendi et puritate conscientiae*)

Speculum verae confessionis (spuria) Mirror of True Confession
(a.k.a. *De modo confitendi et puritate conscientiae*)

Speculum conscientiae (spuria) Mirror of Conscience
(a.k.a. *Tractatus de praeparatione ad Missam*)

Speculum evangelici sermonis (spuria) Mirror of an Evangelical Sermon
(a.k.a. *Soliloquium compassionis*)

Speculum Fratrum Minorum (spuria) Mirror of Lesser Brothers

Speculum religiosorum (spuria) Mirror of Religious
(a.k.a. *Ordinarium vitae religiosae*)

Speculum vitae spiritualis (spuria) Mirror of the Spiritual Life

Speculum vitae Christi (spuria) Mirror of the Life of Christ

Index of Names

Abate, Gius: 140
Accrocca, Felice: 19, 182
Adam: 171-73, 177, 219
Adams, Michael: 80
Aelred of Rievaulx: 253
D'Alatri, Mariano: 102
Albert of Pisa: 24
D'Alençon, Edouard: 194
Agnes of Assisi: 61
Agnes of Prague: 180, 188-91, 193
Agnes of Rome: 189
Alberzoni, Maria Pia: 43
Alexander III: 155
Alexander IV: 45
Alexander of Hales: 25, 245
Andrew of Spello: 196
Angelo Clareno: 30-34, 64, 196
Angelo Tancredi of Rieti: 46, 135
Angenendt, Arnold: 235
Anselm of Canterbury: 20, 158
Anthony of Padua: 19
Antony of Egypt: 20, 157
Ardent, Raoul: 253
Armstrong, Regis J.: 9, 13, 18, 40-41, 91, 94, 113-14, 121, 130, 137, 153, 167, 230
Arnald of Sarrant: 64
Aschenbrenner, George A.: 86, 88
van Asseldonk, Optatus: 79, 81, 102, 109
Auerbach, Erich: 211
Augustine of Hippo: 20, 158, 252-57, 261
Aveling, Harry: 102

Baird, Joseph: 30
Bajetto, F.: 151
Barbaglia, L.: 240
Barlow, C. W.: 184
Bartholomew of Pisa: 176
Becker, M.-F.: 188
Beguin, Pierre: 120
Belting, Hans: 234

Benedetto, Luigi Foscolo: 151
Benedict of Nursia: 20, 70, 158
Berger, Peter: 151
Bernadine of Sienna: 29
Bernard of Besse: 255, 263
Bernard of Clairvaux: 32, 158, 254
Bernard of Quintavalle: 26, 196, 236, 238
Bettelheim, Bruno: 217
Bigaroni, Marino: 67, 114, 234-35
Biller, Peter: 224, 242
Binding, Günther: 234
Blasucci, Antonio: 102
Blume, Dieter: 241-43
Boccali, G.: 188, 196
Bonaventure of Bagnoregio: 22-24, 27-30, 36-37, 49, 54-56, 58-59, 65, 74, 77, 105, 115, 131, 143, 151, 166-67, 169, 172-73, 177, 226, 229, 241, 245, 247-48, 255, 262-63
Boniface VIII: 32
Bonsanti, George: 166
Bosnak, Robert: 217
Boulding, Maria: 252
Bovenmars, Jan G.: 75
Boving, Remigius: 229
Bozzoni, Corrado: 246
Bradley, Rita Mary: 32, 251-52, 254
Brady, Ignatius: 87-88, 91, 94
Brooke, Rosalind: 131
Brown, Colin: 85
Brown, Raphael: 143, 151
Brueggemann, Walter: 198
Brufani, Stefano: 194-95, 200, 236
Brunette, Pierre: 115, 173
Buresh, Vitus: 188
Butler, H. E.: 212
Bynum, Caroline Walker: 66, 220, 223, 226

Cadei, Antonio: 239-40
Caesar Augustus: 77

Index of Subjects

133-51, 163, 171, 189-91, 194, 197, 235
Prayer: 57-59, 65, 76-78, 87-88, 97, 106-08, 110-19, 121-30, 134-36, 139-40, 142-50, 162, 167, 175, 194, 230, 235-36, 238, 241, 245, 247, 259-60
Preaching: 18-21, 36, 51-53, 57-59, 81, 108, 122, 126, 160, 174-75, 177, 234, 236-37, 239-40, 243, 248
Pregnant: 72-73, 238
Prelacy: 132
Preparation: 15, 18, 37, 60, 74, 111, 120, 123, 126, 149-50, 160, 184-85, 199, 250
Presence of God: 107-08, 111, 113, 115-16, 122, 124-28, 133-37, 144, 147-50, 235
Presentation: 35-36, 39, 187, 196, 244
Pre-Socratic: 212
Prestige: 9
Prevention: 114, 198
Pride: 213
Priest: 78, 96, 162
Prime: see Divine Office
Principle: 38, 68, 197
Prison: 114, 196, 206, 221
Private: 21, 179, 188, 198, 232
Privation: 185-86, 189, 193, 199
Problem: 24, 79, 83, 86-87, 92, 94, 100, 121, 129, 131-32, 157, 179-80, 182, 215, 245
Process: 9, 14, 19, 32, 102, 111, 115, 149-50, 171, 175-76, 188, 212, 226-27, 233, 239, 259
Proclamation: 15-17, 19, 21, 24, 32, 38, 42-43, 49, 51, 75, 85, 98, 137, 215, 218, 239, 242, 248
Production: 9, 149, 230-32, 242-43, 245, 248-49
Promise: 36, 44, 53, 55, 57, 108, 120, 138, 140, 142, 146, 163, 190, 192, 201, 237-38, 247-48
Prophet (Prophecy): 10-11, 15-16, 29-33, 35-37, 39-40, 45-49, 55-56, 62-63, 74-75, 88, 177, 259
Protection: 18, 43, 46, 120, 187, 214, 223

Providence: 93
Province: 25, 28, 82
Psychology: 107, 210, 219, 224-25, 227
Psychosomatic: 221, 223
Psycho-Spiritual: 217, 219-20, 225-26
Public: 90, 115, 170, 223, 232
Punishment: 70, 206
Pure (Purity): 34, 42, 58, 77, 116, 134, 140, 156, 159, 173, 215, 252-53, 255, 257-58, 262
Purification: 32-33, 79-80, 84, 133, 253, 255, 258-59

Quaracchi Editors: 92, 95, 183
Queen: 188, 200

Rapture: 61
Rationality (see also Reason): 95, 121, 211
Rays: 155
Reaction: 111, 149, 162, 215
Reality: 9, 53, 68-69, 71, 82, 107, 120, 137, 140-41, 143-45, 149, 162, 177, 199, 221, 231
Realization: 11, 61, 73, 120, 223, 252, 254
Reason: 15, 25, 36, 40, 44, 49, 69, 84, 91, 100, 105, 113, 121, 153, 172, 180, 200, 205, 225-26, 233, 247
Rebellion (see also Revolt): 132-33
Recapitulation: 171
Reconciliation: 19-20, 68, 122, 124, 127, 145-46, 222
Redaction: 91, 97, 188, 192, 250, 257
Redemption: 31, 123, 127-28, 136, 141, 181, 233, 236
Reduction: 210-11, 214, 247
Reflection: 9, 11, 16, 27, 29, 31, 53, 58, 64, 66, 68, 70-73, 84, 88, 99, 107, 109, 111, 130, 143, 154, 166, 175-76, 180, 194-95, 198-99, 202, 252-54, 256-57, 259, 261-62
Reform: 11, 18-19, 21, 25-26, 29, 36, 39, 99, 175, 188, 211, 235, 247, 253, 261-62